TANDEM

R.A.F. Biggin Hill

This is the story of the most famous fighter airfield in the world. Founded in 1917 as a wireless research establishment, Biggin Hill, guarding the southern approaches to London, soon became a key defence station, particularly during the Battle of Britain. On the night of Whit-Sunday, 1918, two pilots of 141 Squadron made Biggin Hill's first kill – a German Gotha – and during the Second World War over 1,600 enemy aircraft were shot down by Hurricanes and Spitfires operating from it.

The reputation of Biggin Hill during World War II is world famous. Among the famous 'aces' who flew from 'Biggin on the Bump' are Michael Crossley, 'Sailor' Malan, Mungo Park, A. C. Deere, Max Aitken, Brian Kingcome – as well as the Free French and U.S. Eagle squadrons.

The story has been told, not only from official records, but from diaries, memories and interviews with the men and women who served there.

R.A.F. Biggin Hill

Graham Wallace

 TANDEM

First published in Great Britain by
Putnam & Co. Ltd.

Published by Universal-Tandem Publishing Co. Ltd, 1969

Reset and Reprinted September 1975

Tandem Books are published by
Tandem Publishing Ltd.,
14 Gloucester Road, London SW7.
A Howard & Wyndham Company

Made and printed in Great Britain by
Hunt Barnard Printing Ltd., Aylesbury, Bucks

Dedicated to the memory of the
men and women of the Royal
and Allied Air Forces who made
the supreme sacrifice whilst
serving at Biggin Hill during
two world wars

ACKNOWLEDGEMENTS

THE author wishes to pay tribute to Group Captain D. G. Smallwood, Officer Commanding R.A.F. Biggin Hill, 1953–5, whose inspiration it was that this book should be written, and to Flight Lieutenant T. A. Lycett, former Education Officer, whose painstaking researches into Air Ministry archives unearthed the greater part of the material on which this history is based. Further valuable help has been afforded by Mr J. C. Nerney and Miss S. I. Brown of the Historical Branch, Air Ministry, and by the official historians of the Royal Canadian Air Force and the United States Air Force. These I wish to thank.

This book could never have been written without the assistance of a great many people who have willingly contributed from their store of memory and who have generously allowed me to quote from their personal papers and diaries. More especially, I would like to thank Dame Felicity Peake, D.B.E.; Air Vice Marshal R. L. Ragg (ret'd); Air Vice Marshal John Worrall; J. M. Furnival; Stanley Mockford; Michael Crossley; Tony Bartley; Johnny Kent; Jamie Rankin; J. W. White; Bill Igoe; D. H. Grice; John W. Hogben; J. Freeman; Brian Kingcome for the diary of the late Tommy Lund; C. D. Stephenson and J. Milner for information and the loan of photographs.

Of the various books I have consulted in compiling the story of Biggin Hill the following are the most important: *Tiger Squadron* by Ira Jones; *Test Pilot* by Neville Duke; *Fly for Your Life* by Larry Forester; *The First and the Last* by Adolf Galland; *The Mouchotte Diaries; The Big Show* by Pierre Clostermann; *Lonely Warrior* edited by V. Houart; *La Vieille Equipe* by Bernard Dupérier; and, lastly, that most invaluable guide and book of reference *Royal Air Force 1939–1945* by Denis Richards and Hilary St. G. Saunders.

CONTENTS

LIST OF ILLUSTRATIONS

INTRODUCTION

'GOOD afternoon to you all and welcome to Biggin Hill. . . .'

The breezy voice of the announcer, booming and crackling from a score of loudspeakers, starts a ripple of expectancy through the vast crowd gathered round the perimeter of this aerodrome perched on top of the North Downs just south of London. His words are half-smothered by the thunder of jets warming-up in the distance. The television and newsreel cameras are ready, boys strain against the barriers to get a better view and in a few minutes a famous film star will declare open yet another Battle of Britain Day at Biggin Hill.

' . . . Before the flying commences, I think it would be in order to remind you of the great history of this station. . . .'

It is the afternoon of 15th September, 1956: the sixteenth anniversary of the victory of 'the Few'. For hours past, cars, buses and coaches have been converging on this small airfield in Kent, bringing over 200,000 people to witness the greatest of the many flying displays given at R.A.F. stations this day. They are Londoners, mostly, with a special affection for 'Biggin on the Bump': twice the capital's bastion of defence against destruction from the air and, later, a sally-port in the liberation of Occupied Europe.

What is Biggin Hill? The name has a homely sound, almost rustic, but there are squadrons in the Royal Air Force as proud of having fought from here as regiments in the Army are of having 'Blenheim' and 'Alamein' emblazoned on their Colours. In itself Biggin Hill is just a fighter station, not very large by jet-age standards, a rather untidy agglomeration of hangars and huts, offices, barrack-blocks and

9

Messes beside an airfield. Some buildings, like the control tower, are modern, others bear the scars of war, patches of raw brick-work and the fading patterns of camouflage, but the eye alone cannot discern the tradition that is Biggin Hill. It lies in dusty files of records and combat reports, in treasured diaries and in the memories of the men, and women, too, who have served here. It was born in the days of the Royal Flying Corps, when the station was a cluster of canvas tents in the corner of a pasture and frail biplanes struggled to make headway against the wind where today the sleek, swept-wing Hawker Hunters flash past at 700 m.p.h.

And during the second World War the squadrons stationed here destroyed more than a thousand of the enemy's aircraft; at the same time over two hundred awards went to its personnel for gallantry and prowess in combat, ranging from almost a score of D.S.O.s to the three M.M.s won by members of the Women's Auxiliary Air Force for their cool courage under bombardment. It is a record unparalleled by any other fighter station. In the neat, austere Chapel of Remembrance, flanked by the immortal Hurricane and Spitfire, are preserved the names of over four hundred pilots who gave their lives in action: men not only from Britain and the Commonwealth, but from Belgium, Czechoslovakia, France, Norway, Poland and the United States.

This is Biggin Hill.

CHAPTER ONE

THE STATION IS BORN

ONE afternoon late in the autumn of 1916 two subalterns in the Royal Flying Corps, a pilot and an experimental scientist, motored southwards out of London to explore a possible site for a new aerodrome. Both men were attached to a unit with the intriguing title of the Wireless Testing Park.

Then stationed at Joyce Green, near Dartford, the Wireless Testing Park was responsible for the testing and approval of all new wireless apparatus for the Royal Flying Corps. Although conveniently close to Woolwich Common where the laboratory work was done by the Signals Experimental Establishment of the Royal Engineers, as an aerodrome Joyce Green had many disadvantages. Being small, lying on waterlogged land bordering the Thames and more often than not blanketed with fog, it was hardly suitable for intensive test-flying. Furthermore, the work was conducted along such strictly military lines that the young enthusiasts of the Royal Flying Corps, agog over the possibilities of wireless, felt exasperated and frustrated by the diehards of Army Signals.

After two years of war the value of wireless in aviation was at last appreciated; now the squadrons overseas were clamouring for more, and improved, equipment. This was desperately slow in forthcoming through the bottleneck of Woolwich and Joyce Green. To speed matters up, the Officer Commanding the Wireless Testing Park, Major Orme, was instructed to move the unit to a better location, if there was one to be found. His pilots searched the environs of London in vain until, one day, Lieutenant Hansard had an inspiration.

By a happy chance his family home was in Limpsfield, a village nestling under the North Downs. On the chalk ridge behind he recalled a high expanse of open grazing that overlooked the Weald of Kent. He felt instinctively that it would make an ideal aerodrome for the Wireless Testing Park; there was even a village nearby, an undistinguished collection of bungalows and cottages with the name of Biggin Hill.

Accompanied by Lieutenant Furnival, a friend on the wireless staff, Hansard borrowed a car from the M.T. officer and drove into the open country beyond Bromley. The road they followed climbed and wound through the oaks and beeches of Keston, all gold and burnished copper in the frosty sunshine, and emerged on to the windswept crest of the North Downs.

It was so tranquil, with the rolling, lightly-wooded landscape of Kent on all sides unmarred by housing estates or factories, that it seemed hardly credible that an hour's driving would bring them to Piccadilly Circus. The field of Hansard's choice was certainly large, all of seventy-five acres, and the turf underfoot was close and buoyant. When the hummocks were levelled and depressions filled, aircraft would be able to take-off and land with ease. With a pilot's eye Hansard noted how the mists of autumn hung low in the valleys on either side, leaving the high ground clear. There were other advantages, too: no sources of electrical interference, altitude to increase the range of wireless signals and, most important, a large house of red brick that would make a fine Officers' Mess.

Strolling towards this, Hansard and Furnival were unexpectedly accosted by a watchman who demanded their business. When they told him, he supplied the startling information that the field was already scheduled as an aerodrome or, more precisely, as a night emergency landing ground. He was paid a niggardly wage by the War Office, he added with justified bitterness, to look after the flares and keep the land free of courting couples tempted by the softness of the grass on a warm summer night.

So more by chance than design, Biggin Hill became an

aerodrome, born in an imbroglio of inter-unit jealousies that had denied the Royal Flying Corps the fruits of brilliant researches into the applications of wireless and aviation.

On the outbreak of war, in the days when opposing airmen engaged each other in gentlemanly combat with revolvers and shot-guns, all communications work for the Royal Flying Corps was in the hands of the Royal Engineers. The unhappy results which followed persuaded the R.F.C. Staff, early in 1915, to organise a small research detachment at Brooklands under Captain (later Major) C. E. Prince. In civil life a well-known Marconi pioneer, Prince had scant respect for the unimaginative thinking of his military rivals. Gathering together the best men he could find, and the Marconi Company was virtually the only source, Prince set the pace in the design of new equipment with a sensational result: air-to-ground wireless telephony.

Aircraft had been used for reconnaissance since August, 1914; at first British General Headquarters were distrustful of intelligence reported by this, then, unorthodox means, but, after the Royal Flying Corps had contributed materially to the victory of the Marne, good use was made of the airmen's godlike power to discern what went on behind enemy lines. There was, however, one drawback: the time elapsed before the pilots and observers landed and reported their observations.

Wireless could obviate this but there were many snags. Wireless telegraphy from an aeroplane was no novelty; as early as 1910 Morse had been transmitted from a machine in flight and received on the ground and, during the battle of the Aisne on 24th September, 1914, wireless-carrying aircraft from No. 4 Squadron were used to good effect as spotters for artillery. This was the era of the cat's whisker and crystal; the spark transmitters employed had an effective range of only ten miles. Increasing this entailed loading the aircraft with heavier gear, while the hapless pilot had simultaneously to tune the set, operate the Morse buzzer and fly, often under fire from 'Archie'. Wireless *telephony*, not wireless *telegraphy*, was the answer: the instantaneous transmission of

13

speech over a useful range with the minimum of effort – but this was 1915 and 'broadcasting' was unknown.

A device already existed which could achieve this and Prince found, to his astonishment, that the military wireless experts, in their ignorance of the principles involved, had condemned it as useless for aircraft. Known as the Round Valve Telephone, it utilised an early form of wireless valve for the amplification of minute electric currents. The inventor Captain Round, another brilliant Marconi engineer, had already shown that the continuous transmission of speech was possible, but in the ideal conditions of a laboratory and not the rough-and-tumble of flying.

Prince mentioned the possibilities of the Round Valve Telephone to an R.F.C. officer who happened to be visiting Brooklands. His name was Dowding. In later years, as Air Chief Marshal Sir Hugh Dowding, he was to make a devastating use of wireless in his direction of the Battle of Britain. Major Dowding was interested in Prince's ideas and requested a demonstration. He foresaw the great tactical importance of wireless telephony and gave Prince his wholehearted support.

Hampered by lack of equipment and money, Prince and his assistants persevered through the summer of 1915 until they had successfully 'crudified' the delicate laboratory apparatus into a robust set where it was only necessary to switch on and talk – the first air-to-ground wireless telephone in the world. By summer's end Prince was able to report: ' . . . It seemed almost beyond hope to achieve really practical Wireless Telephony from an aeroplane, but the difficulties have been overcome, and the new set is by no means a toy, or only of scientific interest. A new and amazing power is conferred by it. . . . '

The first set ready, Dowding arranged for Prince to visit France for a demonstration to the Chiefs-of-Staff. Clear speech was transmitted from an aeroplane and received on the ground twenty miles away. Lord Kitchener was deeply impressed. Military conservatism, however, won the day; the use of air-to-ground telephony was not recommended by the High Command until shortly before the Armistice, leaving the reconnaissance squadrons of the Royal Flying Corps to continue to struggle with wireless telegraphy. Prince returned to Brooklands where he and his assistants resumed their researches. Ground-to-air telephony followed quickly and they were about to tackle the infinitely more difficult problem of air-to-air telephony when the detachment was disbanded.

Their successes had been duly noted by the regular wireless officers of the Royal Engineers, who disliked the 'hostilities only' Marconi men and their unorthodox ways. Prince was drawn into an inter-unit fracas, the research work passed to Woolwich, and the R.F.C. personnel were posted to Joyce Green to become the Wireless Testing Park. Although four-fifths of the R.E. Signals Experimental Establishment's work was for the Royal Flying Corps, only one R.F.C. officer was tolerated on the premises and he was powerless to influence the designs. Out of eleven new sets submitted to the Wireless Testing Park, all were rejected with such revealing comments as 'a monument of incompetence', 'hopelessly bad design' and 'a primitive attempt to get round real difficulties'.

As the indictments accumulated on their desks, it dawned on the 'brass hats' that the Woolwich specialists, competent though they might be in military matters, knew very little about aviation. Nor was it a wise policy to have the Experimental Flight stationed on an aerodrome where the weather, or state of ground, forbade flying for half the days in the year. If the move to Biggin Hill was a partial sop to criticism, it was at least a first step towards giving the Royal Flying Corps (and subsequently the Royal Air Force) its independent wireless research establishment.

Official sanction for the re-siting of the Wireless Testing Park was given on 2nd December, 1916. With one awkward exception, the intricacies of land-ownership and compensation were dealt with swiftly.

The land that had once been presented as a gift to Odo, Bishop of Bayeux, by William the Conqueror and was recorded in Domesday, now formed part of Cudham Lodge farm. Cudham Lodge itself, a pleasant Georgian mansion, was an old and historic landmark, the third house to be built on the foundations of the medieval Manor of Bertray.

There was, of course, no question of outright purchase at this time and local residents willingly accepted the establishment of an aerodrome in their midst. The owner, the Earl of Stanhope, when home on leave from the Front in 1915, had agreed to the use of the largest pasture as a night emergency landing ground. Now his tenant, John Westacott, was required to relinquish even more acres until his own home, Cudham Lodge, came within the bounds of the ever-expanding airfield.

The large house of red brick, so suitable for a Mess, was a case of particular hardship. Named 'Koonowla', it had been bequeathed with a substantial endowment to the Victoria Hospital for Sick Children in Chelsea. It was reserved wholly for the children of the poor, and the hospital trustees were understandably loath to give up the house and forfeit the entailed endowment. As no amicable settlement could be reached, the War Office invoked the Defence of the Realm Act and 'Koonowla' was summarily requisitioned.

Once the land agents and solicitors had folded their title deeds and departed, Major Orme was free to commence the transfer. It was a particularly hard winter that year and the task of preparing the site was most unpopular with the N.C.O.s and men who came by lorry from Joyce Green. One of the early arrivals has recalled the scene:

Inside the entrance to the field I found a C.S.M. with a few R.F.C. personnel in the act of erecting a canvas hangar, and was instantly enrolled into the crew. Under the C.S.M.'s threat of 'Shove the bloody hangar up or no tea, as the first crate arrives tomorrow'! we all got busy. Others were unpacking two large aircraft packing-cases and unloading stores. The cases were then moved to the side of the hangar a few yards from the hedge, one was used for the C.O.'s office and the other for the wireless hut. Farther over on the far side of the field a gang of Labour

Corps were busy with picks and shovels levelling off the bumps and filling in the hollows. Pending the arrival of the rest of the equipment all other ranks were shoved on the 'gardening racket' that day until dark. It was no good being fussy in those days, my enthusiasm for wireless, in common with a few others, was swept aside in the need for more urgent requirements, including the cleaning out and preparation of the red house behind the hedge as the Officers' Mess.[1]

The first aircraft was expected to arrive on 1st January, 1917, but fog over Joyce Green prevented the take-off. Next day Lieutenant Dickie, with Air Mechanic Chadwick as passenger, flew in with an R.E. 7 and was greeted by a fusillade of snowballs as he landed in front of the newly-erected hangar. The ground crew were quickly routed with a shower of icy slush whipped up by the slipstream before Dickie and Chadwick descended to solemnly kiss the ground in mock ritual. They were the first airmen to land at Biggin Hill.

Conditions were grim at first. The officers were quartered comfortably enough in 'Koonowla', but the N.C.O.s and men lived under canvas or in unheated wooden huts, while empty packing-cases had perforce to serve as offices and workshops. The snow thawed and was trampled into freezing, glutinous mud that reminded the 'old sweats', with expressive obscenity, of former days in Flanders.

By 13th February the transfer was complete. The same day Major Orme issued his first Routine Order from the new station, promulgating an address destined to become familiar to many thousands of airmen and airwomen in the years ahead:

On and after the 13th February, 1917, the address of this unit will be:

Biggin Hill Aerodrome,
Near Westerham,
Kent.

[1]Related by W. Wallis.

CHAPTER TWO

WIRELESS MESSAGES

Now settled at Biggin Hill, the Wireless Testing Park not only continued the testing and approval, or rejection, of the Woolwich-produced equipment but undertook an increasing amount of original research. The Chiefs-of-Staff had learnt the value of science in warfare and were receptive to new ideas. Major-General 'Boom' Trenchard, commanding the Royal Flying Corps in the Field, welcomed any innovation that promised his pilots an advantage over the Hun. He urged the wireless officers at Biggin Hill to resume the work begun so auspiciously at Brooklands and, specifically, to develop a practical system of air-to-air wireless telephony.

His requirements were stringent: a one mile all-round range, no adjustments to the transmitter when in use and only one tuning movement allowed on the receiver. A hundred per cent reliability with perfect speech quality was stipulated, and a maximum aerial length of 150 feet, to be superseded by a fixed aerial if practicable.

Preliminary experiments were commenced in the spring of 1917. One set after another was constructed, tested, and abandoned. Microphones were either too sensitive, or too insensitive, and engine vibration played havoc with the carbon granules. The aerials were long wires of copper, weighted at one end and lowered after take-off. Frequently the operator omitted to reel them in before landing, and the trees around Biggin Hill soon became festooned with wires, to the fury of the scientists and the men sent climbing after them.

The difficulties were so great that the project was on the verge of being indefinitely shelved when someone suggested resurrecting the Round-Prince set of 1915 for a final experiment. It was installed in a B.E. 2e, the one remaining Round valve fitted gingerly into place and the operator provided with a microphone of ancient vintage, the 'Hunningscone', swathed in cottonwool inside a cardboard box. To everyone's delight it worked; Prince's original air-to-ground results were reproduced and the operator's voice, albeit distorted, was received in a second aeroplane.

This was heartening, but a long way from Trenchard's requirements. The wireless technicalities proved fairly simple to solve, but all speech remained obstinately distorted and unintelligible. Every type of microphone was tried, with diaphragms of steel, aluminium, celluloid, and mica. Those which gave good results on the ground were inexplicably useless in the air. When, after scores of experiments, some measure of success was achieved, it was discovered that the officer who did all the test-speaking had, with so much practice, trained his voice to get the best out of a microphone – another speaker and the words remained a heart-breaking gibberish. Earphones introduced into the transmitter circuit helped by allowing the operator to hear the sound of his own voice, but they could not be worn with the regulation flying-helmets. The scientists became hatters for a day, designing and sewing new helmets with built-in pockets for microphone and earphones.

One sultry evening in July, as the sun was casting long shadows over Biggin Hill, two Sopwith $1\frac{1}{2}$-Strutters were brought from a hangar and made ready for flight. Shortly after sunset, in the calm air of the twilight hour, they took off and followed divergent courses southwards: along the valley to Sevenoaks and across the ridge of the North Downs towards Edenbridge. Once airborne, Lieutenant Andrews, the operator entrusted with the prototype transmitter, unwound the aerial, switched on the set and started to speak into his microphone.

'One – Two – Three – Four – Five – Six – Dip – your – wing – if – you – receive – me – Seven – Eight – Nine – Ten – Monday – Tuesday – Wednesday. . . . '

In the second Sopwith Lieutenant Furnival briefly tuned the receiver and waited tensely for it to warm up. Suddenly

19

he heard the words spoken by Andrews, distinct and intelligible above the static and crackling interference from the magneto.

'... Thursday – Friday – Saturday – Sunday – Dip – your – wings – if – you – receive – me – January – February – March....'

Furnival leaned forward to give a triumphant 'thumbs up' to his pilot, Captain Peck,[1] who dipped his wings in happy acknowledgement. The distance between the two aircraft increased, but the tinny ghost of Andrews' voice never faltered, never faded. Air-to-air wireless telephony was, at long last, a reality. It was full night when they returned to Biggin Hill, but not too dark for the expectant watchers by the flarepath to see the jubilant waggling of wings against the stars.

Events moved quickly after that; Furnival, Andrews, and Peck repeated and improved their performance until they had sufficient confidence to make a sortie to France with the $1\frac{1}{2}$-Strutters and wireless equipment for a command performance before Trenchard and officers of the Air Staff. They crossed the Channel on a clear, sunny day and landed at Boisdingham, near St Omer, where the demonstration was to take place. It was an unqualified success. The two aircraft circuited the field, one transmitting orders which were carried out by the other. A receiver was provided on the ground so that Trenchard could eavesdrop on the aerial conversation and check that there was no deception by flying to a prearranged plan. Afterwards he grumbled that the transmitter operator had given far too many 'Hullo's'. Individual officers were given the opportunity of flying as passengers so that they, too, could speak and listen for themselves.

Despite the 'Hullo's', Trenchard was delighted and asked for two squadrons to be equipped at once. Air-to-air wireless telephony presaged a revolution in aerial tactics; for the very first time a flight commander could speak to his pilots throughout an action, giving orders that would be instantaneously heard.

[1]Later Air Marshal Sir Richard Peck, K.C.B., O.B.E.

'With regard to the wireless telephone apparatus recently sent here for test', reported Trenchard to the Directorate of Military Aeronautics, 'trials have been made with highly satisfactory results. I am very pleased that this problem appears to have been solved and I consider that it reflects much credit on those who have been engaged in the experimental work and the design of the apparatus.'

Somehow the Germans had got wind of this most secret equipment. Prisoners were captured carrying documents offering a large reward for the salvage of any parts of the set.

'As far as we know', warned Trenchard, 'the enemy has not yet evolved any practical form of wireless telephony, and it is therefore most important to prevent our instruments falling into his hands intact.'

The initial batch of twenty sets was produced by Woolwich in record time and received a thorough testing at Biggin Hill. Furnival returned to France to equip and train No. 11 Squadron, flying Bristol Fighters from Bellevue, on the Arras front. The instructional flights had to be sandwiched in between operations and, with the enemy's eagerness to obtain a set in mind, great care was taken to remove them before the aircraft flew over the trenches. As 11 Squadron was often ordered up three or four times daily, little progress was made until permission was granted for 'A' Flight to be out of the line for a week. The pilots and observers were disgusted. They regarded the wireless telephone as a diabolical box of tricks that kept them from the important business of chasing, and killing, the Hun. Captain Hooper, however, the Australian commander of 'A' Flight, had great faith in the new equipment. He and Furnival persevered with the recalcitrant aircrews until 'Hooper's Circus', flying as one in obedience to his orders by wireless telephone, could perform an immaculate aerobatic drill which became the envy of every squadron in France.

After 11 Squadron had been equipped, Trenchard considered the risk too great to continue the work so close to the Front and sent Furnival home to organise a school of wireless telephony at Biggin Hill.

All of a sudden it seemed to the cynically-minded veterans of wireless research that the whole outcome of the war in the air had come to depend on wireless telephony. Recalling their struggle for apparatus at Brooklands, they marvelled at the flood of new equipment, the nine brand-new B.E. 2es, the hangars that were erected overnight and the way in which experienced wireless officers were snatched from other units to become instructors. A former professional singer Lieutenant Gooch, was seconded as O.C. voice tuition, while a team of Leatherworkers set up a workshop to provide each pupil with a tailored helmet.

By November, 1917, some thirty-six officers a week were passing through the school. The word soon spread to France that a course at 'Biggin on the Bump' meant a cushy billet in the Bell Hotel, Bromley, a chance to visit the girl friend and see the latest West End shows. As Christmas drew near, squadron commanders were overwhelmed with applications for instruction in wireless telephony. Most regrettably, the school closed for the duration of the Christmas holidays!

On one memorable occasion the instructors and pupils were commanded to display their skill before King George V and an assembly of generals on the Horse Guards Parade. At the appointed hour the flight from Biggin Hill swept low over the Horse Guards and dipped wings in a Royal Salute. For the next thirty minutes they banked, climbed and dived in one of the most amazing exhibitions of aerobatics Londoners had ever witnessed. Through a receiving set His Majesty heard the Flight Commander give orders for the 'bombing' of St Paul's and the interception of an 'enemy raider' over the Crystal Palace. Two aircraft peeled off, proceeded to these objectives and returned to report by wireless: 'Missions completed'. His Majesty and the generals were fascinated by the precision of the display, but the Flight Commander was not so easily satisfied. He had detected one pilot lose formation for a few fleeting seconds. While the others were contentedly downing tankards of beer in the Mess at Biggin Hill, this miscreant was kept flying an 'aerial pack-drill' round and round the airfield until his petrol ran out – the order for this penance being given, of course, by air-to-air wireless telephony.

Sooner or later the Germans would lay hands on an intact set and then nothing could stop them listening to our airmen speaking *en clair* as they flew over the Front. The wireless officers at Biggin Hill began to consider the possibilities of a code. Something simple was needed, easy to speak and comprehend, yet meaningless to the enemy. Elaborate tests were made to determine with precision the best words to employ.

Pilots were given long lists of words which they repeated *ad nauseam* in flight, while patient listeners on the ground noted the degrees of clarity and intelligibility.

'Hullo, Dollars.[1] Hullo, Dollars. Pole . . Pole . . Pole . . Bole . . Bole . . Bole . . Toll . . Toll . . Toll . . Pale . . Pale . Pale . . '

The listeners made a careful note. A code containing 'Pole' could use 'Pale' but not 'Bole' or 'Toll'. Through the earphones the voice of the pilot sounded faintly irritable.

'Tale . . Tale . . Tale . I'm thirsty! . . Beer . . Beer . . Beer . . Sorry, as you were . . Moll . . Moll . . Moll . . Male . . Male . . Male . . '

Although in English words the meaning is generally conveyed by the consonants, telephonically speaking these were less dependable than the vowels whose sounds had a greater amplitude. Long vowels and diphthongs proved the best, and words of two syllables lessened the chances of mishearing.

'Hullo, Dollars . . Bolo . . Bolo . . Bolo . . Koodoo . . Koodoo . . Koodoo . . Daily . . Daily . . Daily . . Baby . . Baby . . Baby . . '

There were puzzled faces in the wireless hut. The last two words were indistinguishable.

'Delete "Baby", try "Booty".'

After further exhaustive trials it was agreed that short double-words like 'Dog-rose' and 'Shot-gun' would provide the most effective code. They transmitted clearly and, taken together in a short context, often had a comic meaning of their own guaranteed to flummox the unimaginative Hun.

[1] Call-sign of Biggin Hill.

By the end of 1917 the Wireless Testing Park had grown to such an extent that it was accorded a more distinguished title, becoming the Wireless Experimental Establishment – W.E.E. in short. Major H. T. B. Childs replaced Major Orme as C.O. when the latter obtained a much-desired transfer to an operational station. The sight of fourteen German Gothas flying serenely over Biggin Hill one July morning had been too much for him. 'God damn it,' he yelled in broad Devon accents, 'only one Sopwith Pup and not even a round of live ammo. on the 'drome. I'm finished playing with wireless!'

Every way that wireless could potentially help in the air war was under study. Old equipment was improved, new sets designed and tried out, including spark continuous-wave and W/T transmitters, crystal and valve receivers, valve amplifiers and tonic-train transmitters. Wireless telephony sets were greatly improved by the substitution of the new 'hard' French valves for the imperfectly evacuated Round valves, and the first Home Defence squadron was equipped. Aperfield Court, a spacious mansion with large grounds some two miles from Biggin Hill, was requisitioned and a powerful transmitter installed for the ground-to-air control of fighters defending London against German raiders.

In March, 1918, further important changes took place. Anticipating the fusion of the Royal Flying Corps and the Royal Naval Air Service in to the Royal Air Force, the decision was taken to concentrate all wireless research at Biggin Hill. The R.N.A.S. establishment at Cranwell was closed down; the work being done by the Royal Engineers at Woolwich for the Royal Flying Corps was transferred, and Lt-Col. L. F. Blandy, D.S.O., former O.C. Wireless for the Army in France, assumed overall command of the greatly-expanded Wireless Experimental Establishment.

Simultaneously, work was started on the permanent buildings of the South Camp, as the site of the Wireless Experimental Establishment was known. Plans were drawn up for a new Officers' Mess, together with barrack-blocks, laboratories, workshops, and steel and concrete hangars. It was an

24

ambitious project that was to cost £220,000, and take as long as two years to complete. All building materials were in short supply and a mere wireless research establishment stood low in the scale of priorities. There was friction between the civilian contractors and the newly created Air Ministry. Labourers downed tools on being given orders by uniformed officers, while the airmen resented the British workman's habit of taking Saturday afternoons off with, or without, permission.

Over 600 men were employed on the construction work and Biggin Hill became an El Dorado to the neighbouring villages. As an agricultural labourer a man earned a bare 39s. 6d. a week; for unskilled work on the South Camp he received over £4 in weekly wages. The hours were shorter and the contractors considerately provided a fleet of buses to pick up the men each morning and return them to their cottages at night. Local squires and farmers denounced this mollycoddling and gloomily discussed their labour shortage in the saloon bars; on the other side of the partition their former employees drank their beer contentedly, happy in the security of work at Biggin Hill for many months to come.

When the Wireless Testing Park had first moved in, only fighters were flown; now twin-engined bombers, Handley Page 0/400s and D.H. 10s, were being used and more fields had to be requisitioned for the lengthening runways. It was hard on the farmers but at least it provided some memorable occasions for the other ranks ordered out on the 'gardening racket':

Immediately at the rear of the aerodrome was a fruit farm, with a large acreage devoted to strawberries, bush fruit of every description and numerous well-established apple and other fruit trees.

The owner of this farm was called to the South Camp and informed that the R.A.F. were immediately extending the 'drome to include most of his farm.

The poor bloke was in a highly indignant state as acres and acres of luscious strawberries were to be destroyed,

25

and was given a few days to pick what he could. He asked permission to enrol Service personnel as pickers!

I have never seen such a rush of volunteers for a fatigue party!

Pending developments, the little work required to be done on the 'drome was done in record time on the first day of 'Operation Strawberry' and one then adjourned to the farm where the picking was done on the basis of: 'The best for myself and what I can't eat I'll put in the basket for the farmer'.

By the end of the day the fatigue party had eaten so many strawberries that they were ashamed to look at one another![1]

The Station's nominal roll now mustered 593 persons all told: 68 officers, 297 men and 228 women – W.R.A.F.s who had volunteered for cooking, clerical and M.T. duties. There was even an 'Ancient Mariner', a retired Captain, R.N., who had attached himself to the Mess. Whenever anything had to be moved, a hut, wrecked aircraft or hangar, the cry was raised for 'Barnacle Bill'. With rope, pulleys and rollers he performed prodigious feats of haulage, disdaining a land-lubberly crane or tractor.

In August was given the first demonstration of controlling the movements of a tank from the air by wireless telephone, and two months later the first long-distance flight entirely by wireless navigation. Air-to-tank telephony came too late to be of practical use in the war effort, but the wireless navigational work was of fundamental importance.

It had been known for a long time that a bearing could be taken on a wireless transmitter station by a receiver fitted with a loop aerial tuned to the signal of maximum, or minimum, strength. By plotting the bearings taken in two stations, the position of the receiver could be determined with a fair degree of accuracy, but it was considered impossible to design an airborne D/F set which could pinpoint the position of an aircraft in flight. Encouraged by Blandy, one

[1]Related by W. Wallis.

of his wireless officers, P. P. Eckersley, tackled the problem with such success that, in October, 1918, a Handley Page 0/400, equipped with D/F set and loop aerial, was flown from Biggin Hill to Paris and back again entirely on wireless bearings.

There was a low mist scudding in from the sea on the morning chosen for the flight with ten-tenths cloud overhead. Blandy and the crew of the 0/400 were gleeful when they saw the weather; all landmarks would be hidden and there could be no talk afterwards of cheating with visual sights. Their two passengers, Maj-Gen. Sefton Brancker and an aide, arrived at Biggin Hill in equally high spirits; they regrettably had little faith in wireless as an aid to navigation and confidently expected the flight to be called off. To their surprise, the 0/400 taxied out on schedule and within three minutes was flying through the overcast, out of sight of land.

Near the coast the navigator took bearings on the Marconi stations at Chelmsford and Poldhu, and gave the pilot his course for Boulogne. At the predicted time the 0/400 dipped down through the clouds and there below lay the harbour; Brancker was impressed but not convinced. For the next ninety minutes the flight continued-on over unbroken cloud, flying a course set with bearings taken on transmitters in France. The two passengers were starting to joke pessimistically about being lost and the possibility of landing on the wrong side of the Front when the navigator then passed a confident message: 'Within five minutes we shall be over Paris.' The pilot brought the 0/400 down in a shallow dive through the clouds and there was Le Bourget, with the Eiffel Tower unmistakable in the distance.

They landed at the aerodrome, the crew looking forward to a night's roistering in Paris, but Brancker was in a hurry to return to London. Blandy left them at Le Bourget and drove off in a car, customarily reserved for Winston Churchill, to report to Trenchard on the new D/F equipment. The flight back to Biggin Hill was equally sensational. An accurate course was flown to Boulogne, the Channel crossed in clouds and landfall made at Dungeness at the

27

predicted time. Brancker, by now an enthusiastic convert to the possibilities of wireless D/F, asked if he could satisfy a lifelong ambition and see Brighton from the air. Fresh bearings were taken on the two Marconi stations, a new course worked out and flown until the navigator, stop-watch in hand, signalled the pilot to descend – ahead lay the Brighton pier and inland the domes of the Royal Pavilion.

By the end of the war Britain led the world in the many uses of wireless in the air. The Germans had been unable to develop anything comparable to our systems of wireless telephony and direction-finding, nor, for that matter, had our Allies. The Americans were intensely interested in the work being done at Biggin Hill and requested permission for a party of officers from the U.S. Signals and Aviation Wireless Unit to visit the Station. This was granted as a courtesy between allies, and the visitors spent several instructive days at the Wireless Experimental Establishment.

This visit had a dramatic sequel. On the evening of Friday 16th May, 1919, three Curtiss flying-boats of the U.S. Navy roared out of Trepassey Harbour in Newfoundland to attempt the first crossing of the Atlantic by air. All three aircraft carried D/F sets which had been placed at the disposal of the American Government by the Royal Air Force. For the first leg of the flight, Newfoundland to the Azores, the flying-boats encountered nothing but fog and storms masking the chain of destroyers strung out across the ocean as beacons, and the D/F sets were used continuously to obtain bearings on transatlantic wireless stations. One flying-boat foundered off the Azores, the second limped into Ponta Delgarda after taxi-ing over 200 miles of open sea and only the third, the N.C-4 under the command of Lieutenant Cdr Read, was able to continue the flight. After ten days' delay the N.C-4 flew on to Lisbon, touching down on the Tagus on 27th May to complete the first aerial crossing of the Atlantic which, as Read admitted to the Press, would never have been achieved without the help of the D/F equipment from Biggin Hill.

Some months after the Armistice, when the ban on wartime secrets was relaxed, Major Erskine-Murray, a wireless officer from Biggin Hill, lectured to the Institute of Electrical Engineers on the past four years' developments in wireless for aviation. It was an exciting occasion and few in the audience had an inkling of the great advances made until Erskine-Murray sprang his dramatic surprise. Towards the end of the lecture he glanced at his wrist-watch and requested silence, saying: 'Now one of our aeroplanes has come from Biggin Hill and is going to talk to us.'

A strange voice addressed the assembly from a loud-speaker on the lecture rostrum: 'Hullo! Are you Major Erskine-Murray's audience?'

When the assembled engineers had recovered from their shock, some shouted into the microphone that Erskine-Murray held up: 'We are.'

'Well, we want a few words with you.'

'Where are you?'

'We are circling over Westminster Abbey in a Nieuport machine.'

'How high are you?'

'About 3,000 feet: 80 miles an hour.'

'What are the weather conditions?'

'Delightful just now – on the cool side, don't you know.'

For the next fifteen minutes the audience chatted freely with the pilot and his operator until the latter's voice said rather wearily: 'We're a bit fed up with circling around here – '

'Half a moment,' requested Erskine-Murray into his microphone. 'The audience sends you a vote of thanks.'

The roar of applause was clearly heard by the two airmen before they flew back to Biggin Hill, but not before they had wished everyone by wireless telephone a polite, 'Good Night!'

CHAPTER THREE

DETACHED FLIGHT

THE chain of circumstances which led to the re-siting of the Wireless Testing Park at Biggin Hill in 1916 was soon to have a more enduring consequence. The new aerodrome occupied a unique position guarding the southern approaches to London, hence of great importance in the defence of the capital against air attack.

The Germans had wasted little time in revealing their aptitude for the bombing of towns and cities. On Christmas Eve, 1914, a solitary aeroplane flew over Dover and dropped one bomb, and on Christmas Day two more bombs were dropped on the Thames Estuary. These were but token raids and until Germany's aircraft industry produced a long-range bomber, all serious raiding was done by Zeppelins. The first raid was on the night of 19th January, 1915, when bombs were dropped on several villages in Norfolk. London, at first, was not molested. The Kaiser was unwilling to sanction attacks on the capital, whether from fear of reprisal or qualms of conscience is not recorded. Public opinion in Germany, however, warming to the theme of *Gott strafe England*! soon overcame His Imperial Majesty's scruples and Londoners received their baptism of fire on 26th May when the Zeppelin L.Z. 38 dropped a ton of high explosive, causing seven deaths and thirty-five injuries. During the next two years the Zeppelins ranged freely over England, with London their principle objective, to drop 196 tons of bombs in a total of 51 raids, killing 557 and injuring 1,358 persons.

It was fortunate for the crews of the German airships that our defences were in a state of chaos. The War Office and the Admiralty were at loggerheads over the responsibility for Home Defence. The generals claimed it their duty while the admirals, as traditional defenders of Britain's shores, saw aerial bombardment as an attack on our insularity and therefore their domain. The Navy had little faith in aeroplanes and favoured guns and searchlights, the Army held that the best defence was attack from the air, but lacked the aircraft to substantiate this. A pathetically small number of guns and searchlights was available for the defence of London. Two paddle-steamers, carrying Sopwith seaplanes, were commissioned in readiness to put to sea on nights when a raid seemed likely. The nine trams equipped with searchlights which rattled through London streets after dark amused passers-by, but achieved little else. Great results were expected from a battery of quick-firing, high-angle naval guns mounted on a fleet of lorries. These were stationed at Ken Wood under orders to sally forth to any district threatened by a Zeppelin and there engage the enemy. By the time they had threaded their way through London's traffic the raider had long vanished, but many a timorous citizen was heartened by seeing the bluejackets rumble down the Edgware Road or Pall Mall!

The ground defences and the night-flying pilots of the Royal Flying Corps and the Royal Naval Air Service, who gallantly pressed home their attacks to the point of self-destruction, had just about got the measure of the Zeppelins when the Germans switched to what was ultimately to prove a far more deadly weapon – the heavier-than-air bomber.

The Gotha was passed as ready for operations on 1st February, 1917. It has been said that this aircraft was a development of our Handley Page 0/400, two of which fell into enemy hands when the pilots flew off course on a delivery flight and landed on a German-held airfield. Whether this is true or not, the Gotha was a formidable machine: a twin-engined biplane with a crew of three, carrying 1,000 kg. of bombs at an average speed of 70 m.p.h. Eighteen of these bombers could, so the Germans boasted, carry the same weight as three Zeppelins – and three airships had never succeeded in reaching London at once.

The first mass daylight attack was made on 25th May, 1917, when twenty-one Gothas crossed the Channel *en route* for London. Thick cloud forced them to turn back and scatter their bombs over Kent. One stick fell in a crowded shopping street in Folkestone, killing fifty-six women and children.

Three weeks later, on 13th June, fourteen Gothas flew over London shortly before noon. There were nearly 600 casualties from this one raid.

'The visibility was exceptionally good,' exulted the squadron commander, Hauptmann Brandenburg. 'With perfect clearness the Thames bridges, the railway stations, the City, even the Bank of England could be recognised. Our aircraft circled round and dropped their bombs with no hurry or trouble.'

Ninety-two fighters went up to intercept, few got within range and only one attack was delivered – it failed.

This raid, so soon after the tragedy of Folkestone, provoked a bitter public outcry over the inadequacy of the defences. A conference was hastily summoned by the Chief of the Imperial General Staff, heated debates took place in the War Cabinet and a small committee was formed under the guidance of General Smuts to investigate the whole question of Air Defence and Air Organisation. The great achievement of this committee was to be the formation of the Royal Air Force; of more immediate importance was the establishment of a London Air Defence Area under one command.

Within a few weeks London was enmeshed in a web of defences commanded by Brig.-Gen. (afterwards Maj.-Gen.) E. B. Ashmore. Anti-aircraft batteries were sited on the coasts of Essex and Kent, a close inner ring of guns and searchlights was thrown around the suburbs and a balloon barrage ordered for the dockland boroughs and Essex Marshes. Observer posts were linked to a control room in the Horse Guards, and air raid warnings given by the firing of maroons. At first there were pitifully few squadrons available for Home Defence – six in all. To withdraw more from the Front would be to play into the enemy's hands, but approval was grudgingly given for the recall of two squadrons of Camels.

Although these measures required time to perfect, they had one quick result. After losing three Gothas (two by gunfire, one to an R.N.A.S. pilot) on 22nd August, the Germans abandoned daylight-raiding in favour of attack by moonlight. The Zeppelins had always followed tortuously evasive courses to London; with their limited range the Gothas were forced to take the shortest routes, flying directly over, or very close to, the Wireless Experimental Establishment. As the threat of raids increased with the lengthening hours of darkness, two additional Home Defence squadrons were sanctioned, Nos. 140 and 141, the latter to be stationed at Biggin Hill.

1st January, 1918, was the date authorised for the formation of this squadron; in the meantime south London could not be left defenceless, so an extra flight was formed and detached from 39 Squadron, 49 Wing, and ordered posthaste to Biggin Hill. This squadron, then stationed at Hornchurch and North Weald, was already famous as the first London defence squadron. In 1916 one of its pilots, Lt W. Leefe Robinson, had been awarded the V.C. for bringing down a Schutte-Lanz airship in flames over Essex, the first German airship to fall on British soil.

Ensconced in comfortable headquarters at Upminster Hall, the commander of 49 Wing scorned the existing accommodation, hangars and workshops of the W.E.E. and sent the detached flight to the north end of Biggin Hill, a wintry wilderness of deep snow-drifts. Here the fighter pilots were to enjoy the simple, Spartan life uncontaminated by wireless scientists and other effete characters. The site chosen was that part of the airfield which lay directly behind the 'Salt Box', a cottage famous locally for its resemblance to the kitchen article. It counted for nothing that the assorted aircraft of the Wireless Flight had been using the aerodrome for over ten months. A Sopwith 1½-Strutter was borrowed from Penshurst and only after it had made numerous landings and take-offs in different directions was Biggin Hill accepted

3 33

as being a suitable home for a fighter squadron.

On 1st December, 1917, Biggin Hill became an operational fighter station. Early that morning a ground crew arrived from North Weald to erect two Bessoneau hangars behind the 'Salt Box'. A few hours later 'D' Flight of 39 Squadron flew in from Hornchurch with half a dozen B.E. 2es and B.E. 12s under the command of Captain A. B. Fanstone. The aircraft were housed in one hangar, while the officers moved into bell tents inside the second where they tried in vain to imagine that the reek of their oil lamps was warmth.

Six days later they received their first alert. Shortly before 4 a.m. a field telephone buzzed with hoarse urgency beside the Duty Officer's bed: Gothas were crossing the coast between Ramsgate and Deal. Cursing the Hun for disturbing their sleep, the pilots of the three single-seater B.E. 12s hurriedly pulled flying-suits over pyjamas and stumbled outside. It was bitterly cold. The sky was clear and the moon shone frostily on the snow-covered field. With numbed fingers mechanics were struggling to warm up the congealed engines. A man ran out with a flaming torch to light up the buckets of paraffin and cotton-waste which served as a flarepath.

'Contact!'

The engines coughed, stuttered and roared into life, and for the first time local residents were woken from their sleep by the sound of aero-engines in the night. The mechanics ducked aside nimbly to avoid the icy slipstreams as the B.E. 12s taxied out, blue flames from the exhausts casting weird, flickering shadows of strut and wing on the snow. The ground crew and remaining officers wished the pilots Godspeed as they rolled between the two long rows of ruddily-smoking flares. Only when they saw the three exhausts rise up into the starry sky did they relax and seek the warmth of shelter. They could do nothing but wait.

Once airborne, the night-fighters flew into a strangely different world, three frail biplanes lost in the boundless immensity of the night with only the scattered lights of London to give a dimension of reality. Inside the cockpits the instrument lights glowed softly, the phosphorescent gun-sight a sharp reminder of their mission. Their patrol beat lay between Biggin Hill and the Thames, a great snake of silver in the moonlight. Over the city they could make out the thoroughfares with ease and identify the main-line stations by their naked naphtha flares, but the suburbs were a featureless, confusing mass. The pilots watched the searchlights probe the darkness, hoping to glimpse the elusive silvery flicker that might be a Gotha caught momentarily by the light, but they saw nothing. Away on the horizon they sometimes saw exploding anti-aircraft shells cluster like fire-flies, when the barrage opened up, but never the black silhouette of an enemy bomber. It was a vain endeavour: perhaps seventy night-fighters in all hunting in the sky over London without guidance or sight of their prey.

The searchlights were extinguished one by one. The raid was over and it was time to return to Biggin Hill. It was not easy to pick out the tiny airfield from the moonlit landscape mantled with snow. With one eye on the petrol gauge they searched for the stations, road junctions and chalk pits which were their landmarks until, at last, they saw the flickering 'L' of the flarepath blaze up to beckon them home.

'See any Hunnerinoes, sir?' asked an orderly, handing round steaming mugs of cocoa laced with rum.

'Not a sod!' one of the pilots spat disgustedly. 'I was like a blind bastard in a dark room looking for a nigger who isn't bloody well there!'

Six Gothas got through to London that night. Two were destroyed by the guns, none by the fighters.

On 22nd December there were two more raids. The three B.E. 12s went up on both occasions without sighting a single Hun.

As soon as the little band of officers had converted the hangar where they lived into a snug igloo for the winter, they received a curiously worded order to move:

. . . You will install the Officers' Quarters and the Officers' Mess in the four 60′ Armstrong huts, already completed by hangar, and find that they are much too damp and cold for use in winter. If we get a lot of snow, you will find they are absolutely uninhabitable...

The huts *were* quite uninhabitable, the Bromley-Westerham road was blocked by six-foot snow-drifts and 'Crown Ash' cottage on the far side of the road was hastily requisitioned as a Mess.

Other changes, administrative and personnel, took place. They were renumbered as a detached flight of 78 Squadron, and in a few weeks' time they were to become 141 Squadron. It was all most confusing.

Captain Fanston was posted elsewhere and Lieutenant Stockman became senior officer. Early in December Lieutenant Mockford, Wireless Officer of 39 Squadron, joined the Flight and a few days later an additional pilot arrived, Lieutenant Hardit Singh Malik,[1] a Sikh from Rawalpindi. He turned up late one night, long after the orderlies had gone off-duty, and was given an empty room in the requisitioned cottage. In the morning the other officers were woken by piercing yells, and dashed out of their rooms to see what was happening. A batman, entering the new arrival's room with shaving water, had been startled out of his wits by the turbaned and black-bearded head on the pillow, and fled before a stream of Hindustani invective from the indignant Malik.

A keen cricketer and golfer, Malik was one of the most popular officers at Biggin Hill. He staunchly refused to part with his turban and somehow managed to fit over it an outsize flying-helmet, earning the affectionate nickname of 'flying hobgoblin' from the ground crews.

Despite the unending cold, the snow and the isolation of their camp, the detached flight enjoyed holding the fort until the formation of 141 Squadron. The 'Salt Box' provided an inexhaustible supply of tea, coffee and eggs – day and night. Mr Westacott lent them his guns and horses, and hospitably kept open house at Cudham Lodge where his sisters enter-

[1] H. E. Sardar Hardit Singh Malik, C.I.E., O.B.E.

tained at musical *soirees*. If these palled, there were the pubs on Leaves Green: the 'King's Arms' and the 'Crown' where nightly the rafters rang with:

> Glorious, simply glorious!
> One keg of beer among four of us,
> Praise be to God that there are no more of us,
> For one of us could drink it all alone.

CHAPTER FOUR

'COCK' SQUADRON

SHORTLY after the New Year a start was made with the permanent buildings of the North Camp while 141 Squadron was forming at Rochford. The newly-appointed C.O., Major P. Babington, M.C.,[1] was on sick-leave at the time so the spadework was done by his future 'A' Flight Commander, twenty-year-old Captain N. H. Dimmock. Shuttling between Southend and Rochford in an old 'tin lizzie' Dimmock and the Adjutant, Lieutenant Howard, soon amassed eighty N.C.O.s and other ranks and one Sopwith Dolphin. This was a comparatively new fighter and Lieutenant Langford-Sainsbury,[2] who had just been posted to the squadron, wanted to fly it. He crashed, the Dolphin was written-off and Dimmock had to ring up Babington in hospital and tell him they were out of flying machines for the time being.

The nucleus of the new squadron joined forces with the detached flight at Biggin Hill on 8th February. Babington took command nine days later and the squadron was rapidly brought to strength. Complete strangers at first who had all

[1] Later Air Marshal Sir Philip Babington, K.C.B., M.C., A.F.C.
[2] Later Air Vice Marshal T. A. Langford-Sainsbury, C.B., O.B.E., D.F.C., A.F.C.

volunteered purposefully for the Royal Flying Corps, the original fighter pilots of Biggin Hill included, besides Malik the Sikh, men from Australia, Canada, New Zealand, Rhodesia, the Argentine, as well as the United Kingdom. Their average age was twenty-one. Many had returned as hardened veterans from the Western Front where a pilot's expectancy of life was barely eleven days. They believed whole-heartedly in 'a short life but a merry one', finding relief from the strain of flying in wild, uninhibited play – to the amusement, and discomfort, of local residents. Inevitably a fierce, though friendly, rivalry sprang up between the two camps on Biggin Hill: the fighter pilots and the wireless 'wizards'.

Near to the 'Black Horse' in the village stood a teashop with a monstrously large wooden teapot hanging over the entrance. The temptation was great, a moonlight raiding party was dispatched by 141 Squadron to acquire this trophy and smuggle it privily into the North Camp. In the morning, news of this deed reached the South Camp. The officers of the W.E.E. were furious. As primordial settlers on Biggin Hill they claimed priority on all such spoils of war. A counter-raid was organised and the teapot swiftly abducted; each night it was frenziedly transported to and fro across the airfield until neither side was certain of its whereabouts. A truce was called when the owner of the teashop arrived to collect his property. The teapot, now much battered and chipped, was placed in honour on a lorry and escorted to the shop by a party of officers. High teas for all were ordered, paid for twice over and everybody was happy – for a few hours.

That night the teapot vanished again. This was too much for the proprietor, who called in the local constabulary. The logical suspect was 141 Squadron but, for once, the fighter pilots were innocent; it was the W.E.E. which had taken the initiative. As retribution for this injustice, 141 Squadron planned to steal the motor roller used for keeping the grass apron in front of the South Camp hangars smooth and trim. The operation was conducted at dead of night, but the raiders reckoned without the softness of the airfield. Came the dawn and there, midfield, stood their prize irremovably buried in mud!

For the first month at Biggin Hill 141 Squadron had a mixed bag of aircraft. Besides the B.E. 2es and B.E. 12s, there was a solitary Sopwith Pup,[1] a Bristol Fighter, a Vickers Vampire 3-gun pusher and one flight of Dolphins – a much-disliked machine. Powered by a notoriously unreliable Hispano-Suiza engine, its single cockpit was placed so high between the wings that it could only be entered through the top plane. If a Dolphin turned over on its back in a crash, as once happened to Lieutenant Malik, the pilot was trapped, unable to move, with a fair chance of being burnt alive.

In March the squadron was re-equipped with Bristol Fighters, a first-rate aircraft for its day – the Hurricane of the first World War. With a 250 h.p. Rolls-Royce Falcon engine it could fly at 120 m.p.h. and reach 20,000 feet. Being a two-seater, the squadron's observer strength was increased. Each unit in the Royal Flying Corps had its 'madman'. a pilot who flew with a reckless disregard for his own safety, and 141 Squadron was no exception. It was Lieutenant Essell's particular joy to give observers who had never flown before, their first flight.

'That man,' stammered one observer in the thick accents of Quebec. 'He takey me up . . . He makey ze loop . . . He tell me noddings . . . He is a buggaire!'

Essell roared with laughter and escorted his victim to the Mess for a drink.

Biggin Hill was now a key station in the London Air Defence Area with responsibility for the North Kent sector. As the Germans only ventured to raid during the hours of darkness, 141 became a squadron of night-fighters patrolling a beat between Biggin Hill and the Thames at Joyce Green. When the decision was taken to equip one of the home

[1]Babington regarded the Pup very much as his own 'baby'. Salvaged after being technically written-off, it appeared on no charge lists and therefore had no official existence until the G.O.C. got wind of it and ordered it 'reduced to produce'.

defence squadrons with wireless telephony in an attempt to guide the pilots to the enemy in the dark, it was natural that the squadron sharing Biggin Hill with the W.E.E. should be chosen as 'guinea-pig'.

The scheme was a straightforward development of the work of Lieutenant Furnival and his colleagues in 1917: both ground-to-air and air-to-air telephony were to be employed. Information on the enemy's movements was fed into an Operations Room in the North Camp from coastguard stations, observer posts searchlight and gun sites, as well as patrolling aircraft. This data was sorted and coordinated so that the raiders' positions could be plotted with a fair degree of accuracy. The courses and altitudes that the pilots would have to fly to make an interception were computed and passed to the ground transmitter at Aperfield Court for relaying by wireless telephone to the patrolling Bristol Fighters.[1]

Thus, in all essentials, there was established at Biggin Hill in 1918 the forerunner of the sector control system that played so decisive a role in the Battle of Britain. Ground-to-air control of fighters was a revolutionary concept for 1918 and weeks of hard training were required to perfect the system.

To avoid needless interference with the work of the W.E.E., 141 Squadron's wireless-practice flights were ordered some distance away from Biggin Hill. It had been discovered that excellent meals were to be had at the Railway Hotel, Staplehurst, only a mile from an emergency landing ground at Marden. The practice flights scheduled for the latter part of the morning became suddenly popular and the number of emergency landings rose alarmingly – all at lunch-time! The landlord was trained to count the Bristol Fighters which circled his hotel, multiply by two and dispatch the requisite transport to collect his guests. This admirable arrangement continued for several weeks until the day when the Commander of 49 Wing landed at Marden with engine

[1]Each aircraft carried a receiver, but only the flight commanders had wireless telephone transmitters.

trouble on a flight from the South Coast to Wing H.Q. He was taken aback to find half a dozen Bristol Fighters neatly parked there and enquired the reason from the N.C.O. in charge.

'These Brisfits, sir?' replied the sergeant in all innocence. 'They come 'ere daily, regular as clockwork and usually more than this lot!'

Thereafter it was rissoles and 'Zepps on a cloud' for lunch, taken in the Mess at Biggin Hill.

To ensure close cooperation between the ground defences and 141 Squadron, the Headquarters of No. 17 A.A. Coy of the Royal Engineers moved to the North Camp. This Company had sixteen searchlights deployed over North Kent to illuminate the enemy bombers for the fighters to attack or, failing this, to give an approximate indication of their whereabouts with a concentration of beams. Only on the clearest nights did the searchlight crews attempt to find the raiders by eye; during the winter months, when fog and cloud were prevalent, the order was given: 'Point to sound!' With eyes shut and stethoscopes clamped to their ears, the two operators of the sound detector on each site slowly rotated the four massive trumpets, swivelling in pairs on the horizontal and vertical axes, until they picked up the beat of aeroengines. Listening intently, they balanced the sound between their left and right ears until the two vibrations merged into a single intense pain in the centre of the forehead. They were on target.

'Expose the light!'

The shutter of the searchlight was flung open and a dazzling beam of light leaped skywards. On rare occasions the crew was rewarded with a Gotha caught squarely in the beam; more frequently the light was dissipated by mist and cloud while the raider droned on tauntingly above the overcast. This did not, however, mean total failure. The sound detector continued to track the unseen enemy, flying at 10,000 feet or more, until it passed within range of the next searchlight. The atmosphere played strange tricks with the sound waves: moisture temperature-changes and the wind all combined to falsify the true position of the bomber. Corrections were made and the estimated bearing and altitude passed by telephone to Biggin Hill where one man, simultaneously in touch with all sixteen searchlight sites, recorded the incoming messages on slips of paper for the R.E. officers who, croupier-wise, manipulated aircraft-symbols across the plotting table in the Operations Room – a glorified office in a wooden hut. When their positions had been pinpointed, an R.F.C. officer telephoned the interception courses and altitudes to Aperfield Court for transmission by wireless telephony.

This system worked well in rehearsal with two or three Bristol Fighters simulating Gothas over North Kent, but it broke down disastrously during the first heavy raid. With more than twenty German aircraft converging on London at once, the plotters were overwhelmed by a snowstorm of message-forms and the pilots received their directions long after the bombs had been dropped and the raiders were winging home. Much better results were achieved when the Army's passion for recording every message on paper was ignored and the plotters were given head-sets linking each man directly with a group of searchlight and gun sites.

141 Squadron kept hard at it with endless hours of formation-flying by day and night, improving the technique of interception and exercising the blindfolded operators of the detectors in 'pointing to sound'. These training flights were tedious and uneventful, but the resourceful pilots had their own means of enlivening them:

I remember (recalls Dimmock) doing many formation-flights round the A.A. batteries during the day to give the gunners practice at aiming and to give us practice in formation-flying. Essell and Langford-Sainsbury were always very close on either side of me, but one day I missed Essell. At that time, as 'A' Flight Commander, I had for swank a very long streamer on my tail – about three or four sewn together and that madman Essell was flying below and behind me, trying to catch hold of the end of my streamer. I threw an empty Very cartridge at him which hit his top plane. We used to get very bored flying around all morning in formation, so to pass the time we would pretend to be a band. I would brace up in the front seat and tap the wing prior to conducting, and everyone would go through the motions of playing one instrument or other.

The two R.E. officers[1] from the 17th A.A. Coy who lived in the North Camp were quickly indoctrinated into 141 Squadron. In the eyes of the Army, life with the fighter pilots was the equivalent of active service, so they were able to use field kit and thereby draw field allowances – 'living under false pretences' complained their brother officers roughing it on the bleak and lonely searchlight sites. During their first week at the Mess, they were greatly puzzled at meal times by their immediate neighbours' lack of appetite and insistent refusal of all main courses. The Army had neglected to forward the A.A. Coy's rations and 141 Squadron were politely making sure that their guests, officers and men, did not go hungry.

As 1st April approached, the date set for the formation of the Royal Air Force, the fighter pilot and wireless officers found themselves, for once in complete harmony. Fiercely proud of the traditions of the Royal Flying Corps, they resented the forthcoming merger with the Royal Naval Air Service which was, in their opinion, a circus that flew gas-bags and obsolescent aircraft looking for submarines. It was unthinkable that every one of the 'flying sailors' was to gain in rank in the Royal Air Force simply because the Navy was senior to the Army.

'Just don't let 'em send any of those bell-bottomed buggers to our squadron' was 141's prayer. 'They had better be a very Silent Service if they come near us!'

They scorned the new titles chosen for R.A.F. ranks and ridiculed the motley uniforms they were asked to wear, until the culminating insult of Air Force blue became standardised

[1]Captain F. W. 'Monty' Herring and Lieutenant H. Bellman.

– 'The Final prostitution of the Royal Flying Corps to the amorous advances of the sailor!' was their heartfelt criticism of the new colour.

On the last day of April, Major Babington entered hospital with injuries from a crash-landing one foggy night, and Major B. E. Baker, D.S.O., M.C.,[1] was posted in his place as acting C.O. Babington never returned and a month later Baker was confirmed in his command. Coming from 48 Squadron in France the avowed opponents of the Richthofen Circus, Baker was a great leader and an immensely popular commander. Under him 141 Squadron matured into a highly efficient and very happy unit; the three flights of Bristol Fighters, commanded by Captains Dimmock, Rawson and Slingsby, were now fully operational with wireless telephony, the ground defences smoothly integrated with the Operations Room and everyone was eager to match their prowess against the Hun, who disobligingly refrained from raiding London.

They were the first exponents of a new form of aerial defence and, as pioneers, paid a tragic toll in wrecked aircraft and loss of life. One night, as he was about to take-off in a B.E. 2e for a searchlight exercise, Lieutenant Castle was summoned to the telephone. It was a lovely night for flying and Lieutenant Pownall willingly took his place. Whilst telephoning, Castle heard the roar of the engine fade away into the distance and then swell to a harsh crescendo as Pownall returned and flew low over the North Camp before the beat changed, became sickeningly irregular and abruptly ceased. After an eternity of silence, there came a muffled explosion from the depths of the valley to the west of the aerodrome. Castle ran outside and stared aghast at the ominous red glow pulsing beyond the trees, a plume of black smoke veiling the stars. There was little anyone could do, the aircraft was a twisted mass of glowing wreckage. When the embers had cooled to ash and Pownall's remains had been removed, the small body of a pigeon was found, roasted on the pyre.

[1]Later Air Marshal Sir Brian Baker, K.B.E., C.B., D.S.O., M.C., A.F.C.

All too frequently the squadron marched in slow time to the Funeral March, bearing a coffin for burial in the little graveyard on the road to Keston beneath the airman's cross – a four-bladed wooden propeller cut short, his name and rank engraved on a brass plaque affixed to the boss. The 'Last Post' sounded, they returned at a brisker tempo, swinging along to 'Colonel Bogey', or singing their own cheerful requiem for the dead:

> A brave aviator lay dying
> And as on his death-bed he lay, he lay,
> To his swearing mechanics around him
> These last dying words did he say.
>
> Take the cylinder out of my kidneys,
> The connecting rod out of my brain,
> From the small of my back take the gear-box
> And assemble the engine again.
>
> So gather up quickly the fragments
> And when you've returned them to store,
> Write a letter to Seely[1] and tell him
> His 141st is no more.
>
> When the Court of Enquiry assembles,
> Please tell them the reason I died,
> Was because I forgot twice iota
> Was the maximum angle of glide.
>
> So when I am dead I'll be joining
> The Flying Corps up in the sky.
> Let's hope that they've studied iota
> And the wings that they give me will fly!

The opportunity which 141 Squadron so impatiently awaited came on the night of 19th May, 1918. It was Whit Sunday and conditions were wholly favourable for a raid. A

[1] Major-General Seely, Under Secretary of State for Air.

45

waxing moon shone in a sky that was cloudless from horizon to zenith, and the light breeze scarcely rustled the young leaves on the trees in London squares. The previous night had been equally fine and Trenchard's bombers had struck at railways, barracks and munition plants in Cologne.

Shortly after 10.30 p.m. holiday-makers at Margate heard the beat of a twin-engined aircraft flying in from across the Channel to circle overhead. Several minutes later the throngs on the promenade and swimmers enjoying a moonlight bathe saw a brilliant flare float down over the sea. It was the signal for the attack to commence; within half an hour two streams of bombers were converging on London. For this, the biggest raid of the war, the Germans had mustered forty-three aircraft: thirty-eight Gothas, three Giants and two smaller types. They crossed the coast at five-minute intervals, flying up the Thames Estuary and inland across North Kent. The warning maroons were fired in London, but few Londoners took shelter, preferring to stay above ground and watch the spectacle of the greatly increased defences in action. Innumerable searchlights swept the sky, criss-crossing and sometimes concentrating like a host of accusing fingers. The barrage was incessant; to the spectators the flashes of the guns seemed to weave a protective circle of fire around the capital. They saw the bursting shells as tiny points of light and thrice the sudden kindling of a flame which plunged downwards in a fiery dive. Bombs were scattered widely as the enemy weaved to avoid the fury of the defences. In Sydenham a drunken Irish soldier staggered out of a pub and shouted derisively: 'Go to it, Jerry!' Thirty seconds later he, and eighteen others, lay dead in the roadway.

Within five minutes of the first bomber being detected offshore, the Operations Room at Biggin Hill was alerted and 141 Squadron's Bristol Fighters took-off. After the long weeks of training the control system worked with heartening efficiency. By the radar-controlled standards of the second World War it was primitive enough, but it saved the pilots from an aimless meandering through the darkness and directed them to within a few miles of their slow-flying quarry.

Lieutenants E. E. Turner and H. B. Barwise, pilot and observer respectively of a 'Brisfit' from 141 Squadron, were flying at 12,000 feet over Downe, two miles east of Biggin Hill, when they glanced up and there, masking the moon, was a Gotha. It was returning to Belgium after dropping bombs on Rotherhithe, Peckham and the Old Kent Road. Keeping his eye on the glowing exhausts of the Hun, Turner swung away, climbing to gain altitude and screamed down, pulling up steeply to pour a stream of incendiary tracer and armour-piercing bullets into the Gotha's belly while Barwise raked it from nose to tail with his Lewis gun. Nothing happened. No tongues of flame appeared to start licking the engines and fuselage. Disappointed, Turner manoeuvred swiftly for a second attack but the German pilot, sensing the fighter on his tail, sideslipped steeply to upset it with his slipstream and vanished into the obscurity. With one engine hit and streaming petrol, the Gotha was losing height rapidly when it was attacked again, this time by Major Sowrey, C.O. of 143 Squadron, in a Camel. He fired two drums of tracer and wounded the pilot before his guns jammed. Completely out of control, the Gotha drifted on down and crashed on Harrietsham aerodrome. Pilot and navigator were killed outright, the rear gunner escaped with a broken arm.

There was no victory celebration at Biggin Hill that night. When they landed and reported, Turner and Barwise were greeted with the depressing news that Sowrey had already claimed the Gotha. The whole squadron waited in suspense while Wing H.Q. investigated. Which had attacked first, the 'Brisfit' or the Camel? Twenty-four hours later it was drinks for all in the Mess: Biggin Hill had been accredited its first 'kill'. The Gotha's rear gunner had confirmed that Turner and Barwise had caused the fatal damage. When he could make himself heard above the congratulatory uproar, Major Baker read out a message from the Lord Mayor of London:

The citizens of London are filled with admiration and gratitude for the splendid defensive measures taken by the Air Services against the enemy's attack, and will be glad if their appreciation and thanks may be conveyed to those who gallantly and successfully protected the capital on that occasion.

Both men were awarded the D.F.C. for their victory; Turner received the Gotha's Spandau gun[1] as a memento, Barwise one of the propellers, and the black Maltese cross was hung in the Mess at the North Camp.

Of the forty-three bombers that took-off from the Belgian airfields that night, only nineteen succeeded in reaching the heart of London. Eighty-four night-fighters went up to intercept and the anti-aircraft batteries fired off 30,000 rounds; three raiders were shot down by the fighters, three by the guns and a further two crashed with engine trouble.

This was the last great air raid of the war, the Germans tacitly admitted that the defences had mastered the bomber and hid their chagrin behind a non-committal communique:

Berlin, 20th May, 9.15 p.m.
Last night London, and also Dover and other places on the English coast were successfully attacked with bombs.

With no further enemy activity to occupy the squadron, the summer months passed very slowly. To keep everyone fit and keen, Baker started daily rugger games and cross-country paper-chases. He introduced tight formation-flying, wing-tip inside wing-tip, and borrowed a captured A.E.G. bomber to give the operators of sound detectors practice with German aero-engines. This was the first twin-engined machine that many in the squadron had ever seen. It could carry up to six and, after the confinement of a Bristol Fighter, was greatly in demand for joy-riding until the propeller of one engine flew off while a hilarious game of airborne rummy was being played. The machine went into a

[1]Today still an honoured trophy of 141 Squadron.

48

tight spin but Baker, who was at the controls, cut the second engine and managed to land the badly shaken gamblers. To no one's regret the A.E.G. was then and there condemned to the scrap heap.

The young officers had little to do but dream up ways of making life at Biggin Hill more enjoyable and lively. Flying became more reckless and crashes more frequent. Each aircraft carried a magnificent eight-day watch mounted on the instrument panel and, as might be expected, these swiftly vanished after a crash. One summer evening Lieutenant Aubert, the Equipment Officer, plaintively announced that his deficit of watches had reached serious proportions and something had to be done about it. The obvious solution was to transfer his worries to the W.E.E., so an ambitious clandestine raid was planned. The raiders managed to elude the armed sentries of the W.E.E., enter the locked hangars and unscrew the watches from the aircraft there in total darkness. It was a complete success, though the C.O. was forced to spend several uncomfortable minutes hiding himself in a barrel from a suspicious sentry.

For many there was nothing to do but drink, and each evening saw a rowdy session in the Mess. To curb this, Wing Headquarters instituted a system of payment by voucher but there were ways around that. When the number of broken windows became too great, Baker, as P.M.C., announced a fine of 1s. 6d. per pane. This infuriated a Canadian pilot, Lieutenant Bushe, who walked round the Mess next evening kicking out the remaining glass and chanting: 'One and six, Mr P.M.C. . . . Three shillings, Mr P.M.C. . . . Four and six, Mr P.M.C. . . . ' until he had incurred a fine of several pounds. Someone then decided that he did not like the tone of the hired piano, so the offending instrument was taken outside and swiftly disembowelled. There was, however, a sequel to this critical gesture:

Next day Baker called us together. His spy at H.Q. had told him that word of the smashery had reached the General and he was *en route* to Biggin Hill. We were to remove panes from the cooking and service rooms where the General would be unlikely to go and transfer them to the Mess with the greatest possible speed. The piano case was to be polished up and framed photographs from our bedrooms stood on top. That might prevent the Great Man from looking inside. Let's pray he doesn't touch the keys!

You could have heard the proverbial pin drop as the General edged over towards the piano, looked quizzically at it and decided that he had been misinformed.

The sigh of relief as he got into his car was the signal for a witch-hunt. Who was the sneak? By God! It must be that Clerk of the Works who never did like our habits. Let's deal with him! The mob found him in his little office hut, locked him in and did a war dance round and round it, unwinding reels of barbed wire as they went until the hut looked like a cocoon. How, indeed whether, he ever got out, nobody cared.[1]

The roisterers were most perturbed when a W.R.A.F. officer was posted to the North Camp to take charge of the girls who cooked and served their meals. To be waited on by good-natured, bosomly 'Blondie' and 'Dirty Neck' was fine, but to have a lady officer dining with them would never do. For several weeks the squadron stalwarts held her at bay until she courageously insisted on her rights and took her place in the Officers' Mess. The evening riots became subdued, good-manneredly romps!

Striking while the iron was hot, Baker started a suggestions-book for ways and means of making the Mess more comfortable and attractive. This was a heaven-sent opportunity for the squadron humorists who waited for Baker to read out the latest suggestions after dinner and ask for comments.

'Cannot these everlasting rissoles for breakfast be varied? Signed. R. Suppards.'

In complete silence Baker looked round and inquired:

[1]Related by F. S. Mockford.

'Who is R. Suppards?'

The gale of laughter which greeted his query was the cue for a concerted recitation of 141 Squadron's epic 'Epitaph on the vault of Richard Suppards.'

> A pious mortal and a wise,
> Who never cheated or told lies,
> Beneath this marble tablet lies,
>
>   R. Suppards
>
> Beloved by all the friends he knew,
> He kept an inn and wealthy grew,
> His sign, an angel, grandly flew,
>
>   R. Suppards
>
> Great store of friends he had but that
> He loved the most his tabby cat,
> He kissed and fondled as she sat,
>
>   R. Suppards
>
> But sadly Richard's life was ended,
> By falling from a beam he mended,
> Upon a fence he hung suspended,
>
>   R. Suppards
>
> They took him down, in white arrayed him,
> They shaved his head and tidy made him,
> And sadly in the grass they laid him,
>
>   R. Suppards
>
> And though his form is laid in night,
> And though his bones are out of sight,
> His virtue still will come to light,
>
>   R. Suppards

In France the war was entering on its last, crucial stages and the squadrons there were putting up a magnificent show while those at home fretted at their enforced inactivity with the near certainty of no further raids. To keep up their morale the General Commanding the VIth (London defence) Brigade, Brig.-Gen. T. C. R. Higgins, organised a Squadrons-at-Arms competition. Points were to be awarded for proficiency in formation-flying, aerobatics, wireless telephony and gunnery as well as a *Concours d'Elegance* of aircraft and the appearance and upkeep of airfields and station buildings. The winning squadron would be awarded a silver cup, the title of 'Cock' Squadron and the right to emblazon a fighting cock on their aircraft.

This competition had little appeal for 141 Squadron, aloofly disdaining it as 'kid's stuff'. Only a few days before the eliminating contests Baker suddenly decided that not only were they going to enter, they were going to win! Everyone knew that he meant what he said, all rowdyism ceased as under his drive they worked as never before. The North Camp was still unfinished, the ground littered with debris, but officers and men toiled through the hot September days shovelling earth, cutting turf, making verges neat with white-painted stones. Someone had a great inspiration: they must have trees and shrubs. There were none on the site, but the squadron's experience of midnight pilfering solved that problem. On Inspection Day trees and shrubs grew in profusion where none had stood before; fortunately the adjudicating General had an unsuspicious mind and he failed to detect the sawn-off stems beneath the soil – 141 Squadron received top marks for station upkeep and appearance!

Thus encouraged, the squadron swept through to the finals which took place on 22nd September, 1918, at Sutton's Farm in Essex, an aerodrome belonging to 78 Squadron which had already been knocked out of the competition. The Air Ministry made it a gala occasion with over one hundred aircraft on the field and many distinguished visitors including Lord Weir, Minister of Air, and a galaxy of 'brass hats' from the London Air Defence Area.

At the start things went badly for 141 Squadron, they were outpointed in formation-flying and the race to get airborne from a klaxon signal. Then came gunnery from a diving aircraft at a ground target. Each squadron entered one pilot who was allowed three dives from a maximum height of 1,000 feet. 141 Squadron's opponents made moderate scores and the men from Biggin Hill began to cheer up, confident that Lieutenant Langford-Sainsbury, their chosen marksman, would regain for them the lead in points. After a dozen rounds on the first dive his guns jammed. Baker and the others watched tensely while he circuited and cleared the stoppage. Once again his guns jammed. The squadron was in despair. No one spoke, all eyes were on Langford-Sainsbury as he lined up his Bristol Fighter for the third and final dive. As shallow as possible, he swooped down with Vickers' guns blazing, so low that he ripped the target in twain with his tail skid!

141 Squadron's jubilation was cut short by their rivals' appeal against this unorthodox way of destroying the target. Langford-Sainsbury was ordered to make one more dive on a new target. He riddled this without further incident. The squadron breathed a sigh of relief, they were on top again.

The final event was the test for proficiency in wireless telephony. Each squadron was to put up one flight of six aircraft whose crews had to receive and write down messages transmitted from Aperfield Court. With their experience of wireless telephony 141 Squadron felt certain of winning and so gaining the coveted title of 'Cock' Squadron. General Higgins noticed their boisterous self-confidence. With a sardonic smile he opened a copy of that day's *Times* and selected a real tongue-twisting text:

The Japanese military attache in London has received information to the effect that Blakovestshesk and Alexeievsk were occupied by Japanese cavalry convering from Khabarevsk and Tsitsikhar on 18th September.

Mockford blanched when he heard this, none of his crews could possibly guess these words from the context, but to his consternation they all landed with the message word-perfect. There was an uproar of protest: what 141 Squadron had done was impossible. Mockford was closely questioned, as the squadron's Wireless Officer he was undoubtedy friendly with the Aperfield Court staff but he swore that he did not, and could not, have given his crews the text in advance. Another test was ordered. Once again the crews of 141 Squadron landed with the message almost word-perfect.

They had won the competition. Major Baker received the silver trophy and a live fighting cock from the hands of Lord Weir, and a plaque conferring the soubriquet of 'Cock' Squadron. After celebrating their triumph, they all took-off for Biggin Hill. Captain Harry Slingsby let fire with his Very pistol in a valedictory gesture as he circuited Sutton's Farm. One light fell blazing on to the tent sheltering Lord Weir and his guests, the canvas burst into flames and sent a bevy of 'brass hats' scurrying out into the open.

At Biggin Hill there was no cheering mob of ground crew to greet the 'Cock' Squadron, only a sad flight sergeant with the news that one Bristol Fighter had crashed on the return flight, both the pilot and observer were dead.

With its proximity to London and the reputation of the squadrons stationed there, Biggin Hill has probably received more official and distinguished visitors than any other station in the Royal Air Force. The first of these visits took place shortly after the Squadrons-at-Arms Competition when 'Cock' Squadron was reviewed, ironically enough, by a future enemy but then an ally – Prince Yorihito of Higashi Fushimi. The weather, as so often on these occasions, was atrocious and much of the programme was abandoned. Huddled up in his greatcoat, the diminutive Japanese Prince was shown round the station, inspected the Handley Page 0/400 which had made the first wireless D/F flight to Paris and back, and, despite the low cloud and rain, watched a squadron fly-past with the cock crests in red and gold gleaming proudly through the murk.

Early in the morning of 11th November a drowsy wireless operator at Aperfield Court with nothing better to do, tuned into the Eiffel Tower station and picked up the message:

Marshal Foch to C.-in-C.s
Hostilities will cease on the whole Front as from Nov. 11th at 11 o'clock (French time).

The excited operator told Colonel Blandy who passed on the tidings to Major Baker and the local padres. In a few minutes the bells of Cudham and Westerham were pealing merrily, the first in all Britain to proclaim the end of hostilities. John Westacott heard them in Cudham Lodge and galloped across to the North Camp, sounding the 'View Hulloo' as he rode his hunter round and round the billiard table in the Mess. The Wireless Flight pilots brought out their aircraft and gave joy-rides to all the girls on Biggin Hill. Both Blandy and Baker announced a day's leave for all and soon everyone was heading towards the West End.

Many arrived in London before the news was generally known. The sober residents of the Savoy were scandalised when a party from Biggin Hill burst in, whooping like Indians and demanding champagne at ten in the morning. By eleven all London was caught up in a whirlwind of rejoicing such as had never been seen since Mafeking Night. Officers from 141 Squadron exuberantly dragged the guns in Hyde Park down the Mall and left them lying under the Admiralty Arch. In the Strand they climbed on the roof of a taxi caught in the crowds and danced until it collapsed. Then they drove to the Criterion and jammed the taxi in the entrance where it burst into flames. Mistaking a workman's hut for a Y.M.C.A. coffee bar that wouldn't serve coffee, the 'Cock' Squadron pilots started a bonfire in Trafalgar Square which has left its scars on the base of Nelson's Column to this day. Later that night the two units from Biggin Hill, the fighter pilots and the wireless officers, had a rendezvous at the Savoy. They took over the band and formed a wild crocodile dancing through and over, the tables reserved for generals and 'red tabs'. An elderly guest, watching the fun with a tolerant eye, enjoyed himself so much that he footed the bill for all the broken crockery and glass.

Next day London was out of bounds to all officers and other ranks. Someone pointed out that Croydon was not in London and immediately there was a mass-exodus from Biggin Hill. At the 'Empire' Lieutenant Essell, a 'Ladies' notice around his neck, led a parade through the stalls and on to the stage, blowing loud 'raspberries' through the nozzles of fire hoses. The last two acts of the show were hurriedly cancelled and the curtain rung down on 'Cock' Squadron.

CHAPTER FIVE

INSTRUMENT DESIGN

SOME weeks after the Armistice there occurred one of the more remarkable episodes in the history of Biggin Hill: a mutiny by the men of the Wireless Experimental Establishment.

Now that the war was over, there was little sense of urgency in wireless research and many N.C.O.s and other ranks were impatient to be demobilised. In the return to civilian life, priority was rightfully given to those who had seen active service; as weeks dragged by and no positive announcement was made about their future, the men of the W.E.E. felt they had been altogether forgotten. Thousands of others were discarding their uniforms and taking jobs in 'Civvy street' while they, quite literally, were stuck in the mud on Biggin Hill.

Living conditions at the South Camp were appalling. The civilian contractors had demolished most of the wooden huts, but were doing little to replace them. An atmosphere of apathy and post-war inertia hung over the site and some 500 men were compelled in midwinter to live under canvas, or in the few leaking, indescribably filthy huts that remained. They had no baths, no heating, nowhere to wash and dry clothes. It rained unceasingly, a canvas Bessoneau hangar with its roof in tatters served as a dining hall, the benches and tables were saturated and stood in three inches of mud. The kitchen was an open shed of rusting iron some yards away. All duck-boards had long been burnt as fuel and orderlies had to slither ankle-deep through mud often falling, food and all, into the morass.

One evening in January, 1919, after a particularly foul and unsatisfying meal, the men met to discuss their plight. They had frequently complained to higher authority without effect, now they decided that only strike-action could bring about an improvement. Irishmen and some malcontents who bawled the 'Red Flag' at the tops of their voices demanded a show of violence, but were out-voted by a sober majority who, while regretting the strike, supported it as their only recourse.

At breakfast next morning word was passed round that no one should report for duty. When the Orderly Officer came to inspect the dining hall, he was courteously but firmly turned back by a sergeant and two men who refused to recognise his authority. This was mutiny! The startled officer hurried off to report to the C.O. and the men thoughtfully removed the magnetos from all vehicles including the contractors' so that the labourers, whose indolence was the cause of half the trouble, were forced to walk to the South Camp. At the other end of Biggin Hill 141 Squadron was fully aware of what was going on but declined to interfere in the W.E.E.'s domestic affairs.

On New Year's Day Wing Commander Grenfell, D.S.O., had been posted to command the W.E.E. and was taking over from Colonel Blandy when the men came out on strike. Feeling that the new C.O. could know nothing of the circumstances behind their action, the strikers insisted on seeing Blandy, still resident in 'Koonowla'. After considerately allowing him time to enjoy breakfast, a deputation called to present their case. Blandy, wise man, let his prettiest maid-servant wait on the men before he saw them. Charmed by her smiles, the hot-heads dropped their bellicose plan for marching down Piccadilly, stoning every window they passed, and politely handed in a list of demands to be granted before they returned to discipline.

PROPOSITIONS PUT FORWARD BY THE MEN OF THE W.E.E.

1. NO MAN TO BE VICTIMISED.
2. Unless we receive a satisfactory answer from the Commandant we will put our case before Lord Weir, i.e. our deputation will proceed to his quarters.

   (a) The men state that when they go 'sick' the Medical Officer says that their complaints are due to the disgraceful conditions of the camp food and sanitary arrangements.

   (b) Names of the men who can bear witness to the above statement can be supplied if necessary.

   (c) We demand that Major —— shall be dismissed from this unit.

   (d) Leave to be carried on in the normal way.

   (e) The men demand that they leave the camp until it is put into a habitable condition by the civilian employees.

   (f) Temporary release for those men who have jobs waiting and those who want to get jobs pending discharge. While the men are at home demobilisation must continue, and the men be advised by letter or telegram.

   (g) Abolition of work on Saturday afternoons and Sundays.

   (h) Restrictions placed on Y.M.C.A. to be removed, prices in canteen to be lowered and a full explanation given as to what happens to P.R.I. funds.

   (i) Efficient transport to be provided for officers, N.C.O.s and men.

3. Grievances.
   Sanitary: (a) Wash-house – only 5 basins for 500 men.
   (b) Wet feet – No gum boots issued.
   (c) Dirty and leaking huts.
   (d) NO BATHS.

58

Food:
- (e) Inefficient latrines.
- (a) Shortage.
- (b) Badly cooked.
- (c) Dirty cookhouse staff.
- (d) Dining hall in a disgraceful condition.
- (e) Fully trained cooks should be substituted for present incompetent and inefficient youths.

THESE DEMANDS TO BE CONCEDED BY NOON TODAY

Although no longer his concern, Blandy had been expecting something like this. He had repeatedly reported the conditions at the South Camp but the Air Ministry, harassed by the switch to peacetime conditions and with the future of the Royal Air Force unsettled, had little time for the case of the W.E.E. Speaking from experience, Blandy advised the deputation not to waste the Minister's time but to go direct to the General Commanding the South-East Area which included Biggin Hill, and volunteered to accompany them, *ex-officio*, to support their case. The men accepted his offer, replaced the magnetos in sufficient vehicles and set off for Area H.Q. in Covent Garden. Meanwhile the Camp remained out on strike.

The General was greatly upset when he learned a deputation from Biggin Hill was coming to see him and he refused to have anything to do with them. An officer of the old school, he had little sympathy with the labour unrest sweeping post-war Britain. Discipline must be maintained at all times and he could make no conciliatory gestures. His young and energetic second-in-command, Brig.-Gen. A. C. H. McLean, heard of the mutiny and obtained permission to handle the men in his own way. Without referring to the breach of discipline, he listened to their grievances, confirmed with Blandy that they were substantially true and promised an immediate investigation.

At Biggin Hill the strike committee showed McLean round the South Camp. He was shocked by what he found and interviewed the contractors who glibly promised to put everything right within six weeks, during which time the unfortunate men would presumably continue to live under the same conditions. The committee rejected this and McLean made the builders promise, under threat of cancellation of all contracts, to do their best in ten days. Calling together all the officers and men of the W.E.E. he announced: 'The entire station will go on leave as from noon today, but don't expect to find a "Savoy Hotel" on your return.'

A vote of thanks was passed unanimously and the men returned to discipline. Volunteers helped the Transport Officer prepare the travel warrants and within a few hours the South Camp was deserted except for the labourers who started to work harder than ever before. All in all, it was a very gentlemanly mutiny.

On their return from leave the men found the South Camp greatly improved and there was no more trouble.

The drive for post-war economy forced the Air Ministry to reorganise all research for the Royal Air Force in order to achieve the best results from the smaller resources now available. At the end of the war there were four R.A.F. stations concerned with experimental work of various kinds: Martlesham Heath, Orfordness, Isle of Grain and Biggin Hill. To cut expenditure it was decided to concentrate at one station all research into signals, wireless, instruments, navigation and meteorology. Since Martlesham Heath and Orfordness were already bespoken for other purposes, this meant a choice of Grain or Biggin Hill.

Colonel Blandy, now Deputy Director of Communications at the Air Ministry, was inclined to prefer Grain. Although further from London than Biggin Hill, it already had extensive, solid buildings and ample facilities for seaplanes and flying-boats, but the many wireless stations nearby would undoubtedly interfere with wireless research. Biggin Hill, on the other hand, had a permanent wireless station on the highest ground in the London area, with a large technical laboratory and women's hostel under construction. Its disadvantages were poor access by road and rail, the impossibility of seaplane work and the unsuitability of the grass airfield for heavy aircraft in wintertime. The Director of Research, however, Air Commodore Brooke-Popham,[1] had no hesitation in choosing Biggin Hill, and the Wireless Experimental Establishment was renamed the Instrument Design Establishment – I.D.E. in short.

To make the decision was easy, to get approval for the expenditure was more difficult and a brisk exchange of minutes ensued between the Air Council and the Treasury. The latter suggested that it would be far more economical to have all the research carried out by civilians, either the Department of Scientific and Industrial Research or private firms. They failed to appreciate the amount of flying involved, which could only be done by the Royal Air Force, and the fundamental importance to aviation in general of the projected Instrument Design Establishment. This was emphatically pointed out in a minute by Brooke-Popham:

> . . . If Great Britain is to maintain the lead it at present holds in the production of aeronautical instruments of all kinds and if Air Ministry is to retain the confidence of the aircraft industry there is no alternative but to have a well-equipped establishment such as is proposed at Biggin Hill and to provide a well-paid staff to secure that experiments and researches are conducted on the right lines. The development of civil aviation depends largely on the progress made with aerial navigation, and this in its turn depends largely on the progress made at Biggin Hill in developing and producing aeronautical instruments . . .

'Hullo, Dollars!'
'Hullo, Houses of Parliament!'
One afternoon in August, 1919, greetings by wireless telephone were exchanged between a Wireless Officer at Aperfield Court and an assembly of Peers, Members of Parliament, Treasury officials and high-ranking R.A.F. officers in the House of Lords. The Under Secretary of State for Air, Maj.-Gen. Seely, was dramatising the value of the

[1]Later Air Chief Marshal Sir H. Robert M. Brooke-Popham, G.C.V.O., K.C.B., C.M.G., D.S.O., A.F.C.

work being done at Biggin Hill, hoping to make those in authority amenable to the estimates for future research in the Air Vote. Trenchard was present and, after the initial buzz of excitement had quietened, commanded the distant Wireless Officer to give a recitation.

'He will know "His Master's Voice",' punned Seely in the silence that followed while the unhappy officer racked his brains for some appropriate verses:

> The General got 'is decoration thick
> (The men that backed 'is lies could not complain.)
> The Staff 'ad D.S.O.s till we was sick,
> And the soldier – 'ad the work to do again!

Everyone chuckled at his nerve and the youthful impudence in the voice that spoke out from the great horn facing them.

'These lords and gentlemen want some music,' said Seely into the microphone. 'Put on the gramophone.'

A pause and then the sonorous chords of the 1812 *Overture* shattered the silence. For many this was the first broadcasting they had ever heard and some, convinced that it was a hoax, refused to believe that the music was carried through the atmosphere by wireless waves. Others enthusiastically demanded more music: first a waltz and then a tango disturbed the sacrosanct hush of the Lords.

The voice of the operator at Aperfield Court broke in: 'Sir, the aircraft have just taken off.'

Seely turned to face his audience, playing the showman with understandable, though inaccurate, hyperbole: 'We are now going to have a demonstration which has never before been given in the history of the world!'

They all looked apprehensively at the loudspeaker, not knowing quite what to expect. There was an outburst of discordant whistles and screeches that ceased abruptly as Seely tuned in to the aircrafts' wavelength.

'Hullo, Newport![1] We are the Houses of Parliament. Can you hear us?'

[1] Lieutenant S. G. Newport, a Wireless Officer at Biggin Hill.

'Hullo, Houses of Parliament! We can hear you quite well. My pilot can hear you splendidly, too. We are flying at 8,000 feet, twenty miles away.'

'Mr Speaker is going to talk to you, and there are present here with me a large body of Peers, M.P.s and officials, all listening to you.'

'Please give them all our compliments.'

The Speaker of the House held a brief conversation with Newport who then entertained everyone with a song. Seely returned to the microphone.

'Orders signed by me prevent you from alighting at the House of Commons, but will you come along later and dine with me here?'

'My pilot and I will be delighted, sir,' replied Newport. 'At what time?'

'Come at eight and, look here, bring with you all the pilots and observers who are flying within –'

Seely hesitated, wondering just what he was letting himself in for. ' – Within twenty miles of London at this moment.'

'They have all heard what you say, sir,' Newport informed him, 'and will speak for themselves.'

One voice after another spoke from the loudspeaker, willingly accepting Seely's invitation to dinner.

Doubtless impressed by this pioneer broadcast, the Treasury sanctioned the Instrument Design Establishment. Its task was a formidable one: to maintain the supremacy which Britain had gained during the war in the design of aeronautical instruments and to provide the Royal Air Force with the best possible equipment. The research programme was ambitious and embraced almost every branch of aviation except airframe and engine design. Officers remaining from the W.E.E. continued their development of D/F receivers and transmitters, and tackled the improvement of valves, the deflection of wireless waves and the problem of landing in fog. Signals experts were brought in for long-range and ground-to-air visual signalling, signalling by invisible rays, navigation and recognition lights and audible sound-signalling from aircraft. Aeronautical instruments of all kinds were designed and tested: bomb-sights and gyro-stabilisers, sextants, drift-indicators, course-setting sights, pressure gauges, revolution and airspeed indicators, altimeters and flowmeters were some of the more important devices under study. The safety and comfort of aircrews was another aspect of the I.D.E. programme: safety-belts, anti-glare goggles, oxygen-supply systems, cockpit and clothing heating were all investigated and improved by the technical staff at Biggin Hill. High-speed cinematography was applied for the first time to aeronautical research. Pictures taken at a rate of 450 per second were projected at the standard (silent film) speed of sixteen per second, thus making possible the analysis of movements too rapid for the human eye to register. The behaviour of aircraft on landing and taking-off, the opening of parachutes, movement and vibration of propellers, and the atomisation of petrol jets in carburettors all became the concern of the Photographic Section.

Despite the greatly enlarged scope of the I.D.E. the staff at Biggin Hill was drastically slashed from nearly 600 to 346 persons, including 142 civilians. To fulfil the research programme the Establishment was organised into five sections. New designs, and inventions submitted from outside, passed from the Experimental Section to the Development Section which prepared specifications and drawings, constructed models and samples for manufacturers, and fitted the experimental apparatus into the I.D.E.'s aircraft. The Application Section then took over, testing everything in the air or on the ground, and suggesting alterations and modifications if required. Supporting these sections were the Records Section, responsible for technical reports and a comprehensive reference library, and the Stores Section to supply the other departments with the materials they needed.

It was with difficulty that Brooke-Popham provided a flight of Avro 504Ks for all the test-flying. The five pilots attached to the I.D.E. soon amassed more flying-hours than a full squadron. It was tedious, routine work, flying innumerable short 'hops' to try out each new device from the work-shops. Two of the pilots, Thornton and Traill,[1] devised a game which kept everyone amused except the C.O. They would take up an Avro 504K with one man in control of the joy-stick and throttle, and the other, the rudder. The idea was to try to sell each other a 'pup'. The whole station turned out to watch the crazy flying that resulted, and the crashes.

One day Traill was trying to force a down-wind landing and, when it was obvious they would finish up inside a hangar, opened the throttle and pulled the stick back, just clearing the roof. Traill put on bank and Thornton opposite rudder – a horrifying sight as their speed was so slow. The Avro just side-slipped into the ground, landing on its wing-tip which folded up and eased the impact. Result: two small cuts and a four-month wait for a new Avro.[2]

For nearly two years the Avro 504Ks were the only aircraft flying from Biggin Hill. After a memorable farewell party on 1st March, 1919, 'Cock' Squadron, still defiantly clinging to their khaki R.F.C. uniforms, had left for Tallaght in Ireland. A fortnight later the North Camp was occupied by 39 Squadron who flew in from Stow Maries with Sopwith Camels. The officers of the South Camp decided to initiate the newcomers into the Biggin Hill tradition. Armed with fire-extinguishers, they manned the old tank, left behind from the air-to-tank telephony experiments, and rumbled across the airfield as soon as it was dark. They invaded the North Camp just as 39 Squadron were finishing dinner. In a few seconds the Mess was surrounded and the occupants drenched with foam. A retreat to the tank was ordered before a counter-attack could be organised but the raiders found, to their consternation, that it was no longer there. It had been left in gear and had crawled right through the Camp, miraculously avoiding all buildings, to pitch finally nose-first into a ditch.

39 Squadron remained at Biggin Hill, a part of London's slender fighter defences, until 1921, when it was disbanded

---

[1]Air Vice Marshal T. C. Traill, C.B., O.B.E., D.F.C.
[2]Related by A. L. Gregory, Adjutant of the I.D.E.

and the I.D.E. was left in sole possession of the station.

When more ambitious test-flights had to be made, a Handley Page 0/400 was used as a 'flying laboratory'. In August, 1920, a long-distance experimental flight was carried out from Biggin Hill to assess the comparative worth of all the navigation instruments then in use with the Royal Air Force. The great twin-engined bomber carried two pilots, four scientists and a mechanic. The route encompassed the British Isles, covering all kinds of terrain, flat, hilly and mountainous, as well as a stretch over the sea. After delays due to bad weather and persistent engine trouble, the 0/400 took-off from Biggin Hill on 13th August and returned seven days later, having covered 1,140 miles in nineteen flying-hours. During this time the scientists on board investigated methods of dead reckoning, three types of compass, flares, sextants, the Bygrave slide-rule, a ballistics accelerometer, various chronometers and drift-indicators. From flights such as this the I.D.E. staff were able to make many valuable contributions to the technique of long-distance flying, then of growing importance to the first civil airlines. A chain of occulting light-beacons was established along the route between London and Paris for night-flying aircraft and the I.D.E. then started to tackle the civil pilot's greatest bugbear: landing in foggy weather.

A series of fascinating experiments were carried out at Biggin Hill, forerunners of today's G.C.A.[1] radar, but using sound in place of radio waves. In brief, three sound-detector stations around the aerodrome measured the height, speed and course of the aircraft approaching to land, and reported these to the pilot by wireless. At one end of the airfield was placed a sound transmitter, emitting a narrow cone of sound which could be heard up to 5,000 feet away. On picking up the distinctive note of this transmitter, the pilot throttled down and glided in towards it, keeping as far as possible towards the centre of the beam until he touched down on the runway. The transmitter was an ingenious adaptation by the I.D.E. of the large mirrors developed by the Army for anti-

[1]Ground Control Approach.

aircraft work, using a sound *detector* as a sound *projector*. A gigantic curved concrete disc, twenty feet in diameter and weighing fifteen tons, was constructed to the north of Biggin Hill at a cost of over £2,000. Mounted on trunnions, it could be trained according to the direction of the wind and elevated to the correct angle of glide for the incoming aircraft. A powerful 10 kw. klaxon was placed at the focal centre of this mirror and a narrow beam of sound projected out to guide in the pilot. When in use, the noise on the ground was quite terrifying, shattering the windows in nearby houses and stampeding all livestock for several miles around. Fortunately for the farmers and residents of Biggin Hill these experiments had not been taken very far when the future of the I.D.E. came under review.

The Treasury had never been really convinced of the necessity to have the I.D.E. at Biggin Hill and, early in 1923, proposed that it should be amalgamated with the Royal Aircraft Establishment at Farnborough. Economy was again the excuse. As Biggin Hill was six and a half miles from the nearest railway station, a heavy charge was incurred for the transport of the civilians and airmen who travelled daily to the South Camp; labour was cheaper at Farnborough and overheads could be cut by having a single research establishment. The Air Ministry rejected the Treasury proposal, forecasting, on technical grounds, a lowering in the standards of wireless research if the move were made. The new photographic laboratory, the concrete mirror and other installations at Biggin Hill would be wasted. The War Office, which had a small experimental section in the North Camp, protested they would be left without aircraft, while the I.D.E. staff complained that there was no accommodation for married families in the crowded Aldershot district.

The Treasury officials remained inflexible, their financial arguments unanswerable and the Air Ministry gave in announcing in Weekly Orders:

The Directorate of Research, Air Ministry, will cease to exercise an responsibility for Biggin Hill aerodrome with effect from 1st July, 1922, and control of this station will be vested in the A.O.C. Inland Area.

Thus ended a brilliant phase in the history of Biggin Hill as a research station. The site, however, was too valuable to be left in disuse; with the first expansion of the post-war Air Force at hand important new functions were soon assigned to both the North and South Camps.

CHAPTER SIX

AIR DEFENCE

THE transfer of the Instrument Design Establishment was welcomed by Trenchard who had always been dissatisfied with the dual role of Biggin Hill in research and defence, steadfastly maintaining that it was first and foremost a fighter station. With the scientists moving to Farnborough, Biggin Hill was free to become a key station in shaping the future air defences of Great Britain.

The post-war doldrums had been passed and the Royal Air Force was slowly recovering from the paralysing effects of peacetime economy. In Germany General von Seeckt was already gathering a select cadre of ex-flying officers secreted within the *Reichswehr Ministerium* while in Britain, three and a half years after the Armistice, there were only twenty-four front-line aircraft available for Home Defence. By Cabinet decision the Air Ministry was held responsible for the overall aerial defence of the country, leaving the Army free to provide, organise and train the ground defences that would be employed. Ever since the 17th A.A. Coy of the Royal Engineers moved in to share the North Camp with 141 Squadron, the War Office had retained an active interest in Biggin Hill and now planned, with the Air Ministry's concurrence, to develop it as a centre of anti-aircraft work. Soon both Services were working side by side at Biggin Hill, a happy liaison that was to last until the second world war.

On 15th March, 1922, four high-ranking Air Force and Army officers visited Biggin Hill: Air Vice Marshal P. W. Game; Air Commodore 'Stuffy' Dowding; Colonel Fuller, Deputy Director of Training, War Office; and Colonel Simon, Officer Commanding the School of Anti-Aircraft Artillery and Searchlights on Perham Down. They met on the spot to discuss the concentration there of the A.A. School, a Home Defence squadron and a special Night Flying Flight. In addition, the War Office considered Biggin Hill an ideal location for the Acoustical Section of the Royal Engineers, then developing the technique of aircraft detection by sound.

Their decision was unanimous: in effect Biggin Hill was to become the proving-ground for all the anti-aircraft defences on which one day might depend the security of Britain. It only remained to persuade the Treasury to part with the necessary funds; in the arguments for and against the new scheme the strategic importance of Biggin Hill was strongly emphasised:

> . . . It will enable the problem of air defence to be studied, and personnel to be trained, on one of the aerodromes *most essential* to the aerial defence of London, almost inevitably the principal target of any aerial attack on Great Britain . . .[1]

With Treasury sanction obtained, the Air Ministry proceeded to purchase all the outstanding land which had been held since the end of the war under the Defence of the Realm Act. The entire South Camp was then leased to the War Office and the North Camp reconditioned in readiness for a fighter squadron.

In May, 1923, Biggin Hill again became a fighter station when 56 Squadron flew in from Hawkinge, their Sopwith

[1]Minute from Air Council to Treasury.

Snipes gay with red-and-white checkerboard markings from nose to tail. Shortly before, the Army had occupied the South Camp where the A.A. School started to train personnel in the use of anti-aircraft guns, while the Searchlight Experimental Establishment sought to improve the illumination of aircraft at night for the benefit of both guns and fighters. It was the third Army unit, however, the Acoustical Section, which had the really vital task: obtaining early warning of the raiders' approach. To detect them after the coast had been crossed was no longer sufficient; with the bomber's ever-increasing speed and altitude, warning had to be given before landfall was made.

After the Armistice, experiments had been commenced to find a more sensitive replacement for the 'ear-trumpets' which had served their purpose in the days of the Gotha. For a start, a circular mirror of concrete, ten feet in diameter, was built into the face of a cliff near Broadstairs. Sound waves from an aeroplane flying over the sea were picked up and reflected on to a directional microphone at the mirror's focus. In early trials there was little discrimination between the beat of an aero-engine and the waves breaking on the shore. Later, using a 'Tucker's' microphone selectively tuned to the note of an engine, a trained operator could, under favourable circumstances, detect with an accuracy of two degrees an aircraft flying twenty miles away.

The Acoustical Section took over the giant disc of concrete, left behind at Biggin Hill by the departing I.D.E., with the fervour of astronomers receiving a splendid new telescope. The bigger the mirror, the greater the sensitivity, and, with this outsize in sound-detectors, warning of an aircraft's approach could be guaranteed under most conditions at a range of ten miles. By modern radar standards this was pathetically inadequate, but with the relatively slow-flying aircraft of the early twenties it gave the fighters a precious extra five minutes for interception. The twenty-foot concrete monstrosity remained a landmark, and a hazard to flying, at Biggin Hill until 1926, when it was finally demolished after three aircraft had been written-off in collisions with it.

For the first weeks at Biggin Hill all the cooperation flying with the anti-aircraft units was done by the Snipes of 56 Squadron. On 1st July, 1923, the Night Flying Flight was formed to take over these duties. Equipped with three Vickers Vimys and one Bristol Fighter, the importance of this Flight was out of all proportion to its size. It was always busy, with daytime flying for the Acoustical Section and night flights for the gunners of the A.A. School and to give 56 Squadron practice in night attacks on bombers. Scores of pilots received training in the handling of twin-engined aircraft at night and, for two months each summer, the Flight moved down to Lympne for early-warning exercises over the Channel.

Biggin Hill was still a small grass airfield and the Vimy was a very large aircraft. With a length of forty-three feet, a wing-span of sixty-eight feet and powered by two Rolls-Royce Eagle engines, it had been designed as a bomber capable of flying to Berlin and back from Britain. The Armistice had forestalled its operational use, but the Vimy became famous for three great pioneering long-distance flights made soon after. It was in a Vimy that Alcock and Brown made the first non-stop transatlantic flight from Newfoundland to Ireland on 14th/15th June, 1919. The same year Ross Smith and K. M. Smith flew in a Vimy from England to Australia, and Brand[1] and van Ryneveld to South Africa.

It was some time before the people of Biggin Hill, Cudham and Downe became accustomed to the roar of these great biplanes passing over at night. Many harsh words were spoken in the pubs condemning the Air Force's lack of consideration for their sleep.

Life with the Night Flying Flight followed the somewhat monotonous routine of peacetime service with the Royal Air Force. The happy-go-lucky spirit of the war was frowned upon and the Vimy crews, lacking the cheery *élan* of a

[1] In September, 1923, Squadron Leader Sir Quinton Brand, K.B.E., D.S.O., M.C., was posted Officer Commanding 56 Squadron at Biggin Hill.

fighter squadron, settled down to the tedious grind of anti-aircraft cooperation flying. Reveille was at 06.30 hours followed by P.T. before breakfast. Work began at 08.30 hours. For two weeks before each A.O.C.'s inspection, there was one hour's drill each morning at dawn. Passes were restricted to one 36-hour and one 48-hour pass per month. Apart from the weekly N.A.A.F.I. dance there was no organised entertainment on the camp and only an hourly bus service into Bromley. The penalty for not being in by midnight was a certain three days' C.B.

As a distraction from this humdrum existence, the ground crew invented a novel form of exercise. Tying a bunch of hydrogen-filled balloons to their backs, they would hedge-hop across the fields in a series of gigantic leaps and bounds. The champion, L.A.C. Dodds, could soar effortlessly for a hundred yards, or more, until the day when a balloon burst and he fell to his death on the concrete apron outside the Guard Room.

Despite the restricted area of Biggin Hill, the Flight had only one fatal flying accident during the years it spent there. In the winter of 1924 a film unit visited the station with the blessing of the Air Ministry to re-enact some scenes of derring-do in aerial combat. A Vimy was to be attacked and (apparently) shot down in flames by the fighters of 56 Squadron. The break in daily routine was welcomed by all, and everyone played their roles with enthusiasm. The stirring spectacle was filmed by a cameraman flying in a second Vimy. As the disguised bomber flew over Biggin Hill, the fighters swarmed up from the ground to the attack. With gay abandon they dived and zoomed around the Vimy, coming far too close for the pilot's peace of mind. The cameraman was beside himself with joy and cranked away steadily. The rear gunner in the Vimy flung up his arms in mock agony and hung convincingly 'dead' over the side of the cockpit. The pilot ignited the flares concealed aboard and dived steeply down, black smoke belching from the engines and fuselage, with the fighters in hot pursuit. The ground that day was covered with snow, the pilot of the Vimy misjudged his height and, failing to pull out in time, crashed into a wood near Cudham.

When he landed, the cameraman, not realising what had happened, rushed forwards with loud congratulations on this final touch of realism. He had filmed it all. Both occupants of the front cockpit had been killed outright, but the rear gunner, who had feigned death so well, jumped seconds before the final impact and escaped with a twisted knee.

Of the extra-routine duties carried out by the Night Flying Flight one had a more amusing sequel. To give some much-needed publicity to the Observer Corps, the Air Ministry arranged for a party of newspapermen to be flown over London at night to get the viewpoint of a raider attacking the capital. One elderly journalist, fearful of night flying, bought so much Dutch courage in the bars of Fleet Street and Biggin Hill Mess that he fell asleep as soon as the Vimy took off. He woke up on landing and dashed to the nearest telephone to tell his editor to print the story he had thoughtfully written in advance. It was by far the best of the bunch and described how every detail of London had been clearly visible in the bright moonlight, ending with a magniloquent paragraph on the return to Biggin Hill: 'Like a majestic swan alighting on the water we floated down on to the Kentish airfield whence we had departed. Our lives were safe in the hands of the youthful pilot who flew the mighty aeroplane with unerring skill.'

In reality the visibility over London was so poor that little could be seen. The pilot had overshot the flarepath on his first attempt to land and had only just scraped over the trees on the boundary before trying again. This time he misjudged his height, levelled off too soon and bounced across the field in a series of bone-shaking jolts!

The General Strike was a hectic time for all at Biggin Hill. Leave was cancelled, a cordon of armed sentries was thrown round the station while the three Vimys were used to distribute the *British Gazette*, the Government news-sheet produced to allay false rumours. Each evening an army lorry delivered the papers to Biggin Hill. With the bundles

73

crammed into the rear cockpits and the occupants perched precariously on top, the Vimys took-off on a nightly paper-round, dropping the *British Gazette* over the towns and villages of the South. On the last night but one of the strike, the lorry was intercepted and overturned by a band of strikers. The police telephoned the Station Commander in a panic: the mob was marching on Biggin Hill to destroy the petrol dumps! The station stood-to and manned the fire-hoses. Nothing more exciting happened than the arrest of a harmless civilian taking a short cut home across the airfield in the dark.

The fighter squadron which occupied the North Camp, No. 56, was one of the most renowned in the Royal Air Force. Captain Albert Ball, a great air fighter with forty-three victories to his credit, had gained his V.C. whilst serving with it on the Western Front. Disbanded during the dark days after the war, 56 Squadron was re-formed when the limited expansion of the Royal Air Force was sanctioned early in 1923. The Home Defence units were increased to nine single-seater fighter squadrons in two Wings, north and south of the Thames respectively, and for a year Biggin Hill became Headquarters, No. 5 Wing.

Successively commanded by Squadron Leaders I. T. Lloyd, Sir Quinton Brand, F. J. Vincent and Elliott-Smith, 56 Squadron remained at Biggin Hill for just over four years, carrying out the unexciting duties of a fighter squadron in peacetime: air exercises, cooperation on army manoeuvres and annual gunnery camps. True to the tradition of Biggin Hill the squadron became the 'guinea-pig' for the new R/T[1] sets coming into service. In some respects the Royal Air Force was worse off for wireless equipment than in the days when the Wireless Experimental Establishment was at Biggin Hill and 141 Squadron was pioneering wireless telephony in Home Defence. Fixed aerials had at last replaced the trailing wires which had been such a hindrance to the 'Brisfits' in

[1] By 1923 'Radio Telephony' had become a standard term in the R.A.F. supplanting 'Wireless Telephony'.

aerobatics, but the air-to-air range was only fifty yards and messages had often to be repeated thirty times to be understood. Fighter pilots could never be trained to listen in, claimed the opponents of R.T., who asserted that strict radio silence was necessary during operations quoting, as proof, the Zeppelins which had been detected by overhearing their wireless signals when raiding England.

'What would you do with your R/T set if war comes?' the Chief of Air Staff asked one of his officers.

'Chuck the apparatus right out of my aircraft, sir,' was the uncompromising reply.

Nevertheless, Trenchard, supported by Air Commodore Blandy and others who had served at Biggin Hill during the war, insisted that the single-seater fighter squadrons should have R/T. In due course 56 Squadron was equipped with the latest two-way sets and, rather to the pilots' surprise, became the leading exponent of R/T tactics in the air.

The Sopwith Snipe, introduced as the successor to the famous Camel, was becoming obsolete as a fighter when 56 Squadron moved into Biggin Hill. In 1924 the squadron was re-equipped with the latest single-seater fighter – the Gloster Grebe. Short and tubby, extremely manoeuvrable, with a top speed of 150 m.p.h. and a ceiling of 23,000 feet, the Grebe was the perfect aeroplane for aerobatics. It was strictly forbidden, but the irrepressible pilots of 56 Squadron continued to loop-the-loop after taking off, without climbing to gain altitude. One day Flying Officer Luxmore, thinking the C.O. safely away, set out to beat the squadron record for consecutive loops. He made a quick climbing take-off in his Grebe and went straight into a tight loop over the airfield. As he dived to pick up speed for his second loop the C.O. walked on to the grass. Luxmore ignored the Very signals ordering him to land at once, finished the loop and zoomed up a third time. For an eternity the little Grebe seemed to hang suspended by the spinning propeller, then it flipped over, dived into the ground and burst into flames. In all, the squadron lost six pilots in flying accidents at Biggin Hill.

As part of the training routine of the twenties, each flight in a fighter squadron was nominated 'Battle Flight' for a week, making a two-hour patrol each day, flying fully armed at 10,000 feet. After lunch one 10th November, 'C' Flight took off to carry out this patrol, having waited all morning for the weather to improve. At 10,000 feet it was crystal-clear but, being winter-time, bitterly cold. The flight flew around over the Medway towns for the obligatory two hours and then turned for home. Biggin Hill was covered by a thick blanket of fog, so they split up and searched for an opening. Petrol was running low when one pilot announced over his R/T that he could see the ground. Swearing never to malign R/T again, the others followed him down and bumped to a standstill in a tiny meadow surrounded by tall trees. They set off on foot towards a large mansion a quarter of a mile away and found that they had landed near Edenbridge. It was too dark to think of returning and they gladly accepted the lavish hospitality of the two house-owners – a retired Brigadier-General and an ex-Chairman of Lloyds. In the morning the flight expertly took-off and showed their hosts what the Grebe could do in the way of chimney-trimming before they landed back at Biggin Hill in time for the two minutes' silence.

Another day, when 'B' Flight was Battle Flight of the week, a pilot made a forced landing at the Sussex Flying Club's aerodrome near Worthing and damaged his Grebe. Loudly singing 'I do like to be beside the seaside', the repair party rolled out of the North Camp. A day by the sea was too good to be missed and the C.O. tolerantly let all the ground crew go. The damaged aeroplane was quickly made airworthy and the men were beginning to think of lunch when another of 56 Squadron's Grebes flew overhead. A canvas bag with a long streamer attached plummeted down. The C.O. had thoughtfully sent them their pay. After a grand lunch in the best hotel in Worthing, they set off for Biggin Hill, stopping at every pub on the way. It was dark when they got back but the C.O. was there, waiting to congratulate them on the quick repair of the Grebe. He was not amused, however, by the empty beer bottles which cascaded to his feet when the tailboard of the tender was let down. It was small incidents such as these which made life at 'Biggin on the Bump' so memorable in the otherwise uneventful twenties.

As the public grew increasingly air-minded, flying displays became more and more popular, from the lone airman with his old Avro 504 taking up passengers at 'ten bob a flip' to the great R.A.F. Pageants at Hendon. Each summer more than a hundred thousand people flocked to see all that was latest and best in their Air Force. 56 Squadron took part in several of these displays whilst at Biggin Hill. In 1923 a flight of Snipes made a low-level attack on a tank. Flying out of the sun, they roared a few feet over the Royal Box in line astern to drop practice bombs on the tank which was crawling across the airfield, smothering it in clouds of acrid white smoke. At the 1926 Pageant the Squadron participated in the most exciting event of the day: a mass fly-past and aerobatic display by fifty-four fighters drawn from six squadrons. Taking off in close formation, wing-tip inside wing-tip, they flew past King George V and dipped in salute before giving what was judged the finest display of skilful flying ever seen at Hendon.

Not until 1927 did parachutes become standard equipment in the Royal Air Force. Fighter pilots, accustomed to flying by feel in their buttocks, heartily disliked them. 'It's no use to me,' said one member of 56 Squadron on being issued with his new parachute. 'Who wants to fly sitting on a ruddy football!'

To train the pilots and to give volunteers practice in 'pull-offs' and drops, a Parachute Circus toured R.A.F. stations in a Vickers Vimy. The 'pull-off' procedure was a test of nerve. Two small platforms, eighteen inches square were built around a strut on each wing. When the Vimy was airborne, the two parachutists clambered out of the cockpit, edged their precarious way along the wing and stood on the platforms, held against the strut by the pressure of the airstream. At a signal from the pilot, they moved round behind the struts and clung on for dear life until pulling the ripcord.

When the Vimy reached Biggin Hill, the whole station turned out to watch an expert parachutist, Corporal East, attempt to beat the world record for a delayed drop. No one will ever know why he failed to release his parachute in time. Jumping from 6,000 feet, East struck the road by the 'Salt Box' with his parachute half-opened, falling directly in front of a bus which had drawn up to allow the passengers to watch. Two men fainted and the driver was so overcome that he could not continue the journey.

As the Royal Air Force slowly expanded, it was planned to station a second single-seater fighter squadron at Biggin Hill. More accommodation was needed, the obvious solution being to move the Army from the South Camp and to place the new squadron there, whilst 56 Squadron retained the North Camp. The Air Ministry was in a quandary. In 1923 funds had been obtained from the Treasury for the reconditioning of Biggin Hill on the grounds that, for efficiency, the three anti-aircraft units, the Night Flying Flight and 56 Squadron must all be together. It was now a little late in the day to argue that, as the Army would have to move out in time of war, it might as well do so now. In fact, this point had never occurred to the War Office, quite satisfied with the *status quo*. The Air Ministry cunningly hinted that the Army might prefer to move to a site where live ammunition could be used with impunity. The Army said 'No thank you', Biggin Hill was conveniently close to London and all the Territorial units which were trained at the A.A. School. It was finally decided that the most economical way out of the *impasse* was to enlarge the North Camp. 56 Squadron, now re-equipped with Armstrong Whitworth Siskins, moved to North Weald, leaving the Night Flying Flight as the only R.A.F. unit on Biggin Hill.

The army units, meanwhile, continued to improve the techniques of anti-aircraft defence. As a result of the Acoustical Section's work, a chain of concrete mirrors on the Biggin Hill model was planned for the whole of the south and east coasts, a great 'listening barrier' which would detect all aircraft approaching from the Continent. By 1927 aircraft designers at home and abroad had increased the bomber's performance to such a degree that the Air Council was forced to review the whole problem of early warning. Certain minimum standards to be met were laid down if our fighters were to be alerted in time: enemy aircraft should be detected at a range of twenty-five miles from the coast; at ten miles' distance it must be possible to know approximately their height, speed, course and number; and, finally, as the coast-line was crossed, these factors must be known with exactitude.

These standards were far beyond the powers of the circular mirrors; something even bigger and more sensitive was required. The experts of the Acoustical Section went to work and designed a two-hundred-foot long strip mirror, erecting the prototype near Dungeness. This was considered to be the ultimate in sound detectors, with a chain of these giants at twenty-mile intervals, supplemented by thirty-foot circular mirrors at every eight miles, no enemy aircraft could slip through unheard. Such was the blueprint for Britain's early warning system until the mid-thirties when the magic words 'Radio Direction Finding' and 'Radio-location' were first spoken in secret.

CHAPTER SEVEN

RECONSTRUCTION

THE need for reconstruction and expansion had grown depressingly self-evident ever since the Air Ministry decided to retain Biggin Hill as a permanent station. The airfield was dangerously restricted in area, accommodation in the North Camp was still the temporary wooden huts thrown up in 1917/18, while the Officers' Mess, after a calamitous fire in 1925, had to make-do in a disused workshop-block. Estimates for a complete rebuilding were large, the Lords Commissioners of the Treasury were not amenable to such expenditure and granted funds sufficient only for reconditioning the North Camp: to make it, in the words of a minute, 'comfortable for some years'.

This work, planned for 1927, was delayed by an acrimonious disagreement between the staff of Air Defence of Great Britain and the R.A.F. Building Committee: the bone of contention being the main road from Bromley to Westerham which marched with the western boundary of the aerodrome. The original huts and hangars had been neatly contained within the strip between the road and the grass runways, and it was here that the Building Committee proposed to site the new Officers' and N.C.O.s' Messes, married quarters, barracks and other buildings. The Air Defence staff as practical airmen vetoed this plan, pointing out that any buildings here would menace the southern flying approaches to the field, and suggested that all non-operational premises be situated on the far side of the main road. The idea of a thoroughfare running through the heart of a well-ordered station was anathema to the Building Committee who countered with the suggestion that all living-quarters should be moved to the north, a good two miles from the working area! Fortunately it was discovered that houses built here could not be connected to the main sewerage system, a not unimportant point, and the Building Committee reluctantly accepted the circumstances of having the station bisected by a public highway. This made little difference at the time, but it was to prove highly vexatious during the fifth-column scares of 1940.

Twenty-nine acres of land were required for the new station and had to be purchased piecemeal from several owners. Two landlords, however, held out and refused to allow their property to be engulfed by the expanding aerodrome. One, 'Forge Cottage,' a dilapidated tea-garden, attracted a highly undesirable type of customer whose presence, it was feared, would be prejudicial to discipline. The other was that well-known local landmark, the 'Salt

Box', also a stopping place for refreshments, with a garage and petrol pump which would constitute a very real fire hazard to the new hangars nearby. To have a public highway through Biggin Hill was bad enough, but to have two enclaves of private property was quite unacceptable to the Air Ministry which put up a vigorous case for the compulsory purchase of an 'intolerable nuisance' and a 'real blot':

> It is difficult to translate these factors into a cash value but I should have thought that we could convince the Treasury that they fairly represent the 'ha'p'orth of tar' which will go a long way towards spoiling the station if withheld.

Rather surprisingly, Treasury sanction was granted and negotiations were begun. Ten years later the solicitors were still haggling, the tenants of the offending properties having inflated notions of what was a right and proper compensation for their loss of livelihood and, by the start of the second world war, these two civilian 'islands' had become embedded in the fabric of Biggin Hill. 'Forge Cottage' was destroyed in the blitz of 1940, but the 'Salt Box' lingered on in decay to be finally demolished in 1954. Today a new 'Salt Box' café prospers on a site opposite the original one, perpetuating a tradition of hospitality for airmen that was born in the bitter winter of 1917.

The extension of the airfield itself proved less troublesome. Originally, 117 acres of Cudham Lodge Farm had been taken as the nucleus of Biggin Hill and, since then, more land had been added, a pasture here, a cornfield there, but now faster landing speeds and plans for extensive night flying demanded a doubling in acreage. The tenant of the farm, John Westacott, was understandably reluctant to part with more fields piecemeal so the landlord, Lord Stanhope, proposed an outright purchase of the whole property with, of course, suitable compensation for Westacott.

After some strong bargaining this was agreed to and soon Cudham Lodge, home of many families of note, the

6   81

Mannings, the Brasiers, the Waleys, who had contributed so much to the parish's ancient history, was no more than a memory.

All these delays had one advantage, however; by mid-summer, 1929, when the contractors moved in, sufficient funds had been accumulated to allow a thorough job of re-construction to be done.

For the next three years the only aircraft on Biggin Hill were those of the Night Flying Flight which remained behind to service the Army Anti-Aircraft School in the South Camp.

On Empire Air Day, 1930, quite a crowd turned up expecting to see a non-existent flying display. The embarrassed staff of the Night Flying Flight felt obliged to put up some sort of show and trundled out their only aircraft, a Bristol Berkeley and a Hawker Horsley, together with a hand-operated petrol bowser. There happened to be a Blackburn Dart on the field as well, piloted by a lieutenant, R.N., who had flown over from Gosport on a clandestine visit to his girl friend. No flying was possible, but a Lewis-gun demonstration was given and tea brewed-up for all the visitors before they could be persuaded to go, apparently content with this glimpse of the Royal Air Force at home.

Occasionally a civil aircraft would land, lost or with engine trouble. Once it was a young Japanese who complained that his Gipsy Moth was 'dropping revs'. The Night Flying Flight was away at summer camp and only a small Care and Maintenance party remained: one cook, one pay clerk, two policemen and a wireless operator. They coped with the situation manfully:

> The only thing we could think of was dirty plugs, so we managed to extract them all and give them a good brush-and-clean in petrol. Our Jap was quite satisfied with the result. He then asked for petrol. This stumped us as we had none; then we thought of the 'Salt Box' pump. Man-handling the Moth as near as we could, we filled it up with cans from the garage. The pilot paid up and was

soon on his way to Croydon. I feel sure he thought us a most efficient ground crew as he gave us ten bob, which we spent on a convivial evening in the canteen.[1]

By September, 1932, the builders had finished and departed, leaving the North Camp fit for occupation. The Officers and N.C.O.s' Messes, barrack-blocks, married quarters and offices were replicas in red brick of a hundred other Air Force stations: not luxurious, perhaps, but comfortable with a pleasing, austere dignity. The newly-laid turf was green and trim, the rose terrace outside the Officers' Mess was ready for a gardeners' attention, while the tennis and squash courts lacked only the cries of youthful players.

In the first instance the C.O. of the rebuilt station was Wing Commander G. B. Dacre, D.S.O., who also assumed responsibility for the Night Flying Flight, now re-christened Anti-Aircraft Cooperation Unit. After five months, however, Wing Commander E. O. Grenfell, M.C., D.F.C., A.F.C., took over to remain as Station Commander for the next four years.

Biggin Hill was now ready to become the home of two fighter squadrons, Nos. 23 and 32, then at Kenley which in turn was due for reconstruction. 32 Squadron flew the Bristol Bulldog IIA, adopted by the Royal Air Force in 1929 as its standard day and night fighter. Carrying two Vickers guns, with night-flying equipment, oxygen and, if necessary, four 20-lb. bombs, this versatile little biplane had a top speed of 170 m.p.h. and a duration of nearly four hours. 23 Squadron likewise flew Bulldogs but, in addition, one flight was equipped with the new Hawker Demons as an experiment. They proved so successful that the Bulldogs were soon relinquished and the squadron became the only unit in the Royal Air Force solely to fly these two-seater fighters. No. 23 was also renowned for sensational displays of synchronised aerobatics at the Hendon Air Pageant and other shows, and it was while he was performing some low-level evolutions (strictly forbidden) that one of the squadron's most promising young officers, Douglas Bader, suffered his tragic crash

[1] Related by D. P. Howlett.

83

some months before the move to Biggin Hill.

The reoccupation of the North Camp was carried out with the utmost economy, key-note of the times. An order for new furnishing was even countermanded as being an unnecessary luxury; instead, all the old household furniture, bedding, linen, cutlery, fire-extinguishers and lavatory fittings no longer required at Kenley were taken to Biggin Hill.

By 1st October some 300 R.A.F. personnel were in residence, ready for the ordeal of inspection by a high-ranking officer from Headquarters, Air Defence of Great Britain. His visit nearly ended in tragedy. The inspecting officer, an Air Vice Marshal, had let it be known in advance that all doors and cupboards should be left unlocked. No one could divine what murky secrets he expected to find. However, the inspection went off well – until the Air Marshal reached the top floor of one of the new barrack-blocks and encountered a door which remained obdurately fast.

'Why's this door locked?' he barked. 'My orders were perfectly clear!'

Before the Station Commander could explain, a quaking orderly had gone off at the double to fetch the key.

'Now we'll see . . .'

In front of him yawned a sheer drop of twenty feet. The need for economy had left the building half-finished until further funds were forthcoming.

The inspection terminated in Biggin Hill's new mortuary, the Air Vice Marshal remarking that it seemed an oppropriate place to end his tour.

Life for the squadrons at Biggin Hill was good, their pleasant existence unshadowed by threat of war. The pilots were encouraged to indulge in all the flying their hearts desired, there were games of rugger and cricket to be played against other units, and the night clubs and theatres of London were not far away, providing a pilot officer's bank balance could stand the strain. The country houses of Kent were liberal with weekend hospitality, and full Mess-kit had a gratifying effect on dancing-partners whose fathers lent their guests a gun and dog for a shoot through their coverts.

And then there were the traditional Guest Nights in the Officers' Mess when anything could, and usually did, happen:

A number of Royal Artillery officers from the South Camp were our guests; after dinner some played cards while others retired to the billiard-room. Being 5th November it was not long before some of the younger Air Force officers produced fireworks and started to liven up the game. Later, when the card-room door was locked, a spirited campaign developed to drive out the players with fireworks dropped down the chimney. The problem was to find the right chimney and a party of officers was observed on the roof, still in Mess-kit, forming a human ladder to enable one to reach the chimney-pots. A Flight Lieutenant directed operations from the lawn, there was some initial difficulty in locating the card-room and explosions took place all over the Mess before the target was pinpointed. Once found, a barrage of squibs and thunderflashes was dropped and in a few minutes the room was untenable.

A senior R.A.F. officer, apprehensive of damage to Mess property, asked one of the Pilot Officers whether he had any more fireworks left.

'Rather,' he replied, producing a fistful. 'How many would you like, sir?'

It was a memorable evening and no one felt that the damage charged on their next Mess bills was in any way excessive.[1]

Being so near to London, Biggin Hill was favoured with frequent visits by air attaches and serving officers of other air forces: the French, Danes, Swedes and Italians all came in turn but it was the Chinese for whom the station held special charm, judging by the number of visits they made. A flying display traditionally climaxed these occasions, followed by drinks and a splendid lunch in the Mess.

Taken more seriously, though, were the annual Royal Air Force Displays at Hendon, high-light of the aeronautical

[1]Related by Squadron Leader H. G. Crowe, M.C.

year, at which both 23 and 32 Squadrons performed. Empire Air Day, when R.A.F. stations all over the country were at home to the public, was a more domestic function but the 1936 event brought opprobrium on Biggin Hill for what some in high authority considered to be downright bad taste. The fate of the Emperor of Abyssinia, Haile Selassie, had lately filled the headlines and it was most unfortunate that this tragic figure was chosen as butt of the comedy-turn which the public expected of the day's programme. Two members of the Anti-Aircraft Cooperation Unit, one dressed as a dervish, the other unmistakably the Lion of Judah in pith helmet, black beard and white bed-sheet, drove round the airfield in an ancient Austin Seven while a brother-officer dive-bombed them with sacks of flour from a Hawker Tomtit. As the last 'bomb' fell, a smoke candle was ignited in the Austin and the two fantastic occupants fled ignominiously, leaving their car to career merrily on, belching smoke. The crowd howled for an encore, but in vain: the smoke had rendered 'Haile Selassie' *hors de combat*!

During the summer of 1934, 23 Squadron was chosen to represent Britain at an Aviation Garden Party given by the French Air Ministry to honour the silver jubilee of the first cross-Channel flight by Louis Blériot, though why the organisers chose to celebrate on 23rd June an event which took place on 25th July remains a mystery.

The squadron was away at Andover flying its Hawker Demons against Sidestrand bombers on trials when Squadron Leader Crowe received a most welcome order to take his unit to France. There was no time to work up new aerobatic routines and the pilots had to be content with one rehearsal of their old Hendon formations as they crossed the Channel under the critical eye of the A.O.C., Air Vice Marshal Philip Joubert, watching from his own aircraft. Landing at Le Bourget, Crowe found that *l'Armée de l'Air* had arranged a magnificent lunch for its guests. He begged the Commandant that it should be an 'aviator's lunch', without alcohol, but corks were already popping. There was time, however, for everyone to snatch a much-needed siesta before taking-off for Buc aerodrome where the Garden Party was being held.

In the presence of M. Lebrun, President of the Republic, the British Ambassador and the Air Ministers of both countries, 23 Squadron repeated its Hendon success. The guest of honour, the veteran M. Blériot, was overcome with emotion and suffered a heart attack, but recovered to see the Demons wing over the frail little monoplane in which he had conquered the Channel. This was the first time an R.A.F. squadron had been seen at a French air display, and the frenzied applause that greeted the Demons as they streamed in to land showed they were unquestionably *le clou de la fete.*

There was, of course, a strictly serious side to life at Biggin Hill, a key station in the air defence of London, and its squadrons were kept busy with a continuous round of training and exercises. Each year total mobilisation was practised with the entire personnel, not merely the pilots, moving out to camp under active service conditions as visualised in the early thirties. Every item of equipment and uniform was scrutinised and reported on: ' . . . Two tunics were much too large and one too small . . . Six pairs of boots were very tight and uncomfortable . . . in three instances trousers were from two to four inches too long . . . ' Trivial details, perhaps, but a blistered foot could delay a take-off by vital seconds. The ground crews dismantled and reassembled the Bulldogs and Demons against a stop-watch; leisure-loving administrative personnel sweated out Lewis-gun drill in gas respirators, while the M.T. Section drove hundreds of miles in convoy from one landing ground to another. Within the limited resources allowed the Royal Air Force, everything possible was done to ensure that squadrons were at maximum efficiency, and Nos. 23 and 32 were no exceptions.

Biggin Hill was also of importance to civil aviation as a weather-reporting station on the Croydon-Le Bourget route, its meteorological office remaining open day and night to watch the vagaries of the weather. Six hundred feet above sea level, the airfield was frequently open when Croydon was fog-bound and sometimes a dozen airliners would be parked on the grass outside Station Headquarters. Once an Imperial Airways Hannibal flew in with the American Olympic Games team, including the great Jesse Owens fresh from his triumph in Berlin, another time the station played host to a party of French mannequins bound for a fashion show in London. Stranded passengers were taken to the Officers' Mess and entertained lavishly until the Customs and Immigration officials arrived from Croydon. Few realised that they were temporary guests of a Service Mess and therefore could not pay for all the food and drink they received. To some this meant nothing, others were generously appreciative and presented their involuntary hosts with a piece of plate or cabinet of cigars.

The passing of 1935 marked the end of halcyon years. In July both of Biggin Hill's squadrons took part in the Review of the Royal Air Force at Mildenhall which celebrated the Silver Jubilee of King George V; two corporals of 23 Squadron had the honour of explaining a Demon's equipment to His Majesty. Then, in October, Mussolini and his Fascists commenced their invasion of Abyssinia, an act of war with repercussions even at Biggin Hill. The Demons of 23 Squadron were given major inspections, dismantled and shipped out to the Middle East as part of a strategic reserve being built up lest hostilities should spread. Without aircraft the squadron dwindled away, its pilots were posted and the ground crews employed on routine duties around the station, not to mention a superb overhaul that was carried out on the Station Commander's car. 32 Squadron, however, remained at full strength and for over a year was Biggin Hill's only operational unit. At the 1936 Hendon display the squadron's Bulldogs won applause for a spectacular low-level strafing of 'marauding tribesmen and their baggage-train of loot', but some critics felt that this demonstration of our aerial superiority over 'hostile natives' was both wanton and unnecessary: the real enemy was nearer home. They need not have carped, however, for within a few months 32 Squadron was occupied on work of life-and-death importance to the nation.

88

That 'the bomber will always get through' was a fair assumption in aerial warfare few would deny, but it needed Hitler's cynical repudiation of the Treaty of Versailles and the emergence of the fully-fledged *Luftwaffe* to give this proposition an immediacy that had been lacking since the end of the first world war. Those responsible for planning our defence were only too aware of the truth behind Mr Churchill's words: 'We are a rich and easy prey. No country is so vulnerable, and no country would better repay pillage than our own. With our enormous metropolis here, the greatest target in the world, a kind of tremendous, fat, valuable cow tied up to attract the beast of prey, we are in a position in which we have never been before, and in which no other country is at the present time.'

The greatly increased range and speed of modern bombers, aircraft which Germany was known to be building in large numbers, demanded drastic counter-measures. In May, 1936, the Home Defence Force was reorganised into four functional commands – Bomber, Fighter, Coastal and Training – with Biggin Hill, first and foremost a fighter station, coming under Fighter Command whose Headquarters were opened at Bentley Priory, Stanmore, in July with Air Chief Marshal Sir Hugh Dowding as A.O.C.

His most vexing problem was still that of detecting and giving adequate warning of the enemy's approach. Speed alone made the old acoustical methods, to which Biggin Hill had contributed so much in the twenties, quite useless. Something entirely new was needed: the answer was, of course, radio-location, radar, or radio direction-finding as it was first called – R.D.F. in short. As early as the end of 1934 the Air Ministry had instituted a committee under the chairmanship of Mr H. T. Tizard to explore all possible means of defence, and within a few months R. Watson Watt had staged his now-classic experiment proving that a flying aircraft would reflect wireless waves and that these reflections could be depicted and calibrated on a cathode-ray tube. Research was pushed forwards vigorously, resulting in the planning and eventual construction of a complete chain of coastal radio-location stations from Southampton to the Tyne capable of giving warning of an aircraft up to sixty miles away.

But radio-location by itself could not win battles; the Royal Air Force, and especially Fighter Command, had to learn how to use this new weapon of defence and it was appropriate that Air Chief Marshal Sir Hugh Dowding chose Biggin Hill, with its pioneering experience of ground-controlled interception in the first world war, as the 'guinea-pig' station for this work.

CHAPTER EIGHT

ON THE EVE

ONE day in August, 1936, Squadron Leader R. L. Ragg, a navigation expert attached to the newly-formed Bomber Command, was posted to Biggin Hill for a three-day conference, subject: unspecified. On arrival he naturally reported to the Station Commander, Wing Commander Grenfell, who inquired the reason behind the visit. Ragg replied that he had no idea. They were joined by Dr B. G. Dickens, an Air Ministry scientist; same question, same answer. Then came a Signals officer, Flight Lieutenant W. P. C. Pretty, who was also in the dark, and it was not until Mr H. T. Tizard completed the party that they learnt the real purpose of the meeting.

If they were given by some mysterious means, explained Tizard, information about the movements of an approaching bomber force at, say, one-minute intervals, in the form of altitude, bearing and distance, how would they set about sending up fighters to meet the enemy, to intercept at a predicted point and not just a standing patrol which might, or might not, coincide with the bombers' course? Ragg, as a qualified navigator, was to tackle the interception problem, Pretty would look after communications, while Dickens would advise generally on any scientific snags. They were given three Hawker Harts to simulate the bomber force and the free use of 32 Squadron, at the time the only fighter unit at Biggin Hill, now re-equipped with the new Gloster Gauntlet and highly proficient in R/T procedures – essential to the experiments. No mention was made of radio-location; Tizard's 'mysterious means' were still top-secret.

The object of his briefing was, in essence, very simple: with radio-location able to provide warning of the enemy's approach at distances up to sixty miles, there was no longer any need to keep fighters airborne on extravagant standing patrols as hitherto; now they could remain on the ground until the last minute and then take-off. But in five minutes a modern bomber could travel fifteen miles, so there was little time to work out an interception course with all the paraphernalia of aerial navigation, and a means had to be devised by which the ground controller could give his fighters their course in the minimum time, a minute or less, altering it continuously to match every move of the enemy as detected by radio-location.

The three days allotted to Ragg and his colleagues lengthened into five months. In Biggin Hill's Operations Room they slaved over the chart table with dividers and protractors, pencils and slide-rules suspended on elastic to save seconds by whipping them out of the way when not in use. They devised and constructed gadgets of 'Heath Robinson' complexity, and were visited by high-ranking officers and civilian scientists, Watson Watt and Professor Blackett amongst others, all anxious to learn if progress had been made.

For weeks the problem remained heartbreakingly insoluble. Then came the day when the devices and instruments could be happily discarded; the answer was glaringly simple. Termed the 'Principle of Equal Angles', it reduced the anticipated path of the bombers and the fighters' interception course to the two sides of an isosceles triangle whose base was a straight line drawn between their respective positions at any given moment. As long as the fighters flew a course whose angle to this base is equal to that of the bombers, an interception must follow at the triangle's apex, their advantage in speed always placing the fighters ahead of the enemy. If too far ahead, the ground controller could instruct them by R/T to circle and wait for the bombers to come up with them. Should the enemy 'jink' and alter course, he judged a new isosceles triangle on his plotting table by eye and gave his fighters a revised bearing in the time it takes to speak into a microphone. Today this seems elementary and common-sense but it had to be discovered the hard way.

In their first hundred practical experiments with the Gauntlets and Harts using the 'Principle of Equal Angles' the Biggin Hill team achieved ninety-three successful interceptions. To prove that their system was fool-proof, they tried untrained pilots as controllers and still obtained good results. On days when the weather grounded the aircraft they amused themselves with theoretical exercises with speeds of up to 600 m.p.h., and this in 1936!

A month or so later Ragg was returning to Biggin Hill from a conference at the Air Ministry when he read in an evening paper a report to the effect that the Germans knew we had a means of detecting aircraft with infra-red rays. He casually mentioned this to Tizard next day who burst out laughing: 'Good. Now I can tell you all about it!' He then let them into the great secret. They were naturally ambitious to try their system of interception using radio-location but it was not to be, the group was broken up and posted elsewhere for other duties.

The work they had initiated, however, was carried on under the new Station Commander, Wing Commander H. G. W. 'Fiery' Lock, D.F.C., A.F.C., who replaced Grenfell early in 1937. The experimental radio-location station at Bawdsey was linked with the Biggin Hill Operations Room and civil airliners flying between the Continent and London were used as unsuspecting 'enemy raiders'. 32 Squadron put in hundreds of flying hours on these trials, the early morning

K.L.M. service from Amsterdam becoming their favourite target. The temptation to intercept the daily *Lufthansa* Junkers was strong, but strictly forbidden. The German crew was civilian in name only.

The new experiments were, in general, very successful. Using radio-location alone, 32 Squadron reached the point when it was able to guarantee interception of all airliners flying between six and nine thousand feet, often in ten-tenths cloud. Fighter Command's 'invisible eye' had grown out of the laboratory and was ready to be used as standard defence equipment.

The nerve centre of Biggin Hill as a sector station was, of course, the Operations Room and, parallel with the interception experiments, some work was done to determine the ideal lay-out. The problem was how to display to the best advantage all the information that flowed in from Group Headquarters, the radio-location stations and the Observer Corps so that the controller could see at a glance the relative positions of the enemy and his own fighters in order to apply the 'Principle of Equal Angles'. At first a horizontal blackboard was used on which their positions were drawn in chalk. This had its disadvantages: chalk was messy and smudged, the controller's view was interrupted by the plotters and the angle at which the board lay made it difficult to estimate a course by eye. Once again the answer was simple: use a vertical ground-glass screen on which the plotting is done from behind. The controller has an uninterrupted view from the front, the screen, being vertical, takes up less space than a flat table and the various aircraft formations can be easily displayed with coloured suction discs on the glass. This system remained in use at Biggin Hill until the Operations Room was destroyed by enemy action in September, 1940.

As a consequence of all this work, Biggin Hill became a school for fledgling controllers. On days when the weather made flying impossible, they were trained with dummy interceptions. These still required the cooperation of pilots who, not unnaturally, resented having to work when they could be peaceably drinking beer or watching a 'flick', and so adopted a regrettably light-hearted attitude to these exercises. They involved sitting in the cockpit of a Gauntlet inside a cold, clammy hangar. The trainee controllers gave orders by R/T which the pilot acknowledged and then worked out his theoretical position with a stop-watch and map: so many minutes elapsed equals so many miles flown. The stop-watch was usually forgotten and the pilot made wild guesses.

'Hullo, Red Two. What is your position?'

'Hullo, Daisy. I am now 25,000 feet over Canterbury.'

The controller's voice sounded most indignant. 'How the blazes can you be 25,000 feet over Canterbury, you only took off two minutes ago?'

The pilot then woke up with a start. 'I mean 5,000 feet over Westerham.'

'Make up your mind. Your position is 6,000 feet over Croydon.'

'Ah! That's where I probably am!'

By 1936 the tide of expansion had begun to flow, the Government was at last facing the growing air power of Germany as reality and the Prime Minister, Mr Baldwin, was forced to announce plans for building-up the Royal Air Force on an unprecedented scale; it was none too soon.

Under the newly-formed Fighter Command Great Britain was quartered into four Fighter Groups each of which, in turn, was subdivided into a number of Sectors comprising a main fighter station and satellite airfields. Biggin Hill fell within the orbit of No. 11 Group whose sector stations, Tangmere apart – Debden, North Weald, Hornchurch, Northolt and Kenley – formed a tight defensive ring around London with pride of place given to Biggin Hill, the 'strongest link' that is perpetuated in the station's motto commanding the cornerstone of Britain, a sector reaching from Sheerness to Hastings and inevitably bearing the brunt of an attack across the Channel.

Before the end of the year the few remaining members of 23 Squadron were posted to Northolt where the unit was to be re-formed, leaving No. 32 in sole occupation of the North Camp. Its obsolescent Bristol Bulldogs were replaced by the very latest of biplane fighters: the Gloster Gauntlet II. The Hurricane and Spitfire were still prototypes very much on the secret list. The squadron was kept busy with the interception experiments until March, 1937, when 'B' Flight was split off as the nucleus of one of the new fighter squadrons, No. 79, authorised under the expansion-scheme for the Royal Air Force. The new squadron, equipped with Gauntlets, was also stationed at Biggin Hill. Rivalry between the two was intense, No. 32 protesting disdainfully that it had fathered a 'shocking miscarriage'; nevertheless, they remained a fighting partnership on the 'Bump' until the summer of 1940.

The familiar pattern of flying displays continued and in the blazing sun of Empire Air Day, 1937, nearly 20,000 people visited the station. Nos. 32 and 79 Squadrons competed against each other in a medley of events, honours being equally divided, the most spectacular being the race for altitude. In the wonderfully clear weather the Gauntlets could be seen with the naked eye at 20,000 feet. Highlight of the display, however, was undoubtedly the R/T demonstration where a spectator could, for a sixpenny fee, speak to a pilot flying at 5,000 feet and request any manoeuvre that took his fancy.

Next year the attendance figure broke all records. The public was suddenly taking a very real interest in its Air Force. The bombers that had threatened Vienna during the recent *Anschluss* could so very easily have been over London. This was not the occasion for entertaining demonstrations of our aerial might against 'hostile natives'; the accent was on preparedness for war. In a set-piece the Gauntlets effectively destroyed a dummy torpedo-boat, heavy bombers pinpointed a bridge with smoke-bombs, and the guns of Anti-Aircraft School riddled a towed drogue. There were some present who, whilst admiring the masterpieces of aluminium, fabric and wood that was the Gauntlet, must have thought of the modern Messerschmitt monoplane fighters that Hitler's Condor Legion was using in Spain, and wondered. In the static display armed sentries stood guard over a Hawker Hurricane, the first the public had been allowed to see, while overhead a breathtaking exhibition of aerobatics and power-diving was given by – a Spitfire. It had no time to land, having to show off its paces at five other displays, we had so few.

As the summer of 1938 wore on in increasing uncertainty over the future, life at Biggin Hill changed perceptibly. There was a feeling abroad that the past years had been too happy, too good to last; one could not enjoy such a life without paying. Taxed with such thoughts, however, the young men of 32 and 79 Squadrons would deny any stiffening spirit and maintain that their hours of training – practising interceptions, formation-flying, air-firing, cross-country navigation trips and dummy runs – were not expended for any subtler motive than just a part of the fighter pilot's routine, or fun, or an excuse to clock up more flying hours, or that the Operations Room had thought up some new means on intercepting 'enemy aircraft' that wanted trying out. Later, they were to bless the time they had spent on those 'bloody interceptions'. Despite all modest disclaimers to the contrary, they found themselves taking that little extra bit of trouble to improve their shooting and formation-flying, and putting in some spare time practising Nos. 1, 2 and 3 attacks so that, when Munich came, they felt themselves as ready as any pilot could be with a biplane fighter.

Although nominally day-fighter units, both squadrons put in many hours night flying, being encouraged by 'Stuffy' Dowding who, on his frequent visits to Biggin Hill, always preached: 'I'm only interested in night flying and dirty weather.'

On 12th April 79 Squadron made the first formation-flight at night to be carried out in Fighter Command: nine Gauntlets taking off singly after dark to join up in squadron formation at 6,000 feet over Sevenoaks. Then, wing-tip to wing-tip the pilot's eyes glued on the ruby-red station-keeping lights, they flew north to the Thames, following the silvery ribbon down to Sheerness before swinging in a great arc by way of Hornchurch, Uxbridge, Epsom, Kenley and back to Biggin Hill.

A fortnight later the squadron repeated this feat for the benefit of a torchlight tattoo being staged at Uxbridge. It was so successful that the C.O., Squadron Leader Pritchett, fired with enthusiasm for more nocturnal outings, put up a suggestion that his squadron should fly over London nightly, the Gauntlets carrying fairy lights, to advertise the coming Royal Air Force Display: some very fancy effects would be obtained by changing formation in the dark. This enterprise was, however, vetoed by the Air Ministry on the grounds that 'the element of risk was such as to outweigh the benefits which might be derived therefrom.'

War! War !! War!!!

The atmosphere of war in all its grim horror pervades the usually peaceful station of Biggin Hill. The once cheerful countenances of the pilots are grim and determined as they await the signal to take-off on a dawn patrol. Dead silence reigns. Suddenly a hooter blares out its warning, and all is a hive of activity. Engines splutter into life with a dull roar, white-overall'd pilots sprint for their aeroplanes and within two minutes of the signal the 32nd Fighter Squadron rises in perfect formation from the ground and zooms skywards towards the grey horizon on its errand of death.

Thus the entry for 5th August, 1938, in the diary of 32 Squadron.

1st August was Bank Holiday that year; four days later the code-word 'Diabolo' was flashed to Biggin Hill, cue for Wing Commander Lock to bring his station to a state of 'immediate readiness for war'.

It was a dull, rain-swept afternoon when it happened. The clouds lay on the aerodrome, and hung in the trees and crept under the tall hangar doors. Flying was out of the question, but 32 Squadron was on duty, helping to train some new Controllers with dummy interceptions. 79 Squadron was absent, enjoying a week's leave. Inside 32's hangar it was

Pilot Officer Lance Bowler's turn to sit in his Gauntlet and chatter with the Operations Room by R/T. The other pilots – Michael Crossley, Pete Brothers, 'Grubby' Grice, 'Wooly' Woolaston, Olding and 'Humph' Russell – were waiting in the Flight Commander's office watching a game of 'Battleships' being played out between 'Millie the Moocher' Milner and 'Little Guy' Harris. Next door, in the flight sergeant's office, sat 'Snow' White and 'Henpecked' Hector Proctor, spending the afternoon in writing-up the aircraft log-books: the traditional heritage of all junior sergeant pilots, whether they had neat handwriting, or not.

A dull, damp peace and feeling of lassitude reigned over Biggin Hill.

Suddenly Lance Bowler burst in on the game of 'Battleships', for once in his life looking serious.

'Hey, chaps. We've just been put to "available".'

Cat-calls and derisive whistles greeted this statement. The squadron had been 'available' all afternoon.

'The Wingco said we've got to come to proper "available" immediately,' Bowler shouted above the uproar, 'and we've got to get the machines out and warmed up right away and then go down to the Armoury and make up ammunition belts,' he finished all in one breath. 'I don't quite know what it's all about, but apparently the Germans have walked in somewhere or other where they shouldn't, and it looks like war.'

His announcement of Hitler's march into the Sudetenland was, as it happened, premature.

79 Squadron was immediately recalled from leave, then No. 601 (County of London) Auxiliary Squadron flew in to make Biggin Hill its wartime station, bringing its Hawker Demons to join the Gauntlets. The Auxiliaries, hastily recalled by telegram from summer vacations, offices and clubs, included many who later were to distinguish themselves in the war, pilots like Max Aitken, Whitney Straight, Loel Guinness, Brian Thynne, Roger Bushell and Michael Peacock. Rivalry between them and the regulars of Biggin Hill was fierce and relations were not improved when the

'weekend playboys' beat 32 Squadron at its favourite sport, polo played on old motor bicycles, by using a 'stable' of brand-new Brough Superiors.

The reality of the crisis was brought home vividly to the squadrons by an Air Ministry order that all aircraft were to be camouflaged a drab green and brown. No longer would the Gauntlets be lined up on the tarmac spick and span, their aluminium cowlings polished to a mirror-bright finish, glittering in the sunshine. Sadly each pilot tackled his own machine with paint and brush, reluctantly obliterating the squadron crest which he had emblazoned on the rudder himself: a 'Salamander salient in flames' for No. 79 and a 'Hunting horn stringed in a broad white arrow' for 32 Squadron.

On 11th August Biggin Hill received its first Miles Magister, the low-wing monoplane used as a trainer for the Hawker Hurricanes which were to come. Five weeks later 32 Squadron took delivery of a single Hurricane, two days before Mr Chamberlain flew to his fateful rendezvous at Godesberg. The pilots at first were suspicious of the sleek new fighter, preferring the easy manoeuvrability of the Gauntlets. After a few hours on the Hurricane, however, they were completely captivated. On 30th September the Prime Minister returned home and announced to a cheering crowd from a balcony at No. 10, Downing Street: 'I believe it is peace in our time.'

Noted 32 Squadron's diarist: 'Everyone allowed out.'

The crisis had passed. Life at Biggin Hill had a new, more meaningful urgency. Now one squadron was always kept at 'available', day and night. No one doubted that war was inevitable, but how long was the respite that Mr Chamberlain had gained?

By the end of November both squadrons had received their allotment of Hurricanes, No. 32 getting the first V.H.F. R/T sets with three times the range and far greater clarity. Pilots worked hard converting to the new fighters and men on leave even returned early to get in a few flying hours. There were changes in command, as experienced C.O.s were taken away to form new units: Squadron Leader P. Prickman, 'Mexican Pete', took over 32 Squadron and Squadron Leader G. D. Emms, No. 79. 'Fiery' Lock was replaced by Wing Commander R. Grice, D.F.C., who was to lead and inspire 'Biggin on the Bump' through the Battle of Britain.

The physical appearance of the station changed: trenches and deep shelters were excavated, and windows sand-bagged. Camouflage experts arrived and set about the task of disguising the aerodrome as a wood surrounded by fields and hedges. The glaring white concrete of the aprons and parade ground was toned down with bitumen and granite chippings. Their efforts met with little success. A pilot sent up to observe the result reported that Biggin Hill was clearly visible from 3,000 feet over Sevenoaks and that the orange paint, supposedly disrupting the silhouettes of the hangars, shone like a Belisha beacon in the winter sun. It certainly failed to deceive the sharp-eyed crews of the *Lufthansa* airliners whose route to Croydon passed nearby. Whenever bad weather gave the excuse, a Junkers transport would fly inquisitively over the airfield. Once this proved too much for 32 Squadron who discharged the duty pilot's signal mortar across the airliner's nose. It hastily sheered off, but no complaint was ever lodged.

Christmas that year was white and snow effectively shrouded the worst ravages of camouflage. For a few days everyone pushed all thought of war from their minds, determined to enjoy what might well be, for all they knew, the last Christmas of peace. Then it was back to the daily routine of training and practice, the unspoken feeling of having a definite objective stronger than ever before.

In March the German army occupied the rest of Czechoslovakia, and Biggin Hill was again brought to a state of instant readiness. This crisis passed uneasily and the squadrons took some well-deserved leave. They had been working hard. In addition to routine training, they had made hundreds of flights for interception trials, as well as experiments in smoke-laying from the air and the seeding of airborne minefields. So much extra work was being thrust on Biggin

Hill that Dowding had to intervene finally and point out to the Air Ministry that it was not a research station. Wing Commander Grice and his staff could not cope and carry on with the training programme of an operational fighter station.

And so to August, the last month of peace. Biggin Hill was already at a high state of preparedness, thanks to the foresight and energy of the Station Commander, and everyone took it for granted that they would be the first, if not the sole, objective of the entire *Luftwaffe*. They felt equal to the occasion and ready for almost anything.

Early in the month, about midnight, a policeman in the village telephoned the Guard Room to say that he was sure a gas attack had been launched. He had been gassed in the last war, he said, and knew what he was talking about. There was a sudden tumult of alarms and the entire defence force was deployed, grimly prepared for the descent of parachutists, or they knew not what. Three hours later the same constable rang up to apologise: the source of the gas was a fractured main in a local pub. It was well after breakfast-time when the last tired and angry soldier returned from a fruitless search for phantom Germans.

Another night there was a trial black-out of the London area and Biggin Hill was instructed to send up an aircraft to observe the result. Everyone was in the Mess, except the pilot concerned, the Station Commander leading the choruses of an old Royal Flying Corps song:

> Stand by your glasses, steady –
> This life is a life of woe.
> Here's a toast to the dead already,
> Three cheers for the next man to go!

It was a wild, stormy night with low cloud shrouding the heights of the North Downs. In a break after one verse, they heard the roar of Flying Officer Olding's Hurricane taking-off for the black-out patrol. He circled overhead once, drowning the chorus, then veered off to the South. Suddenly his Merlin engine cut out. Seconds later there was a deep

101

explosion – then silence. Outside a dull red glow flickered ominously, reflected off the low clouds. Grice ordered the crash tender out at once, realising that its crew might never find the wreck in the murk of that night, Flying Officer Woolaston took-off, intending to drop a marker flare by the side of Olding's Hurricane. Those outside the Mess watched expectantly for the glare of burning magnesium to break through the mist. To their horror they heard a second explosion – in the clouds 'Wooly' had crashed into the top of Tatsfield Hill. They found his wrecked aircraft a bare hundred yards from Olding's.

> Here's a toast to the dead already,
> Three cheers for the next man to go!

On 24th August orders went forth for mobilisation and everyone on leave returned post-haste. Wing Commander Grice was delighted when some, who had long left the Air Force, dug out their old uniforms and hastened to Biggin Hill to offer their services. One man, Flying Officer Bill Igoe, formerly of the Anti-Aircraft Cooperation Unit, had resigned his commission after a bad crash. Now he returned to stay and eventually become senior Controller of the station. The Army manned the Ack-Ack defences day and night, and all aircraft were moved out to prepared dispersal points in the event of a sudden bombing raid. The weather was fortunately fine, and the pilots and ground crews were able to sleep in tents by their aircraft.

On the eve of war 601 Squadron returned again, bringing its new Blenheims to join the Hurricanes. Although nominally light bombers, their Blenheims had been adapted for fighter purposes by the addition of a box of four .303 Browning machine-guns under the fuselage and carried an air gunner as well as a pilot.

That evening they saw the impressive sight of the entire London balloon barrage up for the first time. Some felt frightened as they watched the great elephantine shapes rise gleaming in the light; its purpose was so horribly clear.

That evening, too, an old friend and neighbour of Biggin

Hill, Mr Winston Churchill, dropped into the Officers' Mess on his way home to Chartwell. Looking at the fresh youthful faces around him, he said in a tired voice, his expression grim and determined: 'Well, I've no doubt all you young men here will be as brave and eager to defend your country as were your forefathers.'

There was a moment's gloomy silence, then a voice piped up from the back of the room: 'Cheer up, sir. It won't be as bad as all that!'

CHAPTER NINE

TWILIGHT WAR

'I AM speaking to you from the Cabinet Room at No. 10, Downing Street.

'This morning the British Ambassador in Berlin handed the German Government a final Note stating that, unless we heard from them by eleven o'clock that they were prepared at once to withdraw their troops from Poland, a state of war would exist between us . . .'

At Biggin Hill the Hurricanes of 32 and 79 Squadrons, the Blenheims of 601 Squadron, stood dispersed around the perimeter, fuelled and armed, ready for instant take-off. In the Sector Operations Room the controllers and plotters waited patiently, keyed-up for the first indication of enemy action. Round the dispersals the pilots basked in the warm September sunshine and listened to the words of the Prime Minister on that fateful Sunday morning.

'. . . I have to tell you now that no such undertaking has been received and that consequently this country is at war with Germany.

'Now may God bless you all. May He defend the right. It is the evil things that we shall be fighters against – brute force,

103

bad faith, injustice, oppression and persecution – and against these the right will prevail.'

For long seconds no one spoke, each man alone with his thoughts. After the months of indecision and false rumour, of hectic training and improvisation, the dread news was almost welcome.

A little 'erk' cycled past 32 Squadron's temporary dispersal tents, singing at the top of his voice:

> Pack up your Goebbels in your old kit-bag
> And Heil! Heil! Heil!

The tension of the moment dissolved into laughter which ceased as the voice of the Station Commander boomed from the Tannoys: 'As you will all have heard, we are now at war with the Hun . . . '

Scarcely had Wing Commander Grice started to speak when his words were drowned by the banshee wailing of the sirens. Cursing Hitler for wasting no time, some pilots moved irresolutely towards their aircraft, wondering whether to take-off without orders before the sky was darkened by German bombers. Over London the balloons rose with elephantine majesty while thousands of people, impelled by a terrifying vision of *Blitzkrieg*, flocked self-consciously into the shelters.

A telephone rang with sudden urgency in 32 Squadron's dispersal. The airman manning the direct line to the Operations Room replied: '32 Operations . . . Yes, sir . . . Yes, sir . . . Yes, sir . . . What height, sir?'

'Come on chaps. This is it!'

Pilots jumped to their feet, quickly grabbing Mae Wests and parachutes, all eyes on the telephone orderly.

'Yes, sir . . . Right away, sir.' He swung round and shouted: 'Blue Section. Patrol Gravesend 5,000 feet. Scramble!'

Within five minutes three Hurricanes were rocketing up from Biggin Hill like so many startled pheasants.

'Hullo, Sapper[1] control. Sapper control. Jacko[2] Blue Leader calling. All aircraft airborne.'

The voice of the Controller sounded unflurried over the R/T: 'Hullo, Jacko Blue Leader. Vector 045 degrees. Angels five. Unidentified aircraft.'

'Hullo, Sapper control. Blue Leader answering. Message received. Listening out.'

While the Prime Minister addressed the nation, an aeroplane had been flying across the Channel towards the Thames Estuary. When still far from sight, a tell-tale 'blip' on the screens of the cathode-ray tubes in the coastal radiolocation stations gave warning of its approach. Nearer to land, it was picked up by the vigilant watchers of the Observer Corps. Its silhouette was unfamiliar and immediately the intricate defence network sprang to life. In the Operations Rooms at Fighter Command, at 11 Group and at Biggin Hill the suspect was meticulously duplicated by the little symbols the plotters moved across their maps. Air Chief Marshal 'Stuffy' Dowding watched and wondered. An order passed down the chain of command to Biggin Hill – and the Hurricanes took-off. They were recalled a few minutes later. The suspect had landed at Croydon, a French transport bringing a party of Staff Officers to London.

The *Luftwaffe*'s onslaught failed to materialise, the sunny September days dragged lazily on and little happened to make the first month of war at Biggin Hill memorable. 32 Squadron boasted of their first night patrol on 4th September, orbiting for 90 minutes over Canterbury in close formation with navigation lights dimmed and the ground blacked-out below. Encouraged by their Squadron Leader, Brian Thynne, the former 'weekend playboys' of 601 Squadron put in the maximum hours possible on their Blenheims by day and night, training up to the standard of the two Hurricane squadrons. 79 Squadron had the first casualty when Flight Lieutenant R. W. Reynolds crashed his Hurricane in a wood near Biggin Hill after a night exercise. All three squadrons

[1] R/T code name for Biggin Hill.
[2] R/T code name for 32 Squadron.

shot down breakaway barrage balloons – good sport but not combat. A pilot of 79 Squadron decapitated the driver of a motor mower with the wing-tip of his Hurricane. Taxi-ing to a standstill he was confronted by the macabre spectacle of the mower still running with a headless driver bolt upright in the seat.

Towards the end of the month the Station Commander was promoted to the rank of Group Captain. Dick Grice was liked by all; having won his D.F.C. in the first world war, he tackled the often thankless task of Station Commander with the youthful enthusiasm of the Royal Flying Corps. Every section of Biggin Hill was his concern and he possessed the happy knack of making anybody and everybody work for him. A fighter pilot at heart, his slim figure, pipe in mouth, was always at hand in the hectic summer of 1940 to greet returning formations with a crate of beer, nor did he forget the hard-working ground crews. To celebrate his promotion the pilots placed him high in an 'Armadillo' vehicle and paraded him round the dispersals so that all might admire their Station Commander in his new glory.

These weeks of inaction were most welcome to Grice, giving him time to get Biggin Hill's defences into shape. If, and when, the Germans attacked, fighter airfields would be a primary target, and the Polish campaign had demonstrated how devastating dive-bombing could be. Shortly before the declaration of war the 90th A.A. Regiment had deployed its guns around the aerodrome, now Grice insisted that they be moved much closer so they would at least have a chance of hitting the *Stukas*. To defend the station against paratroops and saboteurs the Army provided seventy-four privates of the Queen's Own Royal West Regiment. 'How bloody silly!' snorted Grice and raised his own defence force of seventy airmen armed with rifles.

Relations between the Army and the Air Force had their lighter moments. The Sector Operations Room was the nerve centre of Biggin Hill and it was the 'brown jobs' duty to guard this day and night. The troops were all reservists and their knowledge of the Air Force and its ranks was rudimentary. On his daily visits to the Operations Room, Grice was a little put out by the friendly attitude of the sentries who nodded and smiled at him in a gafferish way, not realising that he was the Station Commander. These elderly soldiers were given some gentle instruction in Air Force manners by the Station Warrant Officer. When next Grice visited the Operations Room, there was a marked improvement. The sentry snapped smartly to attention, inspected his pass and announced that he might enter.

'Don't you feel that I'm entitled to a salute?' tolerantly inquired Grice.

'Oh no, sir. We've learnt that you blokes with gold peaks on your caps, you're Warrant Officers!'

The Group Captain was speechless.

As Sector Station, Biggin Hill had operational control of all the army searchlight units in the area. One night early in September, the C.O. of the Searchlight Company at Maidstone reported that a German aircraft was circling overhead. As no enemy appeared on the plotting table, the Duty Controller rang the Searchlight H.Q. at Knole Park, Sevenoaks, for confirmation. A Territorial Officer replied politely that no such aircraft had been seen or heard. Then Maidstone reported that the sound detectors were still picking up the German. In the Operations Room the staff looked at each other in bewilderment: how had it crossed the coast without being spotted and what was the damn thing doing over Maidstone? As a precaution the anti-aircraft batteries were alerted and Sergeant 'Snow' White of 32 Squadron was ordered up to investigate. Twenty-five minutes later the mystery was solved. The door of a refrigerator had been left open and the Army's new super-sensitive Mark VIII sound detector had picked up the noise of the electric motor!

The Operations Room staff's opinion of their Army colleagues was confirmed a few days later when they visited the Searchlight H.Q. to inspect a new and very secret telephone line linking Biggin Hill and Knole Park. They found it being used for drying the panties and brassières of the A.T.S.

A defence measure which caused great hardship to local residents was the closure of the Bromley/Westerham road to all private cars and pedestrians. This road ran through the station close to two of the most vital buildings, the Operations Room and the power house, the first targets for sabotage. Those whose livelihood depended on transient traffic, the proprietors of garages and teashops, were faced with bankruptcy, as overnight their takings dwindled to a few shillings, while rivals on diversion routes round the aerodrome enjoyed good business. They appealed for compensation and found that Air Ministry Regulations provided for loss of income from all causes except the closing of a road.

October was cold and wet. Fortunately the wooden dispersal huts, office and crew-room, were completed before the weather broke and the squadrons were able to move in from their tents. In Scotland and off the East Coast others in Fighter Command were shooting down their first Huns, but Biggin Hill's pilots had little to do but investigate 'X' raids, as all doubtful aircraft which appeared on the plotting table were labelled. Happily, the watchers of the Observer Corps had as yet little opportunity to become familiar with the appearance of the enemy and any suspect aircraft was promptly reported. The controllers in the Operations Room dared leave nothing to chance:

09.45   Blue Flight, 79 Sq., ordered to intercept doubtful raid No. X 42. No result.

11.38   Yellow Section, 79 Sq., ordered to investigate with caution raid No. X 39. No result.

12.19   Red Section, 79 Sq., ordered to intercept raid No. X 44. No result.

12.56   Red Section, 79 Sq., ordered to intercept raid No. X 40. No result.

So it continued on through the winter of the twilight war.

    The plots that appear on the screen, tra la,
    Have nothing to do with the Hun.

The A.O.C's having a dream, tra la,
And won't send us off in a stream, tra la,
To fight the Hun in the sun,
And that's what I mean when I say and I scream
O bother the plots that appear on the screen![1]

It fell to 79 Squadron to make Biggin Hill's first 'kill' of the war. At 10 a.m. on 21st November Yellow Section was ordered to patrol Hawkinge, the forward airfield of the sector. Only two Hurricanes took-off as the engine of the third failed to start. The pilots, Flying Officer Jimmy Davies, an amiable young American, and Flight Sergeant Brown, did not relish an hour's stooging up and down the South Coast in dirty weather. At 10.20 they were ordered to intercept an 'X' raid over Dover. It was an Anson of Coastal Command. Then the vectors came in thick and fast: at 10.31 back at Hawkinge at 12,000 feet; 10.38 Dover at 15,000 feet; 10.41 the South Foreland. The radio-location operators had a 'blip' on their screens that could only be an enemy aircraft.

There was a hint of excitement in the Controller's voice: 'Hullo, Pansy[2] Yellow Leader. Sapper control. Vector 115 degrees. Angels 15. Buster!'

The two Hurricanes swung on to the new course. Davies and Brown switched on their gun-sights and twisted the safety-rings from 'safe' to 'fire'. At 10.55 they sighted their quarry: 'flying pencil', the Dornier 17, making a weather reconnaissance over the Channel.

'Tally ho!'

The Operations Room staff smiled when they heard Davies's American stammer over the loudspeaker. One of the plotters quickly moved a little red sticker, symbolising the Hurricanes, next to the black, enemy, sticker on the vertical glass map of the sector.

They had an advantage of 3,000 feet over the Dornier. Unseen, the two Hurricanes dived down and opened fire at 600 yards. Davies chortled with delight as he smelt the acrid

[1]Flying Officer 'Grubby' Grice of 32 Squadron.
[2]Code name for 79 Squadron.

cordite fumes seep into his cockpit and saw, for the first time in his life, what eight Browning guns did to an enemy aircraft. Pieces flew off in all directions. With one engine streaming black smoke, the Dornier twisted over and spun into the clouds. Davies and Brown dived after it and emerged from the overcast to see it hit the sea with a wholly satisfying explosion.

Eight days later six Blenheims from 601 Squadron were ordered to Northolt for a most secret operation. No one had an inkling of their mission. Landing at Northolt, they joined the equally mystified crews of six more Blenheims from 25 Squadron. The following day they were briefed. By the end of November magnetic mines had become a serious threat to our shipping. Scientists were working on the de-gaussing apparatus, but had not solved all the problems. Meanwhile German seaplanes were slipping over each night to lay their deadly mines in the Thames Estuary and in the routes of coastal shipping. The Blenheims were to strafe the main seaplane base on Borkum, one of the Friesian Islands. The pilots and air gunners would all be going into action for the first time.

They reached Borkum at dusk. The Germans were caught completely by surprise as the twelve Blenheims dived out of the clouds in sections of three: the second led by Flight Lieutenant Michael Peacock and the fourth by Flying Officer Max Aitken, both of 601 Squadron. For a while the base was in pandemonium as panic-stricken men ran in all directions and jumped into the water to avoid the Blenheims skimming over at less than 100 feet and spraying slipways and hangars with bullets. A ship in the harbour opened up with a pom-pom and was quickly silenced by a Blenheim that flew through a gap in the mole. In five minutes it was all over: five seaplanes wrecked, patrol boats sinking in the harbour and many dead around the machine-gun posts. The Blenheims flew back across the North Sea in darkness and landed at Debden without a single casualty and not a bullet hole to be found on the aircraft. It had been a 'piece of cake'.

In November the first W.A.A.F., Deputy Company Commander M. S. Petrie, reported for duty, paving the way for the many to come. Wearing their blue berets and macs with pride, for few at first had complete uniforms, the W.A.A.F.s set an example which the scarce misogynists of Biggin Hill had to admire. 'No one asked us if we wanted girls but as they're here we'll enjoy them to the utmost,' crowed the pilots and gave a decorous cocktail party to welcome the N.C.O.s. Wives living on the station were not so pleased when they heard they would have to vacate their Married Quarters to become the new 'Waafery'. In the Operations Room the controllers cynically sorted their new assistants into three watches – 'first glamour', 'second glamour' and 'hags' watch, but in their hearts envied the girls' calm ability to pass the long hours of inactivity with knitting or a game of bridge on the plotting table.

December was another quiet month without a round being fired in anger. There were changes in command: Squadron Leader Loel Guinness took over 601 Squadron, and Squadron Leader Chignell the '32nd Pursuit', and on 4th December 79 Squadron escorted the King across the Channel on a visit to France, and again on His Majesty's return. When the royal destroyer was about to enter Dover harbour four Hurricanes swept down, skimming the waves in a bravura 'beat-up' while the King saluted them from the bridge. Back at Biggin Hill the Station Commander was 'tearing a strip' off the guilty pilots for recklessly endangering their aircraft, when a dispatch rider arrived to convey His Majesty's compliments on their low-level display. Seeing that the joke was on him, Group Captain Grice stood the miscreants a round of drinks in the Mess.

The New Year brought with it an upheaval: 601 Squadron to Tangmere, 79 Squadron to Manston and 32 Squadron to Biggin Hill's satellite aerodrome at Gravesend. For the next three months no squadrons operated from the 'Bump', giving the construction gangs an opportunity to excavate deep air raid shelters and lay a short concrete runway. 'The *Luftwaffe* inspected Biggin Hill's new runway today,' announced Lord Haw-Haw, 'and will shortly finish it off!'

Gravesend in peacetime (recorded the diarist of 32 Squadron[1] after the first week there) was an excellent little private flying club with quite a large aerodrome, a useful-sized hangar and a very nice little club house. It was not, however, designed to accommodate about 250 wholetime boarders. The wretched troops lived in the utmost discomfort, sleeping on palliasses on the floor and being fed from a cooking trailer. Characteristically they made the most of it and thoroughly enjoyed themselves. The N.C.O.s also slept on the floor and the less lucky of the officers.

Excitement! Excitement! Excitement! A Heinkel 111 has just flown high over the aerodrome. All aircraft ordered down at once. Ack-Ack batteries opened up. Heinkel didn't notice.

That winter was the severest on record for forty years. How Fighter Command could continue to operate was a mystery to the Germans who knew nothing of the frenzied efforts of pilots, administrative staffs, ground crews and even W.A.A.F.s to keep the runways clear of snow. Deep drifts made Biggin Hill, Hawkinge and Manston unserviceable, but at bleak and unsheltered Gravesend the wind never allowed the snow to settle to any great depth:

1/2/40. No see, no fly! Whole squadron turns out with spades to clear runway of snow-drifts. Method: 'Volunteer', with 'Moocher' as unnecessary passenger in the back, drove the Bedford truck flat out at the drift, and while 99 per cent of the boys carried out a successful flank and rearguard action with snowballs on 'Moocher', 1 per cent dug out the Bedford. Sgt. White and 'Rocky' got in the way and had to be thrown into a snow-drift. Little progress made.

In addition to the air defence of Great Britain, Fighter Command had responsibility for protecting all coastal shipping within a five-mile belt off-shore, and for the three

[1]Flight Lieutenant M. N. Crossley.

months it spent at Gravesend 32 Squadron carried out this onerous and unrewarding task:

> Duty: Escort to shipping.
> Details: Escort train ferry. Height 2,000 feet. No E/A.[1]
> Duty: Convoy patrol.
> Details: Area North Foreland. Height 4,000 to 5,000 feet. No E/A.

Despite the cold, the snow and unspeakable flying conditions, the ground crews and pilots kept the Hurricanes airborne for an average hundred hours a week – a considerable achievement. 'No E/A' was the daily report except once when Green Section sighted the squadron's first Hun, a Dornier 17 at 28,000 feet over Manston, and then the anti-aircraft batteries opened fire on the Hurricanes with such disconcerting accuracy that they were forced to break formation and let the Dornier escape.

By April both home squadrons, 32 and 79, had returned to Biggin Hill where they continued to carry out endless convoy patrols and the fruitless interception of 'X' raids.

> And that's what I mean when I say and I scream
> O bother the plots that appear on the screen
> That have nothing to do with the Hun!

CHAPTER TEN

HURRICANE WEATHER

High Rank, Low Rank, everybody come,
Join us in the Pilot's Room and make yourself at home,
Take off your gloves and flying-boots and light your
   pipes anew,
And let us introduce you to the Fighting 32.

[1] Enemy aircraft.

AT dawn on 10th May, 1940, Hitler invaded the Low Countries. 'Naughty, naughty old Adolph,' admonished 32 Squadron's ebullient diarist. 'You know you said you wouldn't!'

News of this latest *Blitzkrieg* was only a few hours old when 79 Squadron was ordered to France. After three years at Biggin Hill there was no time for a valedictory celebration. Elated at the prospect of meeting the hitherto elusive *Luftwaffe*, the pilots hastily packed their gear and flew their Hurricanes across the Channel. The W.A.A.F.s in the Stores Section were suddenly inundated with bicycles, boxes, pets, radios and unwanted clothing: all to be labelled and sent back to their owners' homes. R.A.F. transports, Bombays and Ensigns, arrived to pick up the ground personnel, stores and equipment, and ferry them to their new base at Merville. That evening the squadron was in action over Belgium. Its place at Biggin Hill was taken by 610 (County of Chester) Squadron which moved down from Prestwick with the first Spitfires to fly from the 'Bump'. By teatime the newcomers, under Squadron Leader A. L. Franks, were comfortably installed in the quarters vacated four hours previously by 79 Squadron.

The older members of the '32nd Pursuit' had no cause to be jealous of the good fortune of the squadron they had fathered in 1937. Within a few days they were to be in the thick of battle.

In Holland one aerodrome after another was reported captured by German paratroops, many disguised as civilians or wearing strange uniforms. The Royal Air Force prepared to strike back with every means at its disposal but the War Cabinet, fearing a massacre of innocent civilians with bombs, restricted attacks to fighters only. On 11th May 32 Squadron was ordered to strafe Ypenburg aerodrome, outside the Hague, reportedly in German hands and packed with troop-carrying aircraft. At 4 p.m. the twelve Hurricanes, led by Squadron Leader J. Worrall,[1] took-off from Manston.

[1]Squadron Leader J. Worrall, former Senior Controller at Biggin Hill, replaced Squadron Leader Chignell as O.C. 32 Squadron on 6.5.40.

Conditions were perfect: clear, sunny weather, visibility thirty miles with scattered, friendly, cumulus clouds. Flying at 10,000 feet they crossed the estuaries of the Scheldt and Maas, all eyes straining ahead in the hope of seeing the swarms of twin-engined Messerschmitt 110 fighters reported by the survivors of another Hurrican squadron which had taken a terrible beating from them that morning. To the starboard lay Rotterdam in flames from end to end, a gigantic column of smoke drifting away to the south-east. Then the Hague, with men and women looking up and waving in friendly greeting.

About the time the squadron sighted the target, 11 Group rang Biggin Hill to demand the instant recall of the Hurricanes. In the Operations Room the Duty Controller checked the time: too late, they were beyond R/T range.

The fields around Ypenburg were dotted with white, the discarded 'chutes of the paratroops. On the concrete apron outside the hangars were some unidentifiable black markings. There were no signs of enemy opposition.

'Echelon Starboard, "A" Flight!'

Five Hurricanes slid obediently into position on the right of Red One, then all six roared down in a steep dive while 'B' Flight stayed aloft to provide cover. As the aerodrome grew larger and larger in the gun-sights, the black marks on the concrete were resolved into the burnt-out wrecks of sixteen Junkers 52's. Only one troop-carrier remained intact.

Flying very fast, 'A' Flight levelled out and swept over the field, streaming incendiary bullets into hangars and other buildings. Then it was 'B' Flight's turn. Some gesticulating mannikins darted out of a hangar when they saw the remaining Junkers burst into flames, and caught the full fury of the attack. Seconds later they lay sprawled grotesquely on the ground.

32 Squadron had fired its guns in anger for the first time. Everyone returned unscathed to Biggin Hill, well-satisfied with the afternoon's work but puzzled by the absence of all opposition.

The B.B.C. news gave the reason that night. During the

day Dutch patriots had recaptured Ypenburg. Cannily biding their time, they had shot-up each troop-carrier as it landed, reserving one for an escape to England.

Depressed by this fiasco, the squadron passed the next few days on fruitless patrols over Belgium and France.

Whew! What a shock. Whole outfit up at 3.15 a.m. Going to France. Everyone amazed. Red Section start for Manston, get D/F'd back in lousy weather. All eventually get off to Manston to find a signal to return immediately. Do so. Later all set off to France, land at Abbeville, refuel, hear dreadful stories, get very frightened, do a patrol, see nothing, feel better, do another, see nothing, feel much better, return to Biggin Hill, feel grand. Everyone has done 5½ hours' flying.[1]

Only once was an enemy aircraft sighted, a Heinkel 111, and then, when he had it fairly in his sights, Flight Lieutenant Crossley found his guns weren't cocked!

On 19th May the squadron's luck changed. Weaving through big banks of cumulus over Cambrai, eleven Hurricanes came face to face with the enemy: nine single-seater Messerschmitt 109 fighters escorting a Dornier 215 bomber.

'Attack, attack . . . GO!'

With no time for precise orders by R/T they swept into the rough-and-tumble of a dog fight, spinning round in tight circles and shooting for all they were worth. Making up for his previous disappointment, Crossley fired a perfect deflection burst at a Messerschmitt which flashed across his nose and saw the bullets rip home. Whipping round in a tight left turn, he watched it slowly roll over and dive to earth. Three seconds wasted in savouring the dreadful elation that comes with the first 'kill', and another Messerschmitt was trying to get on his tail. A quick loop, but it was still there. The Hurricane was the more manoeuvrable: in one and a half turns Crossley got inside the German's orbit. Gaining on the Messerschmitt in a steep climb, Crossley saw out of the corner of his eye, a Hurricane wheeling over on its back, a

[1] Squadron diary.

great sheet of smoke and flame streaming behind. He watched it plummet down until a white parachute blossomed out. Meanwhile his quarry had vanished. Crossley was surprised to find himself alone at 20,000 feet, experiencing for the first time the uncanny sensation of being caught up in a mass of whirling aircraft at one moment and, seconds later, being in a completely empty sky.

Sergeant White, leading Green Section, went straight for the Dornier. A long burst and its tail sheared off. The big bomber went into a smoking spiral from which there could be no recovery. Not one of its crew attempted to bale out. The temptation to make certain of a first 'kill' is irresistible: White was about to follow the Dornier down when he was jumped by three Messerschmitt 110s flying out of the sun. Seeing them diving down, Flight Lieutenant Brothers broke away from another dog fight and was promptly set upon by three 109s. A tight evasive turn brought one across the Hurricane's nose. Brothers fired a two-second burst and sent it tumbling down in flames. Tracers streamed past Brothers from another Messerschmitt on his tail but the German pilot's aim was hopeless. Before he could correct it, Brothers was on his tail as he streaked for the safety of a cloud.

Pilot Officer Daw, having chased another Messerschmitt 109 into the clouds, found himself alone and decided it was time to return to Biggin Hill. Steering by gyro-compass, he set off as hard as he could go through the clouds. After twenty minutes he dropped from cover to check his position. Below was a great expanse of green forest that Daw didn't recollect seeing on the outward patrol. At that moment he spotted three Messerschmitt 110s coming towards him and getting very close indeed. In sudden panic he flew hell-for-leather at the leading one and pressed the 'tit'. The Me. 110 just exploded into a shower of fragments; the other two shot up into the clouds and disappeared. Checking with his magnetic compass Daw found that he had been flying due east for the past twenty minutes, more or less on course for Berlin.

The whole action had lasted, perhaps, five minutes. Within half an hour the Hurricanes were back at Biggin Hill, Group Captain Grice grinned with satisfaction when he saw their victory rolls. One after the other the pilots landed and taxied to the squadron's dispersal where the Intelligence Officer, Flying Officer Sir Richard Leighton, Bart., was waiting to hear their stories: 'Baron' Worrall, 'Red Knight' Crossley, Pete Brothers, 'Polly' Flinders, 'Shag' Eckford, 'Grubby' Grice[1] and, finally, 'Jackdaw' Daw loudly claimed the world speed record from Central Germany to Biggin Hill. Only one Hurricane failed to return: 'Millie the Moocher', Flying Officer Milner, the first pilot of the '32nd Pursuit' to be lost in action. The day's score: seven confirmed, one possible and two doubtful.

'Good show!' said the Station Commander.

Weeks later the squadron received a postcard from a *Kriegsgefangenenlager* in Germany: 'Sorry I left you the other day, I wasn't thinking. Wonder if you are still at the Bump. Do drop in and see me any time you're round these parts – love to everybody and good luck. Millie.'

With its appetite whetted 32 Squadron was in action almost daily during the next week, flying offensive patrols and escorting Blenheim bombers over Northern France in a futile endeavour to stem the German flood. Whenever and wherever possible the *Luftwaffe* avoided combat, preferring the destruction of roads, bridges and troop-concentrations, and the pitiless machine-gunning of refugees. Nevertheless, the squadron shot down another nine Huns for the loss of one Hurricane. By now, all the old hands were 'blooded' but it was Michael Crossley, the tall, debonair Etonian, who took the lead with five destroyed. Always the individualist, with an eventual score of twenty-two victories, he delighted in masking with an impish humour his prowess as one of the outstanding fighter pilots of the war.

Next on the list comes Crossley and he commands 'A' Flight,

[1]No relation to Station Commander, Group Captain R. Grice, D.F.C.

He also leads Red Section, so they christened him 'Red
    Knight'.
He carries out a weather test by standing on a chair
And all the boys from down below cry 'How's the air up
    there?'

To the Hurricane pilots, flying in brilliant sunshine over
the patchwork fields of Artois, the last desperate stages of the
battle being fought out on the ground seemed very remote,
with only the fleeting glimpse of a blazing ammunition dump
or a road crawling with refugees to bring into focus the
reality behind the laconic communiqués of the B.B.C. Those
that baled out, or made a forced-landing found themselves
pitchforked into chaos and, like homing pigeons, struggled
back to the security of Biggin Hill.

While escorting a squadron of Blenheims over Arras, 32
Squadron encountered a lone Henschel 126 – a two-seater
army-cooperation machine. As the terrified partridge seeks
to elude the hawk, the Henschel dropped to earth with
Squadron Leader Worrall and Sergeant North diving after it.
Twisting and turning at tree-top height, the German tried
desperately to shake off the two Hurricanes. After some
minutes Worrall broke away and North fired a long burst at
a hundred yards. The rear gunner of the Henschel replied
with tracer. North was closing to fifty yards when a violent
explosion in the port petrol tank sent the Hurricane lurching
sideways with smoke pouring into the cockpit. Too low to
bale out or even lower the undercarriage, North had perforce
to belly-land in a ploughed field.

Without the roar and vibration of the Merlin engine it
seemed deathly quiet: just the sinister crackle of flames and
the fading sound of the squadron winging its way home to
Biggin Hill. North felt all alone and, momentarily, very
afraid. He knew that he had landed about ten miles south-
east of Arras, but had no idea if the town was still in the
hands of the Allies. After making sure that the Hurricane
would continue to burn, he started walking to Arras and
met a friendly farmer who told him that the Germans were

barely a mile away, advancing towards the canal whose south bank North had reached. The other side, however was still held by the French who had blown up all the bridges. Some miles farther on North came to a sluice-gate guarded by a handful of *poilus*, awaiting the moment when they could drown the greatest number of Germans. Arras had fallen and North was advised to make for Vimy. Tired and hungry, he arrived there at midnight and was thankful to find the British Army in occupation.

All night long the guns roared; the concussion of exploding shells and the vibration of tanks on the move made sleep impossible. At dawn North quit the hayloft where he had sheltered and set off in borrowed army transport for Merville where he knew 79 Squadron had been based. The roads were jammed with an endless stream of refugees; many shouted brave words of encouragement in French when they recognised the sergeant pilot's uniform, others spat and reviled him. North found the aerodrome at Merville abandoned, evidently in a great hurry for thousands of petrol tins, tool-kits, guns and boxes of ammunition littered the field. Sadly he wandered around, looking at the wrecks of Hurricanes belonging to 79 Squadron. He wondered if he would see Biggin Hill again.

From Merville North drove to St Omer where he met another sergeant pilot shot down four days previously. As they reached the aerodrome, a squadron of Dornier 215s flew over to bomb and machine-gun the already deserted field. North and his companion took to the woods and walked to an airstrip on the other side of St Omer, used by an R.A.F. army-cooperation squadron. Here they were bombed by some Heinkel 111s. When an ammunition dump blew up only a hundred yards from their shelter, the two sergeants decided it was time to stop chasing the Royal Air Force and head for Calais. They entered the port at the height of a raid. The *Luftwaffe* had the sky to itself, unmolested by fighters or Ack-Ack fire. Next day North reached Dover on a destroyer, shaken by all the mines which exploded during the crossing. Forty-eight hours after being shot down he reported back to Biggin Hill, convinced that the battlefield was no place for a fighter pilot.

The succession of military disasters in France and the Low Countries brought immediate repercussions to Biggin Hill. R.A.F. transports shuttled back with hundreds of dirty, hungry airmen short of clothing and so very tired. Pilots, who had fought magnificently to protect the B.E.F., landed with but one ambition (after a shave and a pint of beer): to get airborne and take another crack at the *Luftwaffe*. A fortnight after it had flown to France with such *élan*, 79 Squadron returned to Biggin Hill, crossing the Channel like refugees on the S.S. *Biarritz*; many familiar faces were missing, their Hurricanes burnt-out skeletons on Merville aerodrome.

In three days over 800 men were landed on the 'Bump', to be fed, clothed and given shelter. It seemed an impossible task but the Equipment Section, inspired by Squadron Leader Kingham, worked miracles with the slender resources available. Everyone helped to stuff hessian bags with straw for mattresses; fortunately the nights were warm and the weary airmen could sleep in hangars and air raid shelters.

At the same time the station's defences were overhauled and placed under Lieut.-Col Butcher, D.S.O., who commanded the Anti-Aircraft School in the South Camp. Reinforcements began to arrive: half a battalion of the Dorset Regiment and a detachment of the 34th A.A. Battalion with Bofors guns. Any hopes that the local residents entertained for the re-opening of the Bromley/Westerham road were quickly dashed. Even the bus which had been allowed to run through the aerodrome with shuttered windows and an armed sentry on the step was vetoed by Colonel Butcher who had heard that in Norway several important buildings had been captured by a handful of German soldiers, wearing 'civvies', who had boarded buses in ones and twos at previous stopping places.

As the crisis heightened, nerves became tauter and more strained. There were several false alarms and excursions. On the night of 25th May the station stood-to to repel a reported attack by German paratroops. After working eighteen hours a day to keep the fighters airborne, many ground crews were often too tired to return to their billets and dossed down in the shelters at the dispersal-points. The men of 32 Squadron received a rude awakening when the door was flung open and a voice bellowed: 'What are you men doing here? Get up! The country's been invaded!'

'Ah, go f— yourself,' yawned an airman sleepily in the darkness.

'Who said that? I'll have him on charge in the morning.'

Someone shone a torch on the door, revealing an infuriated young subaltern.

'Cripes, he really means it!'

They scrambled into their clothes, grabbed rifles and stumbled out into the night, Corporal Ascot as always with his two Dachshunds. Crouching down in their home-made gun pits, they peered into the darkness, imagining Germans all around. No drill had been worked out for recalling the defenders in the event of a false alarm and it was long after dawn when the disgruntled men returned swearing vengeance on that subaltern.

As the troops of the British Expeditionary Force and the French First Army pulled back towards Dunkirk and the beaches, Biggin Hill prepared for the *débacle*. Ignoring the protests of the Squadron Leaders, 'Stuffy' Dowding sent 32 and 79 Squadrons away for a well-deserved rest: they had been in action more or less continuously since 10th May. 610 Squadron moved with its Spitfires to Gravesend, and three fresh Hurricane squadrons arrived at Biggin Hill: 229 Squadron to replace 610 Squadron in Home Defence, and 213 and 242 Squadrons for Dunkirk. The latter was the first Canadian volunteer squadron in the Royal Air Force, soon to become famous under Squadron Leader Douglas Bader. On the eve of the great evacuation the Biggin Hill sector was ready, the squadrons deployed and pilots cheerfully prepared for their great task.

At 6.57 p.m. on 26th May Vice Admiral Ramsay received orders to commence 'Operation Dynamo' – the evacuation of the B.E.F. from Dunkirk. From then until the last boat had left it was the responsibility of Air Vice Marshal Keith Park, that tall, wiry New Zealander commanding 11 Group, to provide their air cover. Operating at a distance from their bases the Hurricanes and Spitfires could only patrol for forty minutes. With a total of sixteen squadrons at his disposal Park was hard-pressed to keep even one at a time in the air over Dunkirk during the hours of daylight. Inevitably there were times when there was no air cover whatsoever. 'Where was the R.A.F.?' was the bitter accusation of the sorely tried troops on the beaches who knew nothing of the air battles being fought out of their sight.

On the eve of 'Operation Dynamo' no patrols were flown from Biggin Hill, but next day all three squadrons were in action. On their first sortie the pilots of 610 Squadron, flying in their Spitfires at 18,000 feet, sighted a twin-engined Heinkel 111 bomber some 3,000 feet below. Anxious, in this his first combat, to make certain it was a Hun, Squadron Leader Franks dived down and calmly flew alongside taking a good look: the swastika on the tail, the black crosses on the wings were plain to see. Franks ordered Red Two and Red Three to attack. Flying Officer Smith poured all his ammunition into the Heinkel, only breaking off when the starboard engine was enveloped in flames. Sergeant Medway followed him up with a five-second burst, then the three Spitfires of Yellow Section joined in. Blue Section lined up to speed the Heinkel to its doom, but were called off by Franks. Plunging down out of control, the German pilot managed to fire Very signals which brought forty Messerschmitt 109s to avenge him. Undismayed by odds of over three to one, the Spitfire pilots went straight in to attack and sent three Messerschmitts spinning down in flames, with another three 'probables'. From this brief but hectic party Flying Officer Medcalf and Sergeant Medway failed to return. Flying back to Gravesend the squadron sighted a big formation of Junkers 87s and 88s. To their fury the pilots could do nothing about them as all their ammunition was spent.

The two Hurricane squadrons operating from Biggin Hill enjoyed a more modest success that day. On a joint patrol over Gravelines they met ten Messerschmitt 109s and shot down two without loss.

Next day, 28th May, was definitely Hurricane weather. Ironically, the Spitfires of 610 Squadron were twice over Dunkirk when the *Luftwaffe* was on the ground refuelling and bombing-up, and not a single enemy aircraft was sighted.

At 5 a.m. the twelve Hurricanes of 213 Squadron left Biggin Hill to escort a flight of Blenheims on a bombing raid over St Omer. This done, they patrolled between Gravelines and Nieuport, coming under heavy, though fortunately inaccurate fire from our own anti-aircraft guns before they ran into a bunch of Messerschmitt 109s escorting some Heinkel 111s out to bomb the shipping in Dunkirk harbour. The enemy formation was broken up, the Heinkels jettisoned their bombs harmlessly into the sea, one fighter was definitely destroyed and one bomber damaged, but two Hurricanes went down trailing black smoke. The pilot of one, Sergeant Boyd, baled out over the Channel, was picked up and was flying again within twenty-four hours.

After a quick breakfast back at Biggin Hill, the pilots of the remaining ten Hurricanes took-off and flew towards the great pall of black smoke that spiralled up into the sky over Dunkirk. They arrived just as large numbers of Junkers 88s and Heinkel 111s, covered by Messerschmitt 109s started to drop their bombs on the troop-covered beaches. Within five minutes seven German aircraft had been shot-down by the hopelessly outnumbered Hurricanes, several more damaged and the rest scattered to the winds. Three Hurricanes were lost but only one pilot was killed, Pilot Officer Stone, whose body was recovered from the Channel and buried with full naval honours at sea. Sergeant Butterfield had accounted for two 109s, one 110 and a Ju. 88 before he baled out and was picked up by the *Royal Eagle* paddle-steamer. Now down to seven Hurricanes, 213 Squadron was again over Dunkirk in the afternoon, without further success. The Canadians gave an equally good account of themselves, shooting-down three Messerschmitt 109s on their first patrol of the day for the loss of two Hurricanes.

The struggle was carried on for another five days. Each evening saw many more thousands of troops brought back to safety in Britain, but the numbers of Hurricanes and Spitfires dwindled and there were many faces missing from the Mess at Biggin Hill. Every pilot had his experiences. Sergeant Wilson of 610 Squadron baled out from his blazing Spitfire when the wings fell off and landed unhurt in the Channel. Flight Lieutenant Ellis marked the spot and tried to draw the attention of a destroyer to it, only to be nearly shot down by naval pom-poms for his pains. A pilot of 213 Squadron who had crash-landed on a beach north of Dunkirk was prevented from embarking on a ship by an embittered army officer. Another pilot, rescued from the Channel by a destroyer, was abused and insulted by the troops on board. Time and again pilots were heartened by the sight of a lone Hurricane flying over the Channel. They recognised the aircraft by its drooping undercarriage. It was the A.O.C. coming to see for himself. After a very heavy day's patrolling he asked the Canadians to perform an extra task: to locate and destroy a captive balloon over Nieuport spotting for the artillery that was shelling the beaches. There was no sign of the balloon, but the squadron shot down another five enemy aircraft for good measure.

By the evening of 4th June it was all over. 610 Squadron flew a final patrol without meeting a single enemy aircraft. Looking down from 6,000 feet the pilots could see the French soldiers on the beaches wave a friendly *envoi* to the Spitfires as they awaited the coming of the Germans.

In nine days of fighting the Biggin Hill squadrons had accounted for thirty-six German aircraft plus a score of 'possibles' for the loss of only fourteen Hurricanes and Spitfires. Six pilots made their way back to England to fly again.

'We must be careful not to assign to this deliverance the attributes of a victory,' declared the Prime Minister in Parliament. 'Wars are not won by evacuations. But there was a victory inside this deliverance, which should be noted. It was gained by the Royal Air Force.'

CHAPTER ELEVEN

NO LULL BEFORE THE STORM

Our average day is from dawn until dusk
Which doesn't sound much I'll admit,
But when dawn is at three and dusk is at ten,
You'll agree it's a bit of a s—t!

                              32 Squadron

THE emergency over, life at Biggin Hill resumed a more
settled rhythm. In the warm, sun-bathed days of June, 1940,
it was a delightful station. Nestling among the green hills of
Kent, slightly higher than most, Biggin Hill was proud that
its workshops, hangars, sick-bays and living-quarters – all
the multifarious sections of an R.A.F. station, including the
gardens – were in perfect trim. The view across the valley
from the terrace of the Officers' Mess remained as lovely as
ever, an unfailing anodyne for ragged nerves.

The reinforcement squadrons had departed after their days
of glory over Dunkirk; the two which traditionally called
Biggin Hill home were back from brief rests at Wittering and
Digby. The difference between them was striking. 32 Squadron, the senior, had a wholly light-hearted approach to its
duties, squadron discipline was loose and clothing unconventional enough to outrage the more rigid interpreters of
Air Ministry Regulations. Relationships between officers
and other ranks were based on personal worth without for-
mality. 79 Squadron, on the other hand, was very orthodox
with a spit-and-polish approach to life; yet it was the happy-
go-lucky individualists who stood the brunt of combat far
better than the more doctrinaire pilots.

The number of W.A.A.F.s serving on the station had
risen to over 250. There were those whose jobs kept them
always busy: the cooks, telephonists, M.T. drivers and many

others; and there were those who sat around the plotting tables tranquilly waiting for the storm to break. In charge now was Section Officer Nicholl, 'Mrs Nick' to everyone, with twenty-six-year-old Felicity Hanbury as Assistant Section Officer. During the weeks after Dunkirk they were very busy, training the airwomen, seeing to their comfort, giving them air raid and anti-gas drills and preparing as best they could for the uncertain future.

The spirit of the girls was amazing. Long before the first bombs fell on Biggin Hill one young airwoman sent her parents a glowing account of a heavy raid on the station, including a most moving description of the shooting-down of a German aircraft and the subsequent funeral of the pilot at which the Station Commander had ordered all the airmen and airwomen to do the goose-step! This flight of imagination was by no means unique. The girls had volunteered in the spirit of Saint George and when the dragon failed to appear, they gaily invented one.

Not the least of the W.A.A.F. officers' problems was the chivalrous attitude of the Station Commander towards girls brought before him for punishment. It did not help discipline, or please the airmen, if a W.A.A.F who was marched in to the Group Captain on a charge was invited to be seated and offered a cigarette!

There was no respite for Fighter Command after Dunkirk. For another fortnight the armies of France, aided by those British troops remaining across the Channel, ineffectively continued the struggle. The Hurricanes from Biggin Hill were over France daily, escorting Blenheims on bombing raids and covering the British units in their withdrawal to the Channel. At times they encountered only intense Ack-Ack fire, at others they enjoyed sharp, victorious engagements with the *Luftwaffe*.

On 7th June 32 and 79 Squadrons jointly escorted eighteen Blenheims over to Abbeville. While 32 Squadron shepherded the bombers, 79 Squadron took on forty Messerschmitt 109s, shooting-down five. Next day it was the '32nd Pursuit's' turn to celebrate the highest score.

The weather was hot, the sky cloudless and, as there was no urgency behind the mission, the squadron had plenty of time to taxi-out and take-off in good order. 79 Squadron followed behind and together they set course for Beachy Head *en route* for Le Tréport. Orders were to patrol a beat north and south of this harbour for forty minutes to prevent the *Luftwaffe* from harrying the evacuation that was taking place.

Half an hour passed. 32 Squadron was flying at a comfortable 10,000 feet with 79 Squadron three miles behind. The pilots were thinking of lunch at Biggin Hill when a large formation of Heinkel 111s was sighted, 3,000 feet below and apparently unescorted. Black and evil in their war paint, the bombers flew steadily on in section of three, line astern. They presented a perfect target for the classic No. 6 attack in the fighter pilots' manual.

'Line astern!'

Red, Blue and Yellow Sections of 32 Squadron moved into position behind Flight Lieutenant Crossley, flying as Red One.

'Going down to starboard . . . Leader taking port machine . . . Echelon starboard . . . Go!'

Each pilot of Red Section had a Heinkel in his sights.

'Attack, attack . . . GO!'

Crossley pressed his firing button at 300 yards. His Heinkel dropped its undercarriage immediately. The German pilot pulled out of formation and glided to earth, black smoke pouring from his starboard engine.

'Breaking away to port . . . NOW!'

Away went Red Section, leaving the Heinkels clear for Yellow Section to attack. Pilot Officer Daw sent one down in flames, and then another.

As Crossley led his section out of harm's way and turned in parallel to the bombers, he saw his victim make a surprisingly good crash-landing in a field.

Its initial attack completed, 32 Squadron re-formed for the second time.

'Attack, attack . . . GO!'

Crossley picked off another Heinkel and delightedly watched it make a far less dignified landing than his first victim. Pilot Officer Grice, his blood up, went straight for the leader of a Heinkel section instead of an outsider, closed in to point-blank range, pressed the 'tit' – and was shot out of the sky by the cross-fire of the other two. The remainder jettisoned their bombs and dived to safety.

79 Squadron, meanwhile, had attacked the Heinkels' long-overdue escort of Messerschmitt 109s. Those of 32 Squadron with any ammunition left joined in and accounted for three.

The dog fight at 300 m.p.h. took the Hurricanes far to the south. Looking at his fuel gauge Crossley saw with a shock that he had petrol for barely twenty minutes' flying. A second Hurricane flew alongside his, its pilot frantically gesturing that he, too, was running out of fuel. Lost. unable to reach Biggin Hill or even the nearest R.A.F. station across the Channel, they turned northwards and searched for the sinuous course of the Seine. They chose to land at Rouen-Boos, hoping to find the aerodrome there still in Allied hands. It was deserted. There was petrol aplenty, stored in bowsers with no means of siphoning it out. One by one other Hurricanes straggled in; then a Tiger Moth flown by two strange Squadron Leaders with news of refuelling facilities at Drex, some forty miles away.

By lunchtime both squadrons were back at Biggin Hill. More than one pilot had been about to land on an unfamiliar French airfield when he glimpsed the grey-green uniforms of the troops in occupation. It had been a great morning's work: nine enemy aircraft definitely destroyed with another four 'probables', no losses to 79 Squadron but three from 32 Squadron failed to return. For two of the missing pilots this had been their first operational sortie. The third, most unhappily, was twenty-year-old Pilot Officer D. H. Grice who had been with the squadron since the days of peace, one of its most popular and able pilots.

And now we come to Grubby, a pilot of renown
Who flies his Hurricane right way up and also upside
  down.
He flies so close you never have to use R/T,
You just call out 'We'll land now', and he shouts 'O.K.
  by me!'

Grice had crash-landed in a field not far from Rouen
where he met a chilly reception from survivors of an artillery
unit he found sheltering in a wood. They had been bombed
and machine-gunned for more days than they could remember without once seeing an R.A.F. machine. No home mail
for over a month, but they cheered up when Grice promised
to communicate with their families if, and when, he succeeded in reaching Biggin Hill.

'I was in the U.K. only an hour ago,' he remarked, setting
off towards Rouen. 'Spent last night in a pub.'

'Lucky devil!'

Three days later 32 Squadron's diarist was able to record:
'Grubby returns. *Heil* Grubby!'

After a fortnight's uneventful patrolling 79 Squadron lost
two pilots in tragic circumstances. The day began well with
the news that His Majesty the King was to visit Biggin Hill
in the forenoon to hold an investiture. There was, however, a
job to be done first. In the company of three other squadrons
79 took-off from Manston to escort a flight of Blenheims on
a photographic reconnaissance over St Valéry. The outward
journey was without incident. Coming back, 79 Squadron
provided top cover at 10,000 feet. The French coast had just
been crossed when Pilot Officer Parker, flying as 'A. E.
Charles, Esq.',[1] spotted three Messerschmitt 109s diving out
of the sun.

'Hullo, Leader. Weaver calling. Bandits on our tail.
LOOK OUT!'

The warning went unheard: Parker's R/T had broken
down. The Messerschmitts struck and were away at full
throttle before the squadron realised it had been attacked.

[1]'Arse-end Charlie.'

Two Hurricanes went down in flames. Sergeant McQueen was seen to bale out, his Mae West keeping him afloat, apparently unhurt. For the next ninety minutes there was always a Hurricane circling faithfully overhead to mark the spot. When the Rye lifeboat reached it, McQueen was found to be dead.

Biggin Hill was *en fete* for His Majesty. All the officers, airmen and W.A.A.F.s who could be spared from duty were on parade. Standing apart in a small, self-conscious group were the pilots waiting to be 'gonged': the Distinguished Flying Cross for Flight Lieutenant Crossley, Pilot Officers Daw and Grice of 32 Squadron, and Pilot Officer Stone of 79 Squadron; the Distinguished Flying Medal for Sergeants Cartwright and Whitby. Each in turn marched smartly to the table where the King stood with Group Captain Grice. They saluted and remained at attention while the citations were read: ' . . . displayed great qualities of leadership . . . exceptional courage and coolness . . . devotion to duty . . . complete disregard for his own personal safety . . . excellent example to others . . . '

The low-pitched, sententious phrases were belied by the sympathy and understanding in His Majesty's eyes.

At last only one Distinguished Flying Cross lay on the cushion. It was to have been presented to Flight Lieutenant Jimmy Davies of 79 Squadron. Since making Biggin Hill's first 'kill', he had added five 'certainties' to his score. His was the second of the two Hurricanes shot-down that morning. Right up to the end of the ceremony everyone hoped that he would reappear, smiling and nonchalantly apologising for being late on parade.

'What General Weygand called the Battle of France is over. I expect the Battle of Britain is about to begin. Upon this battle depends the survival of Christian civilisation. Upon it depends our own British life, and the long continuity of our institutions and our Empire. The whole fury and might of the enemy must very soon be turned on us. Hitler knows that he will have to break us in this Island or lose the war. If we can stand up to him, all Europe may be free and the life of the world may move forward into broad, sunlit uplands. But if we fail, then the whole world, including the United States, including all that we have known and cared for, will sink into the abyss of a new Dark Age, made more sinister, and perhaps more protracted, by the lights of perverted science. Let us therefore brace ourselves to our duties, and so bear ourselves that, if the British Empire and its Commonwealth last for a thousand years, men will still say: "This was their finest hour".'

At the Station Commander's instigation copies of these much-quoted words were posted up where all might read them. Outwardly the pilots were as carefree and irresponsible as ever, but a new note of firm purpose and resolve underlay their light-hearted banter. A stream of high-ranking visitors stressed the issues at stake, the responsibility that was theirs. The Prime Minister, with his home at Chartwell, naturally took a neighbourly interest in Biggin Hill. Within a fortnight came H.R.H. Group Captain the Duke of Kent, the Secretary and the Under Secretary of State for Air, Air Commandant Trefusis Forbes of the W.A.A.F., and Air Chief Marshal Sir Ludlow Hewitt, Inspector General of the Royal Air Force.

'If only the nobs'd leave us alone to get on with the job,' was the fervent wish of everyone, weary of changing into their best uniforms for V.I.P. parades.

They were more appreciative of the growing numbers of new Hurricanes and Spitfires coming from the aircraft factories. They were grateful, too, for all the efforts of designers and technicians to give them every possible advantage over the *Luftwaffe*. When first introduced into service our eight-gun fighters were fitted with two-pitch propellers. A change to constant-speed (variable-pitch) propellers would make possible a fuller use of the Merlin engines' power, matching the Messerschmitts in climbing, ceiling and power-diving.

On 22nd June the de-Havilland Company received instructions to convert all Hurricanes and Spitfires to constant-speed propellers: a telephone call sufficed, this was no time for formal, written contracts. Within a week one thousand conversion sets had been manufactured: governor units, oil-feed pipes and cockpit controls. Just as soon as the first were ready, twelve de-Havilland engineers set out for the fighter stations.

Mr S. C. Bentley arrived at Biggin Hill on the evening of 25th June expecting to find the Spitfires of 610 Squadron. The squadron, however, was still at Gravesend. Next morning Bentley explained the idea and urgency of the conversion to his assistants, a Flight Sergeant and two fitters, and added that he had no intention of sleeping until the first modified Spitfire was airborne. It was a matter of personal pride to be the first to put an operational constant-speed fighter into the air. Bentley and his team worked all day and through the night, snatching ten-minute breaks for refreshment. At 9 a.m. next day he rang de-Havillands' to ask for a test pilot. He had beaten his colleagues by a margin of several hours. After spending three days more at Gravesend Bentley returned to Biggin Hill to tackle the Hurricanes of 32 Squadron. By the week's end he was a very tired man, but the job was done. In broad daylight, with both eyes open, he walked unseeingly into a wing and knocked himself out!

Across the Channel the Germans were making their preparations for the coming onslaught on Britain. The collapse of France had been unexpectedly sudden; the *Luftwaffe* needed time to reorganise and deploy three immense *Luftflotten*, totalling some 3,500 aircraft, on 400 aerodromes spread out in a menacing arc from France to Norway.

Each day gained was of inestimable value to Fighter Command. Under the dynamic leadership of Lord Beaverbrook the output of aircraft rose steadily; more important still was the increase in the proportion of Hurricanes and Spitfires[1] to strengthen the squadrons at Dowding's disposal. From the Firth of Forth to the Bristol Channel fifty-seven squadrons, 600-odd fighters in all, awaited the six-fold forces of the *Luftwaffe*. Inevitably the fiercest fighting would be borne by

[1]From 331 at the end of Dunkirk to 620 on 10 August.

11 Group defending London and the South-East. The Air Officer Commanding, Air Vice Marshal Keith Park, had only twenty-one squadrons to meet the attack. In the Biggin Hill Sector, keystone of 11 Group, 610 Squadron left Gravesend to join 32 Squadron on the 'Bump', while 79 Squadron, now re-equipped with Spitfires, was withdrawn to Acklington for the defence of Tyneside.

Fresh pilots came from the training units to replace those lost during Dunkirk and the Battle of France. Many were Allies, airmen who had made the hazardous journey from Occupied France to join the Royal Air Force. The '32nd Pursuit' welcomed a Belgian and two Poles. The former, Pilot Officer the Comte de Grunne, had flown with Hitler's Condor Legion in Spain. As an ex-Messerschmitt pilot he was regarded as an expert in German fighter tactics. It was his misfortune to be shot-down on his first encounter with the Me. 109!

The two Poles, Pilot Officers Pniak and Wlasnowalski, dubbed 'Cognac' and 'Vodka' respectively, were magnificent pilots, flying with a fierce hatred of the Hun – on the ground it was another matter. Their disregard for the proper care of aircraft was notorious.

Neither had flown Hurricanes before they came to Biggin Hill, only the gallant biplanes of the Polish Air Force, so Pilot Officer Flinders was deputed to give a brief conversion course. One Hurricane only could be spared for training purposes.

Some hours later, watched by Flinders and a tense Pniak, for the honour of Poland was at stake, Wlasnowalski confidently taxied-out for his first solo. Mechanics working on Spitfires outside the triple-bay hangar dropped tools and stared when they heard the heavy, surging roar of the Hurricane. From the engine note they knew something was wrong. Wlasnowalski, however, kept on at full throttle, struck the boundary fence, cart-wheeled over the main road and came to a grinding halt in the garden of a bungalow. Up went a column of thick, black smoke.

Pniak beat the fire-tender and ambulance to the crash, and arrived to find a doleful Wlasnowalski, amazingly unhurt, shaking his head over the wreckage.

'Coarse pitch! Always the bad luck I have!'

He had made the classic error of trying to take-off with the propeller set in coarse pitch.

Pniak, maddened at the insult to Poland, promptly set about his compatriot so ferociously that when the ambulance did arrive, he had to be taken to the sick-bay for treatment. Honour was satisfied!

For a brief spell in July 141 Squadron returned to Biggin Hill after an absence of twenty-one years. When the order came to move from Turnhouse, near Edinburgh, there were few, if any, in the squadron who knew its origin in that little band of officers and men who spent the winter of 1917/18 in a snowbound canvas hangar on Biggin Hill. To the 'Cock' Squadron of 1940 the name of its new station meant 'somewhere in Kent', therefore near the Channel and, most hearteningly, within shooting range of the *Luftwaffe*.

The squadron flew the Boulton and Paul Defiant, a new fighter from which great results were expected. A slim, Merlin-powered monoplane with a crew of two, pilot and gunner, the Defiant, unlike the Hurricane or Spitfire, carried no forward-firing guns within the wings, being armed instead with a four-gun power turret in mid-fuselage. Only two squadrons had received Defiants: 141 and 264. The latter had scored a great victory at Dunkirk by shooting down 37 enemy aircraft on two successive patrols. This augured well for the new fighter, but the absence of guns fired by the pilot was to prove a tragic flaw in design.

Squadron headquarters were established in the South Camp at Biggin Hill. The Defiants, however, were to operate from the satellite airfield at West Malling where their crews found themselves billeted in a wing of the local mental hospital.

Despite the 'flap' to move south 141 Squadron did not see action until 19th July, shooting in anger for the first time

135

since that night in 1918 when Turner and Barwise brought down their Gotha.

Twelve Defiants were put on readiness at Hawkinge. At 12.30 p.m. nine scrambled to patrol at 5,000 feet 20 miles south of Folkestone, the remainder being grounded by engine trouble.

Flying in sections of three, line astern, they were vectored to a point off Gris Nez. Flight Lieutenant Loudon gave warning of enemy aircraft; twenty Messerschmitts diving out of the sun. If they had tuned in to the Germans' R/T frequency, they would have heard their Defiants being gleefully identified as 'easy meat'.

The squadron broke to port and turned to deliver a beam attack. The wily Huns countered by attacking from below and dead astern, knowing that the Defiants' guns could not be brought to bear on them. Immediately two Defiants were seen to dive vertically into the sea. Realising what was happening, 141 Squadron's pilots whipped into steep left and right turns, giving their gunners split-second chances to get their sights on the Me. 109s. Sergeant Powell was the first to send one down in flames.

A cannon shell smashed into the engine of Pilot Officer McDougall's Defiant. White glycol mingled with black smoke in a long plume as it spun down towards the Channel. McDougall ordered his gunner, Sergeant Wise, to jump and was about to follow when his engine picked up. He circled twice over the water, watching Wise swim strongly towards the coast of France. He was never seen again.

Flight Lieutenant Loudon was caught in the cross-fire of two Messerschmitts. His gunner, Pilot Officer Farnes, got in three bursts before he baled out. Loudon struggled home with his Defiant ablaze and crashed in Hawkinge village. In hospital five bullets were removed from his arms. Farnes was picked up by an air-sea rescue launch. For some reason the new parasuit he was wearing, specially designed for the occupant of a Defiant turret, kept him floating face-down in the water. 'I was bloody glad to feel that boat-hook up my arse!' was his only comment.

Flight Lieutenant Donald and Pilot Officer Hamilton[1] reached Dover, crashed and died in their blazing Defiant. Weeks later members of 141 Squadron saw a newsreel film of the pyre, the commentator exulting: 'There goes another Messerschmitt!'

Only three Defiants returned to Hawkinge. 141 Squadron's first action of the war had ended: six aircraft lost, four pilots and five gunners killed.

At Biggin Hill the rumour spread that the squadron had been completely wiped out. The fitters of other squadrons, hard-pressed to keep their own fighters serviceable, descended on the reserve Defiants and stripped them of everything of use. Before they were reduced to skeletons the R.A.F. police intervened and gathered up the spoils. No disciplinary action, however, was undertaken.

The survivors of 141 Squadron were released from operations. Squadron Leader Richardson was hastily summoned to 11 Group Headquarters to confer on the obvious limitations of the Defiant as a day-fighter. After only eleven days at Biggin Hill the squadron returned to Scotland, posted to Prestwick for conversion to night-fighter duties. 32 and 610 Squadrons were again in partnership on the 'Bump'.

I was leading 610 Squadron, consisting of 7 aircraft, which was ordered to take-off from Hawkinge at 18.37 hrs. While patrolling Dover we saw a destroyer being bombed 2 miles out to sea. I personally did not see the bombers, but saw about 20 Me. 109s at 7,000 ft. so I gave orders for the squadron to attack them. I attacked the last E/A of one section and fired about half my ammunition into him at between 100 and 10 yards' range. I must have taken the section by surprise as they did not break up or adopt any evasive action except gentle turns. My target rolled over and plunged down towards the sea out of control. As I climbed into the clouds after the attack I saw a 109 hit the

[1]Hamilton came from South Rhodesia. Today 141 Squadron's plaque hangs in his memory in the main hall of the Churchill School, Causeway, S. Rhodesia.

sea and believe that this was the one I attacked. After this I cruised around just in the cloud where it was possible to see clearly downwards. While doing this I sighted another section of 4 Me. 109s in line astern. I dived down below this section and carried out again a climbing attack on the last E/A. I emptied the remainder of my ammunition into him at point-blank range, and he fell out of the sky burning furiously and hit the sea.

In the unemotional, almost banal, wording of his combat report Flight Lieutenant Ellis described his part on the battle of seven Spitfires against twenty Messerschmitt 109s. The rules of victory were stringent: 'Did you see it crash?', 'Did it break up in mid-air?', 'Had it caught fire with no possible chance of survival?' were the questions the Intelligence Officer asked the pilots on their return. If there was any doubt, a 'probable' or a 'damaged' was their award. On this occasion, 610's pilots writing their reports under the sceptical eye of the squadron 'Spy', were granted five 'confirmed' for no loss. They had amply revenged their Squadron Leader, 'Big Bill' Smith, killed when trying to land his badly shot-up Spitfire after another engagement earlier that afternoon.

This action was typical of many hundreds fought out over the Channel during the weeks preceding the Battle of Britain. 10th August was the day nominated by Hitler and Goering as *Adler Tag*, the 'Eagle Day' which was to commence the annihilation of the Royal Air Force as a necessary pre-liminary to the invasion of Britain. In the meantime, using only a tithe of its strength, the *Luftwaffe* probed our defences with small raids at night and daylight tip-and-run raids on the Channel ports and coastal convoys. Little material damage was achieved by these attacks but they forced Fighter Command on to the defensive, flying up to 600 sorties a day. In four weeks 227 enemy aircraft were destroyed for a loss of only 96 of our fighters. Coastwise shipping was particularly difficult to protect as it sailed up the Channel within sight of the hostile cliffs of France. It was just too easy for a formation of *Stukas*, escorted by

Messerschmitts, to take-off, dive-bomb the convoy and flee for home before our fighters could give battle. From Hawkinge, the Sector's forward base near Folkestone, the Biggin Hill pilots often saw the white geysers of near-misses erupting around the ships before they heard the 'Scramble!'

Great morning, noisy afternoon. Hawkinge again responsible. Squadron patrol Dover below low cloud. Red Knight unwisely said he saw something above cloud. Green Section went to see. Didn't. Pancake all. Just doing so when we saw a barbecue in progress over Dover. Interest immediately revived and we tore back to have a 'butcher's'. Red Section nominated a Me. Jaguar, chased it through spray and tipped it into the sea. Received unwelcome attention of another Jaguar.

Later we intercepted, without any exaggeration, a total of at least 20,000 assorted Huns. The following tipped stuff into the Drink: Hector, Pete B, Sgt Higgins, Humph and Red Knight. The Mandarin converted three non-smoking Ju. 87s into smoking 87s but earned the attention of at least 4 squadrons of 109s to such an extent that he just couldn't make the 'drome (fan stopped). He force-landed in a field, 2532 caught fire and burnt-out. Mandarin jumped out with cuts and a string of language which did justice to his high position.[1]

Squadron Leader Worrall's account was more circumstantial:

I was leading Green Section on a convoy patrol off Dover from 17.00 to 18.00 hours. At 17.40 Sapper told me Blue Section was joining me, also E/A between 10,000 and 20,000 feet were approaching the convoy. Almost at once I spotted them and, ordering Green Section line astern, attacked the first Ju. 87 just as he was starting his dive. Despite the fact that I had throttled right back I overtook him after a two-second burst. I turned and took on another but had to break off as I was attacked by a 110. I then lost the 110 and saw the Ju. 87s bombing a

[1] 32 Squadron's diary, 20.7.40.

139

destroyer. They finished bombing and made for home. I attacked the nearest who started smoking. I had to break off as I was attacked by a 109. I could not find the 109 so attacked another 87 which was near. He started to smoke and again I was attacked by a 109. I broke away. The 109 was not in view so I attacked a third 87 which also started to smoke. I was just about to fire another burst when I saw tracer going over my port wing. I immediately broke away and felt bullets entering the A/C from behind which were stopped by armour-plating. Then two cannon shells hit, one in the engine and one in the gravity tank. I turned for home and the engine petered out just too far away from Hawkinge. I had to make a crash-landing in a small field ½-mile to the east of the drome. Almost immediately she went up in a slow fire, giving me ½-minute to get out.

Neither squadron diary nor combat report reveal the strain of those July days with sixteen hours of daylight to aid the *Luftwaffe* in its attacks on our Channel shipping. At 3.45 a.m. pilots woke to their batman's cheerful reveille: 'On readiness Hawkinge, 05.00 hours, sir', followed by the long hours of waiting, slumped on deck-chairs in the sun, subconsciously alert for the telephone's ring which, for a moment, made the world stand still – a demand for payment of some forgotten Mess bill, or 'Squadron scramble!' Then the sprint to the aircraft, the hurried take-off and the fleeting minutes of combat over the Channel. Three scrambles a day were common, often more. During July the Biggin Hill squadrons shot down twenty-seven Ju. 87s and Me. 109s.

As the date of *Adler Tag* drew near, the *Luftwaffe* intensified its attacks but, inexplicably, neither 32 nor 610 Squadron made contact during the first ten days of August. The sudden inactivity was welcome. The '32nd Pursuit' had little to do but pose for photographers from the Press and Ministry of Information – 'line-shooting' it heartily disliked. Only one Hun was encountered, a Heinkel seaplane bearing Red Cross markings. A section of 610 Squadron was ordered to attack at once.[1] After the swarms of Messerschmitts and *Stukas* the lone seaplane seemed too much of a sitting duck. The attack was half-hearted and the surprised German pilot was allowed to flee over the wave-tops to sanctuary in Boulogne harbour.

Unseasonable weather ruined Goering's hopes of commencing the annihilation of the Royal Air Force on 10th August. Next day conditions were again impossible, so it was not until 12th August that the curtain rose on the Battle of Britain.

CHAPTER TWELVE

THE STORM BREAKS

'MONDAY, 12th August, 1940. Grouse shooting begins: ends 10th December', thus the heading for the opening day of the Battle of Britain in many a diary, to which scores of fighter pilots added their personal paraphrase: 'Hun shooting continues: ends?'

Sunrise was at 5.38 a.m. At Biggin Hill it was 610 Squadron's turn for dawn readiness. Well before it was light the billets were resounding with ringing telephones and the thud of flying boots running. Outside it was cold and clear. Feet scraped impatiently on gravel while the pilots shiveringly awaited the shooting brake to take them to their dispersal-point. A few knowingly inspected the sky.

'Blitzy morning.'

Inside the brake they sat in silence, rubbing their hands

[1] Besides rescuing German aircrews shot down in the Channel, the Heinkel 59s with Red Cross insignia were undoubtedly used for reconnaissance purposes to report the movements of shipping. After a protest against this improper use of Red Cross immunity had been made without effect, the Government authorised the shooting-down of all such aircraft encountered.

and huddling together for warmth. The squadron's Spitfires loomed large in the half-light of dawn, with undercarriages weirdly truncated by the layer of white mist that blanketed the field. Ground crews were already at work, stripping off engine-covers and trundling out starter-batteries.

The windows of the dispersal hut were blacked-out. In the crew-room a few shaded bulbs shone dimly on the luscious 'pin-ups' and aircraft silhouettes which decorated the walls. A Flight Sergeant reported to Squadron Leader Ellis that all twelve Spitfires were serviceable.

'No non-runners today, sir.'

'Good show.'

Ellis went to a blackboard and chalked up the order of flying, allotting each pilot and aircraft a position in Red, Yellow, Blue and Green Sections. They sorted out their parachutes, helmets and gloves from an untidy heap of kit lying in a corner and took them out to the Spitfires. Parachutes were placed in readiness with the harness laid out to save precious seconds lost in fumbling when the order to scramble came. Swollen with flying suits and Mae Wests, everyone returned to the crew-room to catch up on sleep, lying on beds, or slouching in broken-down armchairs round the stove. They had nothing to do but wait, and hope that the kitchen staff would hurry up with breakfast.

Across the Channel, a hundred miles or so from Biggin Hill, the *Luftwaffe* was preparing to launch the first assault of Hitler's long-awaited *Adlerangriff*. On airfields in Normandy and the Pas de Calais, which two months ago had harboured Hurricanes of the Royal Air Force, German ground crews were servicing Messerschmitt fighters, 109s and 110s, whilst on airfields farther inland the bomb-trains were rolling towards the waiting Dornier 215s, Heinkel 111s and Junkers 87s – the much-publicised *Stuka* dive-bomber which was to take such a terrific beating from our Hurricanes and Spitfires. In briefing-rooms the bomber crews listened eagerly to Goering's orders. At last they were to strike in force against the mainland of Britain. Attacks on coastal shipping and the Channel ports were to continue, but the paramount objectives for 12th August were the three air-fields on the Kentish coast, Manston, Lympne and Haw-kinge, and the radio-location stations which had so successfully thwarted the *Luftwaffe*'s efforts to operate undetected over the Channel. With these knocked out, the way to London would be clear.

In 610 Squadron's dispersal hut the black-out shutters were taken down, letting warm sunlight flood the room. The ringing of the telephone brought the drowsing pilots instantly to their feet. The duty corporal answered it, tantalisingly spinning out the agony. 'Yes, sir . . . certainly, sir . . . right away, sir . . .'

Poker-faced, he replaced the receiver and announced, 'Breakfast's on the way over.'

A tornado of cushions and kit sent him ducking under the table.

Shortly before 7 a.m. radio-location operators on the South Coast detected the build-up of a large formation over the Pas de Calais. From that instant the enemy's movements were inexorably followed by the plotters at Fighter Command Headquarters, 11 Group and the seven Sector Stations, including Biggin Hill. Underground in his Operations Room at Group Headquarters, Air Vice Marshal Park studied the plotting table, trying to divine the *Luftwaffe*'s intentions: a feint, or a mass attack?

At 7.20 a.m. puzzled members of the Observer Corps, searching the Channel from the ramparts of Dover Castle, saw a small enemy formation, flying too high to be identified, approach the coast and discharge, not the expected bombs, but clouds of thick white smoke. This screen was ineffective. Six minutes later the observers reported that eleven waves of bombers, heavily escorted by fighters, were crossing the Channel. Park instantly gave orders for their interception. His Group Controller spoke crisply to his opposite numbers at Biggin Hill and Manston. Four and a half minutes after the enemy had been sighted the first fighters were taxi-ing out.

In 610 Squadron's dispersal the telephone rang a second

143

time. The orderly poked his head round the door of the crew-room and yelled: 'Squadron, scramble! Dungeness, 10,000 feet.'

As the pilots raced to their Spitfires the Intelligence Officer noted down the precise time: 7.31 a.m., and smiled.

Entering the dispersal hut, 'Spy' picked up the telephone to speak to the Operations Room. He was forced to shout above the crescendo of the Merlin engines.

'Dog-rose A Flight taken-off . . . Dog-rose B Flight taken-off.'

When the last Spitfire rose into the air he glanced at his wrist-watch: not too bad, three minutes, twenty-five seconds for the scramble.

Already the Tannoys were clamouring: '32 Squadron to readiness.'

Before the undercarriage had folded into the wings of his Spitfire Squadron Leader Ellis was reporting by R/T: 'Dog-rose Red Leader calling Sapper. Am airborne.'

The Biggin Hill Controller might have been a captain giving advice to a batsman before sending him out to the wicket. 'Hullo, Dog-rose Red Leader. Receiving you loud and clear. Vector 120 degrees. Nine bandits approaching Dungeness. Angels 10. Good hunting.'

'Thanks a million,' replied Ellis. 'Message received and understood.'

The squadron climbed steadily at three-quarter throttle. Ellis glanced round at the others. His No. 2 and No. 3 were tucked in nice and close, steady as rocks; on the left was Yellow Section in a tight vee, a little behind and on the right were Blue and Green Sections. Below lay the familiar patchwork of hopfields and pastures disected by that long, straight railway he had come to know so well since the squadron moved down to Biggin Hill. Under his port wing lay Ashford. 'Why does it always look so smug and peaceful?' he wondered.

The Controller interrupted his thoughts. 'Hullo, Dog-rose Red Leader. The bombers are all yours. Leave the fighters to Bulldog Squadron.'

144

Bristol Fighters of 141 Squadron flying past
Prince Yorihito of Japan, October 1918

A neighbour and old friend, Winston Churchill

'Cock' Squadron, No. 141, celebrating their victory in the
Squadrons-at-Arms Contest, 1918

Hurricanes of 32 Squadron flown by Sgt. Proctor, P/O Grice,
F/Lt. Connolly and F/O Milner, Biggin Hill,
Empire Air Day, 1939

The *Luftwaffe* over Biggin Hill

Bristol Bulldogs of 32 Squadron

'O.K., received and understood.'

Now they were approaching Romney Marsh. At any moment the bombers would be in sight. Twelve pairs of eyes searched the haze over the Channel. It was Ellis who gave the 'Tally ho!' when he noticed white fountains from a falling stick of bombs spurt up in the sea off New Romney. High above were nine tightly-packed black specks flying towards Rye. Dornier 215s! The sun struck little glints of grey and silver from the weaving escort of Messerschmitt 109s.

Ellis looked round for the squadron promised by the Controller. There were no other aircraft in sight.

'Hullo, squadron. Bandits one o'clock. 6,000 feet above. Watch the 109s.'

'O.K., Leader.'

The twelve Spitfires climbed at full boost. Reflector sights were switched on, gun-rings turned to 'fire'. They were barely a thousand yards from their prey when the Me. 109s pounced.

'Look out, Leader!' screamed the 'weaver'. '109s at six o'clock.'

'Break and give 'em hell!' Ellis' voice was quietly authoritative. 'NOW!'

The squadron whipped round in tight left and right turns to meet the attack head-on.

Ellis picked out a lone Me. 109 and followed it into a fast, shallow dive. It grew larger and larger. Now it almost filled his sights. A slight touch of left rudder brought the Spitfire dead astern. He pressed the gun button and felt the smooth shudder of eight synchronised guns. Relentlessly Ellis followed him down into a vertical dive, firing burst after burst, only breaking away when he was convinced his adversary was hopelessly out of control.

Back at 15,000 feet over Dungeness Ellis spotted another Me. 109 climbing to safety in the sun, and caught it at 20,000 feet. A single burst started it spinning down, a tricky target, but Ellis managed to keep it in his sights almost to sea level, using up his ammunition with deadly effect.

Sergeant Gardner chased a Me. 109 all the way to France and tipped it flaming into the sea a mile off the coast. Returning to the fray, he passed a Spitfire scrapping with another Me. 109 and joined in. The German was experienced. He tried steep climbing turns, stall turns and rolls to shake off his pursuers. Gardner remained glued to his tail, fired four short bursts in quick succession, and left him gliding gently towards France, with his propeller idling and glycol streaming from the radiator.

Looking for more trouble, Gardner tangled in a dog fight over Lympne at 10,000 feet. Quickly climbing up-sun, he chose his victim and dived, holding fire until the range was twenty yards. Pieces of the Me. 109 flew off and smashed against the Spitfire's canopy, 'Christ!' Gardner swore, ducking involuntarily. 'Too bloody close!' He pulled away above and to the right, glimpsing for a ghastly instant the lifeless pilot slumped in his harness as the Me. 109 rolled on its back and went tumbling down.

Meanwhile the Dornier 215s, saved from the fury of 610 Squadron by the escorting Me. 109s, bombed their target, the radio-location station on Dungeness.

For twenty minutes the fight raged. Fresh squadrons of Me. 109s joined in but the Biggin Hill pilots were undismayed.

Sergeant Chandler flew straight at a formation of forty and shot-up six. Entranced by a Me. 109 belching smoke and flames, Pilot Officer Rees jerked awake when he heard: 'Look out, Taffy! For Christ's sake, behind you!' Before he could take evasive action his attacker was shot-down by Pilot Officer Cox who finished his ammunition on a second Me. 109 that drifted into his sights. Pilot Officer Pegge saw six Me. 109s flying in a tight defensive circle below him. He dived out of the sun and slapped one down. Back at 23,000 feet he was amazed to see the remaining five still circling round. 'Stupid bastards,' he thought, sending a second crashing into the Channel. 'Will they never learn?'

Suddenly there were no more enemy aircraft to be

attacked. The survivors were all streaking back to France.[1]

Eleven Spitfires winged home to Biggin Hill.

The pilot of the twelfth, Flight Lieutenant Smith, had a lucky escape. Closing in on a Me. 109, intent on the 'kill', he felt his Spitfire shudder uncontrollably as cannon shells smashed home. The engine stopped dead in a terrifying silence. The cockpit filled with white smoke. Little tongues of flame started to play round the instrument panel. 'God! I've got to get out', was Smith's instant reaction. He let go of the stick and heaved back on the hood. It wouldn't budge. The Spitfire dived sickeningly, the wind whistled past like hurricane. Smith jerked his feet off the rudder and braced them, tugging desperately at the hood. Still it wouldn't open. Flames were licking his face and neck. 'This is what it's like to die,' he thought, 'choking and blinding and can't get out.' With the thought his presence of mind returned. The Spitfire was diving too fast. Reduced speed. He seized the stick and pulled it back savagely. The hood slid open without difficulty. Release the seat harness. Now over on your back and push the stick forwards. The Spitfire rolled and, before he knew where he was, Smith was outside it.

His aircraft, which had seemed so large and important, so full of smoke and flames, vanished. Smith was tumbled head over heels alone. 'Pull your ripcord before you pass out,' the instructors had dinned into him. Obediently he pulled. It seemed a very long time before his parachute opened. He had quite decided it wouldn't when he felt a tremendous jerk and found himself swinging gently. Half a mile away he saw a Me. 109, probably the one that had shot him down, being chased by a Spitfire.

In a moment they were out of sight. Smith could hear nothing except a slight silken rustle from above. The world

[1]It must be remembered that the Germans were operating at a greater distance from their bases than were the British. Writing of the Me. 109 during the Battle of Britain, Adolf Galland in his autobiography *The First and the Last* states: 'It used to take us roughly half an hour from take-off to crossing the English coast at the narrowest part of the Channel. Having a tactical flying time of only eighty minutes, we therefore had about twenty minutes to complete our task. . . .'

with all its familiar sounds was very far away. There were no birds to sing, no humming insects, and no railway engines cheerfully hooting.

Ten minutes later he was floating in the Channel, buoyed up by his Mae West, and relishing the cool salt water that allayed the agony of his burns.

At Biggin Hill Group Captain Grice stood alone outside 610 Squadron's dispersal. Fifty-four minutes after take-off the first Spitfire was in sight. The Station Commander listened for the whistle of the guns; one could always tell if they had been fired. He puffed his pipe contentedly when he heard it, a rise and fall like the sound of a flute, infinitely soft and melancholy in the wind.

'Tell N.A.A.F.I. to hurry up with the tea waggon,' he instructed the telephone orderly. 'It's late.'

Subconsciously tallying their number, Grice waited to see that each pilot had his mug of tea or cocoa, sandwich or sausage roll.

'Come and make your reports, chaps,' pleaded the Intelligence Officer. 'Group wants them at once.'

Clumsy with flying-kit Squadron Leader Ellis and the others crowded inside the dispersal office, all talking at once and boisterously re-enacting their experiences like excited schoolboys. Their average age was, in fact, a few months short of twenty-one.

'Well, Ellis?' asked Grice when there was a moment's lull.

'A grand show, sir. Went through them like a dose of salts.'

'Oh, it was simply wizard,' chimed in a youngster, unawed by the Group Captain's rank. 'You never saw so many Jerries in . . .'

He broke off abruptly. Everyone was watching a Spitfire coming in to land with a frightening, crab-like approach. It struck the ground, bounced heavily and taxied jerkily to a stop. Ground crew were already dashing towards it. They had seen the port aileron hanging limply, the tell-tale streaks of leaking petrol. The pilot, Flying Officer Gardiner, had to be helped down out of the cockpit, wounded in the leg by an exploding cannon shell.

'What's the score, Spy?' demanded Grice after he had seen Gardiner off in an ambulance.

The Intelligence Officer checked his reports. 'Sir, it looks like two confirmed destroyed, six unconfirmed, two probables and one damaged. There's no news of Flight Lieutenant Smith. The boys saw him bale out over the Channel.'

Grice irritably knocked the dottle from his pipe. He hated to lose a single pilot from his command.

'Of course,' added 'Spy' placatingly. 'We should hear more about those 'unconfirmed' when the reports come through from Ack-Ack and Observer liaison.'

Just then the telephone rang. It was a message to say that the missing man was safe in hospital at Dover.

The Station Commander beamed, and rammed his pipe full of fresh tobacco.

*   *   *

No further demands were made on Biggin Hill for some hours. Such news of the morning's raids as filtered through was none too good. Despite its losses the *Luftwaffe* had scored heavily: five of the all-important radio-location stations put out of action, in the Thames Estuary two convoys dive-bombed and, shortly before noon, Portsmouth heavily raided by 150 aircraft which cannily sneaked through the gap in the balloon barrage formed by the harbour entrance.

The situation would become serious if the Germans resumed their offensive during the afternoon. Temporarily bereft of long-range, early warning by radio-location, Fighter Command fell back on visual reporting by the Observer Corps. The margin of time left for interception was very, very small. No one at Biggin Hill was surprised when, at lunchtime, 32 Squadron was ordered down to the sector's forward base, Hawkinge. Only by keeping at least one squadron in the air on continuous patrol could Air Vice

Marshal Park hope to beat off the raiders before their bombs fell on target.

At 2.30 p.m. 32 Squadron was scrambled to patrol Dover / Hawkinge at 8,000 feet; no enemy aircraft sighted. While the Hurricanes were on the ground refuelling and the pilots snatched a breather, Spitfires from Manston kept watch. The squadron was airborne again at 4.50 p.m. Five minutes before the patrol was scheduled to end the enemy was sighted, a formation of Dornier 215s escorted by Messerschmitt 109s heading for Dover.

'Coo! What a Blitz!' was Michael Crossley's light-hearted account of the ensuing battle. 'All of a sudden we sighted a cloud of Huns, and moved unwillingly towards them. Then another cloud a bit nearer, complete with mosquitoes. We moved even more unwillingly towards that one and attacked. 32 versus the world, it seemed. Hell of a lot of zizzing. Very hectic.'

Undeterred by the barrage thrown up by the Dover guns, the Hurricanes attacked before the Controller had time to utter a word on the R/T. Led by Michael Crossley, his actions belying that 'unwillingly', the '32nd Pursuit' tore into the enemy – twelve Hurricanes pitted against eighty Huns, each man for himself and the devil take the hindmost. From Dover to Whitstable the sky was vibrant with vicious, snarling dog fights as the Biggin Hill fighters harried and scattered the enemy. They claimed eleven victims, their highest score to date. Only one man was shot-down, Pilot Officer Barton. That evening he was happily recounting his experience over a can of beer in the Mess.

Hawkinge, meanwhile, had 'copped a packet'. Returning for fuel and ammunition Michael Crossley and four others from 32 Squadron looked down aghast at the smoking skeletons of two hangars and the grass cratered by bombs. The station's R/T installation was fortunately undamaged, and was at once jammed with urgent questions and answers. No one had petrol enough to reach Biggin Hill. Manston? Impossible, bombed out of action for the time being. Lympne? Lympne was in the same state as Hawkinge.

Michael Crossley's cool drawl cut across the babel. 'Hullo, Sparrow[1] Control. Jacko Red Leader calling. So sorry to trouble you. Afraid we simply must pancake.'

'Hullo, Jacko Red Leader. We've had a spot of bother here,' the Controller apologised. 'Permission to pancake granted. Good luck.'

Crews manning the fire-tenders and ambulances cursed obscenely when they saw the Hurricanes coming in to land. There were a score of unexploded bombs lying on the airfield. They needn't have worried. The fighters touched down almost daintily, as if they sensed that the slightest shock might set off an explosion, and weaved to a halt between the craters. The pilots were hardly out of the cockpits when they heard the hum of approaching aircraft. Ground crews, already at work on the Hurricanes, looked up apprehensively at a small formation of twin-engined machines which had just appeared over the far side of the field.

'Blenheims?' hazarded a voice.

'Blenheims be buggered! Them's Jerries.'

Everyone dashed for cover except the visitors from Biggin Hill, more accustomed to meeting bombers at 15,000 feet. They felt themselves trapped in the fighter pilot's nightmare, on the ground with their aircraft unfuelled and unarmed.

'Don't stand there like a bunch of ruddy clots!' the Controller roared over the Tannoy, his voice half-drowned by the crash of exploding bombs.

They fled.

Five minutes later Michael Crossley and the others emerged from shelter and hurriedly inspected their Hurricanes. Miraculously, not one had been hit. Incendiaries spluttered and blazed all over the place. Here and there ominous bulges broke up the thyme-scented turf. While waiting for their aircraft to be serviced, one or two of the pilots inquisitively poked at these outsize molehills.

'Please don't do that, sir,' a young 'erk' implored. 'It's a delayed-action bomb.'

The field cleared like lightning.

[1]Code name for Hawkinge.

151

Sunset was at 8.31 p.m. Half an hour before both 32 and 610 Squadrons were released from readiness. Their pilots, off duty until the coming dawn, set off in search of beer, a blonde or a seat at the 'flicks'.

The Station Intelligence Officer sent through his final summing-up of the day by teleprinter to Group Headquarters: ' . . . Operational sorties: 36. Enemy casualties: 5 confirmed, 16 unconfirmed, 4 probables and damaged. All pilots safe. 1 in hospital.'

Later that night Fleet Street editors read the Air Ministry communiqué and drafted the headlines for the morning papers:

The Battle of Britain is on.
Hitler launches the biggest raids of all.
Official: more than 39[1] down.

CHAPTER THIRTEEN

BLITZY DAYS

Boiled eggs and tea at 3.30 a.m.
With the thought of a Blitz shortly after
(And your tum making noises like Foden's brass band)
Is hardly conducive of laughter.

32 Squadron

FOR ten weeks ahead there was no respite for the squadrons of Biggin Hill; by the end of the Battle of Britain six in all had fought from this small airfield in Kent, making it the top-scoring station in Fighter Command. Inspired by Group Captain Grice, staff and ground crews toiled selflessly to keep their aerodrome serviceable and aircraft flying – noth-

[1]Post-war analysis of German records has revealed the true figure as 36, against a loss of 22 R.A.F. machines.

ing else mattered. Parades, leave and inessential routine were cheerfully ignored, yet discipline was never so high. For weeks no one was brought before the Station Commander on charge; the mere threat of posting an airman away from Biggin Hill for some minor offence ensured that it did not happen again. One administrative officer, pleading a trayful of 'bumf' as an excuse for not meeting a squadron returning from combat, found himself posted forthwith to the Shetlands!

After the fighting of 12th August the next twenty-four hours were a welcome anticlimax: five patrols and not a single Hun sighted. Then, the following noon, 610 Squadron tangled with a gaggle of *Stukas* and escorting Me. 109s off Folkestone, claiming six 'confirmed' and seven 'probables' in as many minutes. 32 Squadron had no such luck. 'A' Flight, caught unawares by Me. 109s lurking in the sun over Dover, lost three Hurricanes. Their pilots, however, escaped unhurt, Pilot Officer Barton for the second time in three days.

Then came Thursday, 15th August, 1940, the day which saw the heaviest fighting of the entire battle. Using 1,800 aircraft in five massive assaults, the *Luftwaffe* made an all-out effort to smash the Royal Air Force and bring Britain to her knees – and failed.

The early hours were unusually quiet. At Biggin Hill both squadrons waited at '15 minutes available'. Not until 11.20 a.m. did the Tannoys call them to 'top-line readiness'. The enemy's first onslaught was under way against south-east England. Spitfires from Hornchurch, Hurricanes from Gravesend, parried and repulsed the raiders without calling on Biggin Hill for assistance.

Like a pendulum the attack swung to the north-east where formations of He. 111s, escorted by long-range Me. 110s, aimed for Tyneside. True to the hard-hitting tradition of the 'Bump', 79 Squadron, now at Acklington, savaged the Heinkels over the North Sea so effectively, destroying eighteen without loss, that the *Luftwaffe* never again ventured a mass attack on the north-east coast by daylight.

At 2.20 p.m. the third assault commenced with streams of heavily-escorted bombers converging on Felixstowe and two thrusts across the Channel towards Deal and Dover. 32 Squadron was already at Hawkinge, awaiting the 'scramble!' From the ground the pilots could discern their enemy as silvery motes high over the coast. At 11 Group Headquarters the controllers, usually so accurate, became confused by the many simultaneous threats and feints and sent 32 Squadron winging to Harwich, sixty miles away, to intercept a handful of Me. 109s streaking home.

The German pilots, low in fuel, declined to stay and fight. Climbing, twisting, rolling, they beat every trick of the Hurricanes, never remaining in the gun-sights for even the split second reflex of jabbing a firing button. It was infuriating for the Biggin Hill pilots, but worse was to come. One Hun, suddenly aggressive, turned and caught Pilot Officer Grice with a murderous burst, sending him down in flames.

In the Operations Room at Biggin Hill the R/T loudspeaker blared: 'Christ Almighty! They've got Grubby!' A W.A.A.F. cypher officer blanched. Hiding her anguish beneath a mask of routine efficiency, she carried on until news came through that her fiancé was safe. 'Grubby' Grice had baled out into the sea off Harwich, had been picked up by an M.T.B. and was now in the naval hospital at Shottley suffering from burns.

Wlasnowalski was quick to avenge him. Slamming his throttle wide open, he tore after the fleeing Me. 109s and caught up with a straggler. Hurricane and Messerschmitt circled dizzily at 300 m.p.h. The German's nerve broke and he foolishly dived to sea level. Instantly the Pole was after him, pouring 800 rounds into the hated black-cross'd fuselage. The Messerschmitt exploded like a rotten puffball. Without warning, Wlasnowalski's Merlin engine faltered and died. The glycol temperature was high over the danger line. 'Full boost for too long,' he thought and prepared for a forced-landing in an Essex cornfield.

'Kurva Jagomasy!' he swore, ruefully inspecting his wrecked undercarriage and imagining the reproachful

expressions of his fitter and rigger when they heard the news.

Chagrined, the rest of 32 Squadron straggled back to refuel and re-arm.

Ninety minutes later the squadron, two Hurricanes short, was scrambled to Selsey Bill. The fourth attack had started, aimed at targets in Hampshire and Dorset. With Portsmouth beneath his starboard wing, Crossley exultantly gave the 'Tally ho!' Ahead over the Channel were three hundred of the enemy, echelons of bombers and fighters stepped-up like a gigantic escalator. Leading Red Section at the nearest Junkers 88s, Crossley promptly sent two down with port engines ablaze.

Watching from the ground, a *Daily Express* reporter described the battle: 'To see these fighters diving through great masses of enemy planes, to see them tear, one after the other, out of the sky and rise again to dive back, is the most heroic and inspiring thing I have ever seen in my life. There are no words to express their fury and their bravery.'

32 Squadron was not alone. Nearly one hundred and fifty Hurricanes and Spitfires had been thrown into the fray, the greatest force so far scrambled by Fighter Command.

The coastal radio-location stations detected the build-up of the fifth, and last, assault at 6.15 p.m. In Biggin Hill's small, rather old-fashioned Operations Room the atmosphere was hot and close. W.A.A.F.s, tunics off and sleeves rolled up, contrived to remain trimly feminine as they stood by telephones and teleprinters, or waited, head-sets lightly ruffling their hair, to plot the coming battle on the glass sector map that divided the room. The Duty Controller and his aides sat enthroned on a dais; to them the enemy was a cluster of black rubber suckers, labelled '60+', midway between Calais and Dungeness. Obedient to the whisper in her headphones, a W.A.A.F. placed four red suckers–squadrons ordered up by 11 Group – in opposition and then moved one black a foot over the coastline of Kent: twelve inches on the map, six miles in reality.

The Controller glanced at the board giving the state of his

squadrons: 'Jacko' had nine Hurricanes serviceable, 'Dog-rose' eight Spitfires.

The leading enemy formation was now fifteen miles north-east of Dover. As the menacing black symbol was shifted even farther inland, Group came through on the direct line from the great underground Control Room in Uxbridge where Air Vice Marshal Park and his staff watched every move the enemy made.

'Sapper Control.'

'Group speaking. Raid 51, forty-plus south-east of Maidstone.'

'Got it.'

'It's all yours. One squadron only.'

The eyes of the Controller had never left the sector map, his mind transmuting the abstraction of symbols into orders calculated to bring one of his squadrons into contact with the enemy. Beside him the Ops. B. officer stood, telephone in hand, ready to speak to the dispersals.

'Scramble Dog-rose!' The Controller paused fractionally, laying off the course by eye, 'Vector 095 degrees. Angels 10.'

Ops. B. relayed his instructions.

Three minutes, fifty seconds later Flight Lieutenant Warner, leading 610 Squadron, reported by R/T: 'Dog-rose Blue Leader calling. Squadron airborne.'

The black symbols were thrusting towards London in a two-pronged threat. One spearhead was aligned on Biggin Hill.

'Hullo, Dog-rose Blue Leader. Sapper Control speaking. Vector 130 degrees. Twenty-plus bandits, now Angels 12. Buster!'

Ten miles south-east of Biggin Hill the eight Spitfires met the Dornier 215s with their escorting Messerschmitt 109s 10,000 feet above, too high for effective cover. The bomber pilots scattered like terrified quail, thankful for the haze of that summer evening which made pursuit so difficult. Warner sent one Dornier plunging earthwards, Pilot Officer Cox another. Sergeants Arnfield and Corfe both started 'smokers' before running out of ammunition, then kept up feint attacks so ferociously that the Huns turned back.

A second enemy formation, however, sneaked through to its objective – Croydon airport. The raid came with appalling suddenness. People in the streets looked up and saw for the first time the evil insignia of Nazi Germany winging overhead. Bombs rained down before the sirens had finished their wailing. Workers on the aerodrome fell flat as a hail of bullets swept the hangars. One man had both shoes ripped off by blast and ran to shelter in stockinged feet. The Hurricanes of 111 Squadron, Croydon's own, were quick to attack. Thinking it a Jerry, passengers on a bus cheered wildly when one tumbled flaming from the sky. Only the 'clippie' recognised the fighter. With tears in her eyes she made the sign of the Cross. Orbiting Biggin Hill at 5,000 feet, 32 Squadron could see the rising pall of smoke and dust.

> We turned and beat it for Croydon as fast as we could. Sure enough when we approached, we saw a large party in progress. Masses of Me. 110s were dive-bombing the place. As they did not appear to notice our approach, we steered straight past them with the object of getting between them and the sun.[1]

The ruse was successful and 'Red Knight' Crossley opened in classic style.

> I attacked a Dornier 17 from astern and opened fire at 200 yards, setting the port engine on fire. I broke away, Red Two closed in and shot some pieces off it. He then gave way to Red Three who also hit it. We followed. The fire appeared to go out, giving place to two streams of white smoke. Red Two and Three went in and knocked it about so badly that it crashed E. of Sevenoaks.[2]

Green and Blue Sections followed Red Sections into the *mêlée* over Croydon. In ten glorious hectic minutes they tackled all-comers and chased them back to the Channel. Three Do. 17s, two Ju. 88s and four Me. 109s were con-

[1]32 Squadron diary.
[2]Combat report.

firmed destroyed, one apiece for the Biggin Hill pilots. The '32nd Pursuit' was back in form. It was a fine parting gift to the squadron leader, 'Baron' Worrall, due next morning to hand over the reins to Crossley and resume his former duty as Senior Sector Controller.

The Croydon raid was the last before sunset. During that memorable day all twenty-one of 11 Group's squadrons had been in action, some, like No. 32, three times.

The B.B.C. gave news of victory at nine o'clock: 182 enemy aircraft[1] destroyed for a loss of only 34 of our fighters. That evening the bar of the 'White Hart', down in Brasted, was packed. As usual 32 Squadron was there in force, with sufficient of 610 Squadron to give spice to the interminable argument of Hurricane *v.* Spitfire.

They heard the Air Ministry communiqué in astonished silence, never imagining the score would be so high, then it was 'drinks all round!' for every man, and woman, too, for that matter, wearing Air Force blue. An American journalist, visiting the 'White Hart' in search of copy, sipped his beer and marvelled at the British. It was incredible to him that these noisy youngsters were, in fact, front-line troops even then in the thick of battle. He pondered the poignant contrasts of their life: the fleeting emotions of exhilaration and sorrow, hatred and fear, which crowded their cockpits, followed by this boisterous laughter and horseplay in the cheerful atmosphere of an English pub.

The pilots celebrated after their fashion; at the same time other men were hard at work in the blacked-out hangars on Biggin Hill. Hurricanes and Spitfires were coming back so shot-up that life for the harassed engineer officers and ground crews became an unending struggle to inspect, patch, mend and somehow turn out a complete squadron every morning. Holes shot through the propellers were plugged with wax and, as long as the hydraulics weren't leaking, the control wires not fraying, and there was plenty of grease where it was needed, an aircraft *had* to be considered fit to fly. Fitters

[1]The scale and confusion of the day's fighting undoubtedly contributed to this exaggerated estimate. The *Luftwaffe*'s true loss was 76 aircraft.

and riggers downed tools only when the imminence of closing time lured them through the perimeter hedge for a quick pint in the 'Old Jail'. A night's sleep in billets was out of the question. They dossed down on blankets in the hangars whenever and wherever they could.

Friday, 16th August was another good day for Biggin Hill with 32 Squadron claiming nine 'destroyed' after four patrols, and 610 three 'probables'. Before the last dog fight was over, Group Captain Grice was telephoned by an irate councillor of Sevenoaks complaining that the town had received more than its fair share of jettisoned bombs. Would the Station Commander please arrange to intercept the Germans elsewhere?

By sunset the fields of Kent were littered with the wreckage of enemy aircraft and many villages could boast at least one Nazi prisoner. There were a couple in the Guard Room at Biggin Hill, fretting under the watchful eye of Sergeant Herring of the R.A.F. Police. 32 Squadron 'liberated' one and bore him off to the Mess for a drink. Blond and very sullen, he was furiously indignant that he, a *Hauptmann*, had been placed in the charge of an N.C.O.! After a few Westerham ales, however, he cheered up and admitted to being the pilot of an Me. 110. Then someone tried to slip a gin into his tankard unnoticed and he shut up like a clam.

After supper he was taken to the squadron's dispersal hut. Surveying the disorder of tattered armchairs, Esquire girls, trophies and assorted flying-kit which 32 Squadron fondly called 'home', he haughtily pronounced it: *'Sehr primitiv.'*

'We know it's not the Ritz, old boy, but there is a war on, in case you hadn't noticed.'

'Bitte?'

The sight of Pniak the Pole chalking 'Made in Germany, finished in England' over the squadron's trophies – a machine-gun from a Ju. 88, the fin of a Heinkel, a gas mask – elicited the vehement denial that they were of German origin at all! This was too much for his hosts who had a strong suspicion that not only were they German, but had until very recently been the property of the *Luftwaffe.*

The second prisoner, a cheerful little rear gunner, was entertained by some of 610 Squadron. He regarded his captivity as a purely temporary misfortune. After several drinks, he punctiliously inquired the names and ranks of his hosts. He was most anxious, he explained, to make certain that they received equally courteous treatment after Hitler's forthcoming and inevitably victorious invasion of Britain!

The gale of laughter which greeted him drowned out the nasal crowings of Lord Haw-Haw on the wireless. An elderly Intelligence Officer was trying to pick up the latest 'gen' from Berlin: 'This is Germany calling, Germany calling . . . yesterday our mighty *Luftwaffe* bombed Croydon from the map, soon it will be your turn, Kenley and Biggin Hill . . .'

Two evenings later the same officer stood outside Station Headquarters and looked round at Biggin Hill. He cursed Haw-Haw and all that he stood for. Everywhere red flags flutteringly marked the position of unexploded bombs, while men in blue toiled side by side with men in khaki, frenziedly attempting to fill in all the craters before nightfall. He remembered the *Lufthansa* airliner which had flown over Biggin Hill with such persistence during the last days of peace and wondered if the same pilot had guided the bombers that morning.

The attack took no one by surprise. It was a Sunday and in Kent people were leaving church when the sirens wailed their warning of approaching aircraft.

On Biggin Hill both squadrons were at 'top-line readiness'. In the Operations Room the Duty Controller studied the tracks of the enemy across south-east England. It was too early to divine his intentions. Group Headquarters remained mute, giving no orders for interception.

Several large formations were well inland, flying inexorably towards London.

A telephone shrilled. Ops. B. snatched it up and listened tensely. Slamming it down, he reported: 'That was Kenley, sir. Jerry's right on top. Bombs falling all over the place.'

The Controller winced, visualising the destruction that

must be taking place at that very moment only a few miles away. Kenley, so pleasant with its lawns, flowerbeds and neat peacetime buildings, was, like Biggin Hill, one of the vital Section Stations in 11 Group holding the southern approaches to London.

Spitfires from 64 Squadron partnered by Hurricanes from No. 111, roared to the defence of Kenley, but the *Luftwaffe* pilots courageously pressed home their attack leaving six Hurricanes smoking wrecks on the ground, every hangar except one destroyed, the runways bombed to blazes and communications so badly damaged that the Operations Room had to be transferred to a butcher's shop in Caterham.

Biggin Hill's fighters remained on the ground. Group's orders had been: 'hold fast.'

Ten minutes after Kenley, Croydon was attacked.

The Controller reached for his steel helmet and purpose-fully tightened the chin strap.

'Hats on everybody, please.'

Some wore them defiantly at a jaunty angle, others a trifle shame-facedly, as if the wearing of a steel helmet was a sign of cowardice or fear. W.A.A.F.s awkwardly slipped them on over head-sets, put out at this marriage of their habitual chic.

Then it was the turn of West Malling, a satellite of Biggin Hill, to be blitzed.

Every man and woman in the Operations Block had the same thought: Kenley, Croydon and now West Malling – was Biggin Hill also on Goering's schedule?

There was no doubt in the Controller's mind. The plot showed '50+' near Tunbridge Wells. If they continued on course, the bombers would be overhead in twelve minutes' time. He reached for the telephone linking him with the dispersals.

'Jacko Squadron, scramble! Dog-rose Squadron, scramble! Protect base.'

Twelve Hurricanes of 32 Squadron were first away, climb-ing as they had never climbed before. Then fifteen Spitfires rocketed up, outpacing the Hurricanes in the race for alti-tude. Minutes later, a lone Hurricane taxied-out from the maintenance hangars and took-off. Pilot Officer 'Polly' Flinders, in charge of 32 Squadron's training flight, was not going to miss the fun if he could help it.

The Station Commander stood quietly behind the Controller, watching all that went on.

'All our aircraft are now airborne, sir,' Ops. B told him. 'If Jerry comes our way, he's in for a surprise.'

'Groupy' Grice puffed his pipe and eyed the plot speculatively: the enemy was very very close. With sudden decision he stabbed the button that sent the alarm raucously hooting from the Tannoys, then spoke reassuringly into the microphone.

'This is your Station Commander speaking. At any moment we may be attacked. I want all personnel except those engaged on essential services to take cover immediately.'

Mechanics working on aircraft reluctantly quit and strolled to the trenches. Before leaving, the kitchen staff were careful to switch off the gas beneath Biggin Hill's Sunday dinners. From offices and stores W.A.A.F.s scuttled, chattering excitedly, down into the airwomen's shelters. Around the perimeter army gunners leaped to their Bofors and stared into the sun for the first sign of a target. On Leaves Green a company of Local Defence Volunteers enthusiastically slipped clips of live ammunition into their aged rifles. Few were in uniform, the majority wore L.D.V. armlets proudly over civilian clothes.

'Enemy approaching base,' the Controller warned his airborne squadrons. 'Enemy approaching base. Angels 12. Attack on base imminent.'

'You haven't a thing to worry about,' Squadron Leader Ellis's voice rasped confidently over the R/T, then savagely exultant: 'Tally ho!'

The first bombs fell on the east side of the aerodrome, well away from the station buildings. In one of the airwomen's trenches Section Officer Hanbury listened as the explosions drew nearer. One bomb fell just outside. 'I suppose one feels like this in an earthquake,' she thought. Other W.A.A.F.s felt their limbs must surely be torn apart by the blast and concussion. The noise outside was indescribable and yet, through it, the girls could hear the heartening stutter of the Hurricanes' and Spitfires' guns.

Stick after stick of bombs rained down. On the airfield earthen geysers were in continuous eruption. One bomb fell squarely on the M.T. sheds, fortunately empty. Another fell close by a Bofors gun, killing one of the crew and wounding others.

Only one Dornier 215 ventured low. Gliding in over Leaves Green, it met a defiant fusillade from the Local Defence Volunteers. To their utter amazement the bomber burst into flames, rolled over and crashed on the far side of Biggin Hill. Their cheers were heard even in the shelters!

Overhead, the fighters cut an angry swathe through the Huns; they had been ordered up none too soon. Outnumbered five to one by Do. 215s and Ju. 88s, with Me. 110s stepped-up in the rear, the Hurricanes met the enemy over Sevenoaks. A quick climb for altitude, a steep turn, then 'Red Knight' Crossley took his squadron into a head-on attack. A Ju. 88 filled his sights. A five-second burst from 100 yards triggered a violent internal explosion. Pulling away steeply to avoid the pieces flying off in all directions, Crossley saw the Ju. 88 jettison its bombs harmlessly before crashing near Ashford. Back in the thick of it, he got in a quick squirt at an Me. 110 that flashed across his sights. White smoke streamed from its port engine – only a 'probable'.

Tight behind Crossley, 'Shag' Eckford took the middle line of bombers, selecting a Do. 215 for a two-second burst. Sliding beneath it, he glanced back and saw it break formation in a steep spiral dive. Then he was in amongst the Me. 110s, trapped in their cross-fire. The emergency panel of his hood flew open, the draught sucking off his helmet. Grabbing hold of it as it whistled away in the slipstream, Eckford dropped 5,000 feet before he had it on again.

The sound of bombs exploding on their home station, faintly audible over the R/T, spurred them on. The Belgian, de Grunne, bagged two 'probables', and Wlasnowalski a Do. 215. Flight Lieutenant Pete Brothers, leading Blue Section, found several Me. 110s on his tail. Whipping round to meet them head-on, he let fly with all he had before his engine stalled and he flicked over in a spin. Pulling out at 8,000 feet, he pounced on a lone Do. 215. Two Spitfires forestalled him, then considerately allowed him to finish it off. After a frantic climb in the old training Hurricane 'Polly' Flinders caught up with his squadron at 12,000 feet, in time to get in a squirt at a Do. 215. Smiling happily, he watched black smoke and flames mingle in a long streamer as it fell out of the sky.

Leaving the bombers to 32 Squadron, Ellis took his Spitfires roaring up at full boost to 31,000 feet where the escorting Me. 109s were waiting. There was no time to manoeuvre, it was every man for himself. Five Huns fell in flames, the rest fled.

The Squadron Leader's voice held a fierce joy as he called over the R/T: 'O.K. All Dog-rose fighters. Let's join the party below.'

The Spitfires re-formed and the pack fell in a screaming power dive to help the Hurricanes. Ellis tackled six He. 111s and chased one all the way to the Channel, sending it into the sea off Dungeness. Pulling out too steeply, Pilot Officer Cox blacked-out, stalled and spun down. Coming to, he found himself immediately below a Do. 215 and emptied his ammunition into it. Caught by surprise, its crew hurriedly baled out but their aircraft flew on unmanned. Sergeant Else got two Do. 215s, Sergeant Chandler another; Pilot Officer Rees set a Ju. 88 on fire, and Pilot Officer Pegge an He. 111. So it went on, more and more enemy aircraft being shot down or crippled until their attack was finally broken.

The raid lasted barely ten minutes, then it was strangely quiet. Men and women emerged dazedly from the shelters and stared in surprise. Driving towards them across the razor-sharp hot shrapnel that carpeted the ground came a Salvation Army mobile canteen. 'Tea and wads' were never more welcome.

The injured were taken to the Decontam. Centre for medical attention. A young subaltern, wounded when the Bofors site was hit, was carried in on a stretcher. W.A.A.F. orderlies did their best to make him comfortable until the doctor arrived. Then the crew of the Dornier which had been shot-down were brought in under guard. Their captain, a young *Leutnant*, stepped forward and spat in the face of the wounded gunner.

'We felt like shooting the lot,' a W.A.A.F. told the doctor.

Throughout the raid those on duty remained steadfast at their posts. Sergeant Joan Mortimer was in the Armoury when the alarm sounded. Although surrounded by several tons of high explosive, she remained at her telephone switchboard, relaying messages to the defence posts around the airfield as if sitting on a volcano that might erupt at any instance was the most natural thing in the world. Then, before the 'All Clear', this middle-aged W.A.A.F Sergeant picked up a bundle of red flags and hurried out to mark the numerous unexploded bombs. Even when one went off close by, she carried on, to the terror of the quaking 'erks' shamed into helping her.

This courageous act was recognised with the first of three Military Medals awarded to W.A.A.F.s at Biggin Hill that summer.[1] Stated the citation: ' . . . This airwoman displayed exceptional courage and coolness which had a great moral effect on all those with whom she came into contact . . . '

One by one the fighters with empty magazines came back, weaving warily through the bomb craters and red flags.

Those with any ammunition left kept up the fight. Sergeant Parsons of 610 Squadron chased a formation of Do. 17s at 15,000 feet. They went into a tight defensive circle as he approached so he climbed up-sun and waited patiently. Five minutes later one rashly broke formation. Instantly Parsons jumped him, attacking from astern and killing the rear gunner.

[1] During the entire war only six M.M.s were awarded to members of the Women's Auxiliary Air Force. This tribute to the girls of Biggin Hill is unequalled.

Compressed air hissed in his empty breech block meant no more ammunition, but Parsons continued feinting and succeeded in forcing the Dornier down. Its pilot prudently lowered the undercarriage before making a perfect landing on Romney Marsh – one Do. 17 intact, taken by an unarmed Spitfire!

Having made certain of his Do. 17, 'Polly' Flinders started after a Do. 215 in a wild hare-and-hound chase. The Dornier was flying at 12,000 feet when its pilot saw the aged Hurricane on his tail. He dived to 300 feet and looked round. Flinders was still there. With little ammunition left he could only afford one burst. Dornier and Hurricane roared over West Malling at 200 feet. Airmen filling in the bomb craters waved encouragement. The German dropped lower. Flinders strained his Hurricane to the last pound of boost pressure to catch up. They swept over Detling aerodrome, the Dornier making frantic barrel rolls. Two miles north of Canterbury, Flinders got his opportunity. Pulling up to avoid some trees, the Dornier lost speed. The Hurricane closed to 150 yards and Flinders let fly with his remaining rounds. They were sufficient.

For some months past Flight Lieutenant 'Humph' Russell had been seconded to the Operations Room; this was his first operational sortie after rejoining 32 Squadron. Having bagged an Me. 110, he was delightedly reporting his success by R/T when a cannon shell exploded inside his cockpit. He baled out and found that he had been shot through the leg. Blood was streaming from the wound, yet, somehow, as he floated down, he contrived a tourniquet. The doctors in Edenbridge hospital congratulated him on a professional job, suspended in the air at 10,000 feet!

Compared with Kenley, Biggin Hill got off lightly: 500 bombs dropped, including 90 D.A.s; one direct hit on the M.T. sheds, no other damage to buildings; no damage to aircraft or vehicles on the ground; casualties were two killed and three wounded.

The raid over, everyone not urgently required, officers and men, Air Force and Army, set-to to fill in the hundreds of craters that pock-marked the airfield. Picks, shovels, even household brooms were commandeered; many used their bare hands. A bomb disposal squad arrived and found to their disgust that some of the unexploded bombs were, in fact, British, captured during the Battle of France: several dated from the early twenties.

The raid was a great leveller. Before, the airmen had been somewhat 'toffee-nosed' towards the 'brown jobs' billeted in the South Camp, thereafter they were inseparable.

Two high-ranking W.A.A.F. officers from 11 Group hurried down to see how Biggin Hill's girls had fared. After praising them for their superb example to the whole Women's Auxiliary Air Force, one cheerfully remarked: 'Well, now you know what it's like it won't be nearly so bad the next time.'

Not one of the audience could agree with her. It was precisely 'knowing what it was like' that made the next time seem so very much harder to take.

There was no resting on laurels, however, for the pilots. Early that evening the *Luftwaffe* sent a strong force against the Thames Estuary airfields, and 32 Squadron was detailed to intercept the Huns on their way home. The nine Hurricanes caught thirty of the bombers' escorting fighters over Herne Bay and shot down five Me. 109s.

Alone, Squadron Leader Crossley was flying back to Biggin Hill, thinking happily of the Me. 109 he had just 'bagged' which brought his score to twenty-one, when he spotted another eight in line astern below. He reckoned he could pick off the German 'tail-end Charlie' and get away before the others noticed. Flicking his Hurricane over in a quick half-roll, he dived. The leading 109s saw him, turned and attacked with everything they had. Crossley ignored them, kept on after his chosen victim, opened fire – and missed. A great hollow bang shook his aircraft, but it continued to fly. The Huns vanished homewards. Then Crossley's Merlin engine started juddering, white smoke pouring from the exhausts. Hell and damnation! A glycol leak!

Detling, however, was not far away and he had 8,000 feet in hand.

The white smoke turned black, streaked with red. Disconnecting his helmet and loosening his harness, Crossley feverishly tried to recall the drill for baling out. He felt very insecure without his straps. 'Don't turn over on your back or you'll fall out,' he thought and roared with laughter as he realised that this was exactly the drill.

Floating down, he sadly watched his beloved 'F' make her last dive, a long sheet of flame trailing behind. She was the best Hurricane he had ever flown.

He landed in some allotments near Gillingham where a reception committee was waiting with pitchforks and shotguns. They seemed rather disappointed that he was not a Nazi!

Then, for the next five days, heavy cloud blanketed western Europe and the *Luftwaffe* stayed home. The weather was a godsend to Biggin Hill. It meant a rest for weary bodies and taut nerves, time to repair damaged aircraft adequately, and time, too, to teach the tricks of combat flying to the replacement pilots, brashly over-confident after only a few hours' flying on single-seater fighters in the Operational Training Units.

Decorations came through quickly: the D.S.O. for Squadron Leader Crossley, D.F.C.s for Flying Officers Gardiner, Humpherson and Smythe and, of course, the M.M. for W.A.A.F. Sergeant Mortimer. The surest way to incur the Station Commander's wrath was to keep him in ignorance of when a pilot had scored his fifth victory. Then he would at once send a recommendation for an immediate award to Fighter Command. His interest in the civilians working on his station was equally heartfelt. When the N.A.A.F.I. manageress, perhaps more responsible than anyone for morale, showed signs of strain, Grice ignored her tearful pleading to be allowed to carry on and brusquely sent her packing on four days' leave. She left behind a gay jumper, souvenir of pre-war holidays abroad, embroidered with the names of European capitals. He dropped a hint to his

W.A.A.F. Section. On returning from her leave the manageress found the words 'Biggin Hill' emblazoned in scarlet across the back. She was delighted with this accolade.

The shortage of aircraft was becoming serious: on 18th August 32 Squadron alone lost six Hurricanes. Despite the great-hearted efforts of the aircraft industry, there were not enough to go round. Just as soon as they had been flight-tested and armed, new fighters were flown to the battle-front. Hard-pressed pilots at Biggin Hill had long ceased to be surprised at seeing a girl wearing the overalls of the A.T.A. step from the cockpit of a new Hurricane or Spitfire to demand a signature for its delivery.

With both squadrons below strength, the work of the ground crews became even more important. Some pilots, careless through lack of sleep and nervous strain, were sadly unappreciative. One evening, just after the raid, Wlasnowalski was told to collect a Hurricane that had been serviced in the hangars. The fitters had worked from dawn to dusk repairing the engine. They pushed the Hurricane out of the hangar just as it was growing dark. Wlasnowalski arrived, signed the chit and climbed into the cockpit. The mechanics started up the engine and stood listening to its healthy roar as he vanished across the field. They were contemplating a few well-deserved pints in the 'Old Jail' when they heard the engine suddenly stop. Curses all round: someone would have to trundle the heavy starting-battery out to the aircraft. No one moved. Let Wlasnowalski walk back: that would teach him not to stall his engine. Soon he appeared, shaking his head bemusedly over the cussedness of all aircraft.

'Always the bad luck I have!'

'Cor! Chase my Polish Aunt Fanny round the mulberry bush!' snorted a fitter disgustedly, staring at the Hurricane nose-down in a crater.

During this lull the squadrons were not completely idle; there were tiresome 'X' raids to be investigated which proved to be nothing more alarming than a thunderstorm or flock of migrant birds picked up by radio-location, and there were escort patrols to be flown over the gallant convoys of coasters running the Channel gauntlet. Sometimes these could be amusing:

> We were escorting an eastbound convoy just off Dover and were flying at about 5,000 feet just under the clouds when all of a sudden four colossal spurts of white rose up in quick succession about half a mile to seaward of the convoy. We immediately thought the Hun had sneaked up on us and was bombing the convoy. We nipped up over the clouds to have a look, at the same time cursing Control for not warning us the enemy was in the vicinity. There was nothing above the clouds so we came down again just in time to see four more columns of water shoot-up, a little nearer this time. We were mystified and annoyed. There we were for the purpose of discouraging just such enemy tactics, and we might have been flying a squadron of Moth trainers for all the good we were doing. Suddenly someone piped up: 'I rather think they're shelling the convoy from Gris Nez. I've just seen four flashes.' Sure enough four more water spouts appeared.[1]

They reported the shelling and, within twenty minutes, a squadron of Blenheims flew under the Hurricanes bound for Gris Nez.

The weather cleared on Saturday, 24th August, and the *Luftwaffe* resumed its attacks in full force. Three of 11 Group's airfields were blitzed – Debden, Hornchurch and North Weald – and, as if bombing was not enough, the enemy started lobbing shells that evening at Hawkinge, Biggin Hill's forward base.

Both squadrons were in action at the time, fiercely engaging Me. 109s over the Channel. Taking Flight Lieutenant Osmond, Sectors Signals Officer, with him, Group Captain Grice took Biggin Hill's Magister and flew down to Hawkinge to inspect the damage.

In the Operations Room the staff were intent on the battle as it was reported by R/T. During a moment's lull, the Observer Corps' liaison officer said: 'There is a Maggie being

[1] 32 Squadron diary.

chased by a couple of Messerschmitts.'

Grice and Osmond were on their way back from Hawkinge when they were attacked. Grice, who was piloting the unarmed Magister, dived for a wood and flew round and round it for so long that they both got dizzy. Every time he looked up, there were the two Messerschmitts, wickedly awaiting their opportunity to kill. Twisting and turning through the trees, clipping hedgerows with the tail wheel, Grice made off across the countryside towards Biggin Hill, knowing that the Huns dare not fly so low.

On landing he went straight to the Operations Room to see how his squadrons had fared. Squadron Leader Worrall was able to give him some good news: the Spitfires had bagged four Me. 109s and another 'probable', bringing their day's total to ten. The Hurricanes, however, had been outfought and could only claim three aircraft destroyed for which they had to pay dearly with two pilots crashing in flames and two more having to bale out.

'And I almost forgot to tell you, sir,' Worrall added. 'Somebloody fool in a Maggie was being chased by a couple of Messerschmitts.'

Grice laughed, still breathless. 'I was that bloody fool, but thanks to the courtesy of the local populace in opening the gates, I was able to elude them!'

'32 on the move?'
'Yes.'
'Where to?'
'Acklington.'
'Blitzy?'
'Not very.'
'Good!'

The rumour was true and on 25th August the '32nd Pursuit' heard officially that it was to change places with its peacetime brother squadron, No. 79. It was time to rest, though the move broke up a partnership which had made the name of Biggin Hill anathema to every *Luftwaffe* pilot across the Channel. Since Dunkirk the squadron had been in action almost daily. They hotly denied it but the pilots were tired, so very tired, and their nerves were strained to a point when nothing seemed to matter any more: life and death were one. Their successes had forced the *Luftwaffe* to fly higher and higher and the Hurricanes were becoming less effective; over 18,000 feet 79 Squadron's Spitfires would be more deadly.

That afternoon Michael Crossley led the squadron on its last patrol from the 'Bump' to intercept a dozen Do. 215s, escorted by thirty-six Me. 109s, over Dover. One of each were shot-down, but the '32nd Pursuit' lost two pilots killed. It was a melancholy farewell.

For nine arduous and successful years 32 Squadron had been at Biggin Hill. It was now the top-scoring squadron in Fighter Command with 102 enemy aircraft confirmed destroyed, with one D.S.O. and five D.F.C.s to its credit; of the pilots, five had lost their lives and one was a prisoner of war. Before leaving, the living contributed a gay *envoi* to their squadron diary:

Well, old Biggin Hill, 32 (F) Squadron bids you farewell. You brought us honour, excitement, fear, depression, happiness, tragedy, laughs, new associations, thrills – in short, every sentiment a man can experience in quick jumbled succession. Do we regret leaving you? Do the happiness and elation you brought us outweigh the sorrow and pain, and the indescribable 'eat, drink and be merry for tomorrow we die' sensation that each day brought? We don't know. We think perhaps not.

No, we wouldn't have you again for worlds, but we wouldn't have missed you! You made men out of boys and we're grateful. So long, Biggin Hill. 32 Squadron will never forget you.

CHAPTER FOURTEEN

AT THE FRONT

I wish to thank and congratulate all ranks, R.A.F. and W.A.A.F., for the spirit of calm courage and fortitude shown while our station was under heavy bombardment by the enemy, also for the fine display of initiative shown by all for getting the runways and station serviceable once again.

(signed) G/Cpt. R. Grice.

THE Channel was as smooth as the proverbial mill-pond, the atmosphere so clear that men of the Observer Corps atop the chalk cliffs could easily discern the cranes of Calais harbour. Smoking a cigar, Mr Churchill stood with the Mayor of Dover on the castle ramparts observing the antics of a German seaplane through binoculars.

For several days seaplanes, He. 59s, had been coyly playing games in mid-Channel, skimming over the water between Calais and Gris Nez, then wheeling about and beating it for home.

While Mr Churchill and the Mayor watched, four Spitfires flashed overhead and flew to sea. Three stayed aloft as cover, the fourth pounced on the unsuspecting seaplane which had about as much chance as a pelican against a sea hawk. Two short bursts and the Heinkel, its engines stopped, flopped awkwardly into the water and broke up in a flurry of spray.

79 Squadron, which had unknowingly staged this *divertissement* for the Prime Minister, wasted no time in celebrating its return to Biggin Hill. At first light that morning Squadron Leader J. H. Heyworth brought the Spitfires down from Acklington to replace 32 Squadron's Hurricanes. Scarcely had they been refuelled when they were ordered to Hawkinge, auspiciously collecting four 'probables' *en route*.

There followed this episode of the seaplane and, as added entertainment for Dover's Mayor and his guest, a second and equally successful attack on another He. 59 half an hour later. The shooting-up of the two E-boats which raced out from Calais to pick up the survivors, if any, completed the morning's work.

Pilots who had been with the squadron eight weeks, or more, found Biggin Hill very changed from the station they had left at the end of June. The difference was one of atmosphere, for the bombing had left few permanent scars. The continuing spell of fine weather brought the threat of invasion nearer. In June the fields around had been green with growing corn, now they were golden – but the harvest-makers carried steel helmets. Nerves were frayed and fifth column activity was imagined in the most innocent events. Trigger-quick perimeter guards were authorised to fire at any lights showing in the village or the valley below; local residents riposted by complaining of careless talk by airmen who frequented the 'Ace' and 'Welcome' cafés and the 'Black Horse' inn. In the minds of everyone was the certainty that Biggin Hill would be attacked again.

Time was running short if Hitler's cherished 'Operation Sealion' was to be launched before autumnal gales made it impossible. Repeatedly, Goering emphasised to his commanders that the elimination of the Royal Air Force was the first prerequisite to invasion. Having failed to drive the Hurricanes and Spitfires from the skies, the alternative was to destroy their bases. The Battle of Britain had entered its most deadly phase.

Shortly before noon on Friday, 30th August, 150 German bombers, escorted by a similar number of fighters, swept over Kent and fanned out towards the inner ring of airfields around the capital. Radio-location and the Observer Corps gave ample warning; at Biggin Hill the Controller was able to get his squadrons airborne in time to tear the guts out of a formation sent to wipe the 'Bump' from the map. Between them, 79 and 610 Squadrons shared ten victories: Flying Officer Morris claiming one 'destroyed by collision'

174

Inevitably, some of the raiders got through but the majority of bombs fell wide of the airfield, causing much damage in the villages of Biggin Hill and Keston.

At six o'clock that evening the *Luftwaffe* returned and, for once, caught Biggin Hill unawares.

The warning went just as a stream of airmen came pouring from their Mess. They glanced up and saw a small formation bearing down on them from the east. Any doubts as to their identity were dispelled by the crackle of machine-gun fire. The men dashed for the nearest shelter, but there was not room for all. Those left outside were the lucky ones. Five minutes later all that was left of the shelter was a monstrous gaping crater, littered with fragments of uniform and mangled flesh.

Section Officer Felicity Hanbury was walking to Station Headquarters when the alarm sent her at the double into the nearest trench. Amongst those inside she recognised the Padre, and wondered if this was an ominous sign. Squadron Leader Crossley was there, down for the day from Acklington. Through the pandemonium of Ack-Ack fire and exploding bombs outside he heard Spitfires taking off. He cursed his luck: twenty-four hours ago they would have been the Hurricanes of 32 Squadron.

Six of 79 Squadron managed to get off and claimed two 'probables'. 610 Squadron was already airborne, too high and too far away to defend its base.

Although only nine Ju. 88s were attacking Biggin Hill, the havoc they wrought was appalling. The Workshops, some of the cookhouses and the N.A.A.F.I. were all wrecked; the Sergeants' Mess, the 'Waafery' and the airmen's barracks were made uninhabitable; ninety per cent of the station's transport, so carefully dispersed, was damaged or destroyed; one hangar received a direct hit; two aircraft were burnt-out and all electricity, water and gas mains cut.

Some of the Control staff, off duty, climbed on to the roof of the Officers' Mess and blazed defiance with a Lewis gun – a *beau geste* but totally ineffective.

In the airwomen's trench W.A.A.F.s were packed like sardines – with steel helmets. 'I think we're being dive-bombed,' said a girl who still had her voice. No one contradicted her. They were remarkably calm: no panic, no hysteria, even when the entrance blew in and a hot blast bowled them over like ninepins.

Another bomb fell, closer still, and the concrete walls of the shelter caved in with a terrifying slow motion. Those inside were crushed, smothered with stones and chalky earth. A girl sobbed uncontrollably in the silence that followed. As the choking dust settled, they heard Flight Sergeant Gartside exclaim in a muffled voice: 'My heavens! I've broken my back!' Someone giggled, then everyone laughed aloud as their Flight Sergeant added: 'And I've broken my false teeth, too!' Now cheerful and unafraid, they lay in a heap in the darkness, waiting to be dug out.

In another shelter Felicity Hanbury listened to the head-splitting inferno outside: the sharp crack of lightweight bombs punctuated by the deep, vibrant roar of a thousand pounds of high explosive. Everyone sat quietly with their hands folded. A W.A.A.F. soundlessly repeated the Lord's Prayer, over and over. Crossley hummed the refrain of 'It's only a Paper Moon' and mimed the strumming of a ukelele.

Then there was a lull, broken only by the sound of Spitfires returning. A breathless messenger arrived to say that a trench had been hit and would the Padre please come at once.

They climbed out over the earth and rubble and into a lovely summer evening. It was very quiet, strangely unreal. The 'All Clear' had not yet sounded. Lighting a cigarette, Felicity Hanbury thought of her airwomen and made her way through the craters towards the W.A.A.F. Guard Room, or what was left of it. She noticed a strong smell of gas.

'Put that cigarette out before you blow the place to bits!' a voice shouted with unintentional irony.

Hastily she complied, then noticed two men gently laying the body of a girl wearing N.A.A.F.I. uniform in the shade of a hedge. She started towards them to see if she could help.

'Don't bother, miss,' a young airman caught her arm. 'The poor thing's dead.'

The N.A.A.F.I. girl was the first dead person the young W.A.A.F. officer had ever seen. It occurred to her that she would have to get used to the sight.

Airmen, helped by an old countryman who cared for the garden of the Officers' Mess were already digging fiercely to reach the entombed W.A.A.F.s. Pilots leaped down from their cockpits to help. Ambulances and stretcher-parties were standing-by. As the 'All Clear' sounded, the shelter was uncovered. Everyone braced themselves for a shambles within. One by one the bodies were brought out. Some were hardly recognisable through the dirt and blood on their faces, others were dazed and badly bruised, but all were alive save one: Corporal Lena Button, a nursing orderly from Tasmania.

Flight Sergeant Gartside was one of the last to be brought out. 'Don't worry about me, ma'am,' she pleaded with Felicity Hanbury. 'I'm quite all right. Look after the others.'

When she had done all she could, seen the wounded off to hospital, tucked the others up in blankets with a cup of tea laced with whisky, provided by the C.O.'s batman, Felicity Hanbury started off for the ruined 'Waafery'. As she passed by the dead N.A.A.F.I. girl she saw that someone had covered her with a blanket. It struck her as being so very casual, and yet so final.

Darkness fell, but they carried on digging by the light of headlamps focused on the crater that had been the airmen's shelter. The death roll was over forty.

Helped by local post office engineers, Flight Lieutenant Osmond and his Signals Section toiled all night to restore the vital nerves of Biggin Hill – the telephone links with 11 Group Headquarters, the Observer Corps, the R/T transmitter and receiver. By morning a temporary lash-up was complete and the Operations Room was back on the air.

There was no gas, electricity or water, yet somehow the

W.A.A.F. cooks magically produced delicious sausages and mash for a cheerful queue of airmen and soldiers. Now that it was over, they could laugh at their experiences and the freak effects of the bombing.

One 500-pounder had crashed through the roof of the triple-bay hangar and exploded outside the open door of a wireless room. None of the delicate apparatus within was broken, only the dartboard! That morning an officer had painstakingly camouflaged his Morris Minor and left it outside a hangar under a tree to dry. After the raid the car had gone and so had the tree. The officer found it back inside the hangar with its wheels in the air. A large hole in the roof exactly reproduced its shape in profile!

Late into the night Group Captain Grice sat up, telegraphing the parents of those who had been killed an invitation to a funeral service to be held the following Sunday. Away in the distance a cow mooed plaintively, as if in agony. The sound rasped Grice's nerves and he wondered if it had been wounded. He supposed he should do something about it, but there were so many things to be done.

Dawn held all the promise of another heavenly summer day. From the terrace of the Officers' Mess where he had slept, having relinquished his house to the bombed-out W.A.A.F. officers, Grice looked across the valley. Birds were singing and a rising mist showed that it would be very hot. With a sigh he turned and faced the chaos of ruins that was his station.

At the dispersals Spitfires were being given their pre-flight checks, soon they would be flying north away from the battle-field. Like 32 Squadron, No. 610 had been ordered to Acklington for a well-deserved rest.

When news came through that we were moving to Acklington, we had mixed feelings about it. While we felt that it would be pleasant to be a bit further from Jerry for a while, we were secretly proud to be in the thick of it; we all felt that we were doing a vital job as well as, or perhaps a bit better, than any other squadron in the

R.A.F. Also it was very gratifying to see the look that appeared on the faces of visiting airmen when they first caught sight of Biggin Hill.[1]

Punctually, the *Luftwaffe* paid another visit to Biggin Hill at noon. The pilots of 610 Squadron had already flown off with their Spitfires, the equipment had been loaded on to a 'Queen Mary' and was now on the road, only the ground crews remained. Festooned with kit, they straggled over to the North Camp to await the buses taking them to Bromley station. Everyone was in high spirits, cigarettes were passed round – then the Ack-Ack guns opened up. It was the last straw! The men fled in all directions, leaving kit-bags and haversacks strewn over the roadway. An officer dashed up, brandishing a revolver and yelling that he'd shoot the first man who started running! No one heeded him. They were all in the woods, dodging the hail of machine-gun bullets which brought the leaves drifting down. Any sentimental regrets they had on leaving the 'Bump' were quickly dissipated!

One pilot failed to leave with the others, his Spitfire needing some last-minute repairs. During a lull in the bombing he looked out from a shelter and saw his aircraft blazing.

'Those . . . Jerries have set fire to my . . . Spit!' he shouted in fury.

There was a deathly hush inside, then someone murmured: 'Steady on, sir. There's a lady present.'

The petrol tanks exploded with a cascade of searing flame and the pilot hastily ducked back, tears streaming down his face. A young N.A.A.F.I. girl pulled him close, comforting him over the loss of his beloved Spitfire.

Quite a small formation of Dornier 215s was responsible for this attack, dropping their bombs from the safety of 12,000 feet. Many fell wide of their mark but the runways were so badly cratered that 79 Squadron, returning from a scrap over Dover, had to be diverted to Croydon. The Station Commander set every available man and woman to

[1]Related by Sergeant J. E. Wilson.

work and by teatime one runway was back in use; the Spit-fires of 72 Squadron, down from Acklington, were able to land at their new base.

Accommodation was now the most pressing problem. During the afternoon Felicity Hanbury, with a fellow W.A.A.F. officer, Pam Beecroft, set out to find billets for the airwomen whose quarters had been demolished. The attitude of local householders came as a bitter shock. Some slammed doors in their faces, others made them stand and listen to their views on the R.A.F. in general and Biggin Hill in particular. Had it not been for Biggin Hill, they whined, their lives would not have been endangered! This was almost more than the two W.A.A.F. officers could bear. Fortunately the faint-hearted were in a minority and sufficient billets were found. With their faith in human nature somewhat restored, they started back to Station Headquarters:

> As we approached the aerodrome, the sirens sounded and all the preliminary noises of the day before began again. We crammed on our tin hats and moved to take cover in a nearby wood. As we did so, a policeman's bell-shelter at the crossroads opened and a voice said: 'You'd better come in here.' It was a tight squeeze and became tighter when a bus driver banged on the door and was also admitted. We waited in that bell-shelter for what seemed an eternity, practically suffocating and listening to the thunderous noise outside. Eventually we emerged weighing, I am sure, much less than when we entered.[1]

The *Luftwaffe* was keeping to a rigid schedule for the strafing of Biggin Hill, timing each day's second blitz to coincide with the six o'clock news. For the previous half-hour there had been sporadic raids over Kent and the Duty Controller, Squadron Leader Roger Frankland, had his

[1]Related by Dame Felicity Peake, M.B.E., who, as Section Officer Hanbury, was awarded the M.B.E., for 'setting a magnificent example of courage and devotion to duty during the very heavy bombing attacks experienced by the station. The calm behaviour of the W.A.A.F. during enemy action was outstanding and was largely due to the splendid example set by this officer'.

hands full with both 72 and 79 Squadrons airborne. As 'Baron' Worrall joined him to assist, they noticed a small formation of enemy bombers being plotted up the line of the Ashford-Redhill railway. The Huns' tactics were good: south of Kenley they suddenly swung north-east and headed straight for Biggin Hill, flying up-sun. With the Spitfires away, scrapping over the Channel, the ten Junkers 88s had a clear run to do as they pleased.

In five minutes' concentrated bombing the runways were plastered and the few buildings still intact were all hit. Old as it was, the Operations Block at Biggin Hill had no re-assuring roof of reinforced concrete and several feet of earth. Everyone not urgently required inside was ordered to shelter: many refused to go. Sergeant Helen Turner, a W.R.A.F. veteran of the first world war, remained at her telephone switchboard, alone in a little cubicle outside the Operations Room proper. By an appalling mischance a bomb fell squarely on the temporary lash-up of cables and lines out-side, severing all save the direct line to 11 Group Head-quarters, deep underground at Uxbridge. Sergeant Turner sat on unmoved, her hands busy with plugs and switches, seeking in vain to establish contact with the rest of Biggin Hill.

No further controlling or plotting was possible and every-one dived for the floor, unashamedly crawling under the flimsiest tables and chairs. A burly Warrant Officer grabbed hold of Sergeant Turner and dragged her down protesting – just in time. A 500-pounder plunged through the roof, bounced off a safe and exploded in the Defence Teleprinter Network room. Razor-edged fragments of steel ripped through the switchboard where Sergeant Turner had been sitting, seconds before. Blast bowled over Corporal Elspeth Henderson, still tenaciously manning the line to 11 Group Headquarters. Slivers of glass from the shattered plotting screen ricocheted everywhere, catching Group Captain Grice in the face and arms as he came in to see how his Ops. staff was faring. The shock sent his pipe flying. Cursing blas-phemously, half-blinded by blood from a cut on his forehead,

181

he groped around and found it – blessedly undamaged. Cramming it full of tobacco, he lit up and helped Corporal Henderson to her feet with congratulations on her composure.

'There wasn't much else I could do anyway, was there, sir?' she replied, forcing a shaky smile. 'After all, I joined the W.A.A.F.s 'cause I wanted to see a bit of life.'

Miraculously, there were no immediate casualties. Several days later, however, a young bugler, a lad borrowed from the local Boys' Brigade for emergency signal duties, died from blast injuries to his lungs.

Without panic, but bruised and shaken, the Ops. staff climbed out through a shattered window; Biggin Hill was indeed a sorry sight. The Station Armoury was ablaze, four Spitfires were burnt-out and, oddly enough, a foam fire-tender. A distant clanging of bells heralded the arrival of ambulances and fire-engines racing up from Bromley and Westerham. The road through the camp was impassable with craters and there was no way round. Grice ordered everyone still on their feet into action, to fight the raging fires with buckets of water and carry the wounded out, painfully over the heaps of rubble.

While giving chase to a Dornier streaking for home and safety after unloading its bombs on Biggin Hill, Pilot Officer Millington of 79 Squadron was himself jumped by two Me. 109s. Shaking one off, he fought the other down to 3,000 feet and sent it keeling over to crash on Romney Marsh. Five seconds wasted in watching its pilot crawl out of the wreckage, then Millington felt the full weight of the second Messerschmitt's cannon strike home. Shells smashed through his Spitfire's radiator and Merlin, mangling fuel pipes and wiring, and starting a flicker of flame that reached back greedily into its cockpit. Choking and retching, blinded by scalding oil, Millington forced the hood back and prepared to jump. A sudden draught cleared his eyes. Below was a small town – Tenterden, he guessed. There were villages all around. The Spitfire, out of control, could bring sudden tragedy to any one of these. Fighting back the urge to save his life at any cost, Millington righted his Spitfire and brought it gliding down to crash-land in an open field. Wounded in the head, agonisingly burnt, he dragged himself clear seconds before the tanks exploded.

'I considered it unwise to bale out,' he remarked drily in hospital, 'as my machine would probably have crashed in a small village.'

Next day was a Sunday. The funeral of those who had been killed during the raids was held at noon in the little cemetery beyond the boundary of the airfield. Over fifty coffins lay beside the rows of newly-dug graves, but there were not sufficient Union Jacks to cover all. The station was represented by Group Captain Grice and Section Officer Hanbury, for few could be spared while Biggin Hill carried on the bitter business of war, but there were many civilians present, friends and relatives of the dead.

As the Padre commenced the service the civil warning drowned his words with its hideous wailing, reinforced by the station's klaxons and the thunder of starting Merlins. The mourners looked hesitantly skywards, expressions of sadness mingling with a sudden, pitiful uncertainty. Some had travelled all night to be present at this service.

Handing his steel helmet to one mother and Felicity Hanbury's to another, Grice insisted on all taking cover. Only when he was satisfied that everyone was as safe as could be expected under the circumstances, did he allow the Padre to continue.

Bare-headed, standing to attention beside the graves, the Station Commander and his W.A.A.F. officer tried to listen calmly to his words. Overhead they heard the all too-familiar sounds of enemy aircraft approaching, bombs whistling down and the crump-crump of anti-aircraft shells. Shrapnel pinged crisply off the gravestones but the Padre never faltered, just glanced upwards once or twice, that was all. In an agony of mind Felicity Hanbury heard the screech of an aircraft diving with gathering speed. Then the crash: ours or theirs? At last the 'All Clear', the mourners returned and the dead were buried in peace.

This was Biggin Hill's fifth raid in forty-eight hours. By now there was little left for the enemy to destroy save the unquenchable spirit of its personnel. Their ordeal was to continue for another four days, and each evening Grice took pride in reporting to Fighter Command: 'Airfield still operational!' Under the circumstances he thought the mark of exclamation well-justified.

The warm September weather was a godsend, making the task of dispersing the various bombed-out sections very much easier. In the village an emergency Operations Room was improvised in a shop where the controllers and plotters carried on with the aid of a school blackboard and chalks until such time as a requisitioned country house, 'Towerfields' was converted into a new Operations Block. The workshop equipment was salvaged from the ruins and installed in the stables of Keston Riding School, while a belated effort was made to camouflage the runways with tar, rather futile, so everyone thought, when there were two conspicuous chalkpits on the southern slopes of Biggin Hill – beacons for friend and foe alike. To reinforce the defences Ack-Ack Command provided more Bofors guns and sent down a party of Labour Corps to dig the emplacements. When the gunners arrived, they found that these had been neatly filled in again by the conscientious airmen who dealt with bomb craters!

The ground crews adopted an unconventional, troglodyte existence and it was with determination rather than enthusiasm that they emerged from the shelters to re-arm and refuel the fighters, yet not one was grounded by lack of servicing. Without water, shaving and clean clothes were ideals of the past, and airmen luxuriated in stubble beards and a congenial grubbiness. When their condition became too offensive, parties were sent into Bromley for a bath – a welcome break until the bathers noticed the glass roof of the bath-house. To feed everyone at the dispersals was another problem. The Army helped with field kitchens set up in the South Camp. Taking it in turns, two volunteers distributed hot meals for all in one of the only vehicles still running – a full petrol bowser. It could be an exciting chore when caught in the middle of the airfield by a sudden blitz!

Of the thousand-odd beings who lived on the 'Bump', the two hundred W.A.A.F.s suffered more than most with their belongings buried beneath their wrecked quarters, no water to wash the clothes they wore and those cut to shreds by the rubble that lay everywhere. Small wonder that three new girls, posted to Biggin Hill as replacements, were found standing tearfully in the blazing sun by the ruins of what had once been the W.A.A.F. Guard Room. They were hot, tired and very scared. They hadn't wanted to come to Biggin Hill, they sobbed to their C.O., could she please send them elsewhere?

After the eighth raid one of the few buildings still intact, but only just, was the Clothing Equipment Store. Helped by some willing airmen, Felicity Hanbury set to and gave out all the clothing she could lay her hands on. Within twenty-four hours the store, now empty, had become a smouldering heap of charred wood and brickwork. The Air Ministry, however, showed little gratitude for her foresight. Months later an equipment officer arrived with bundles of dockets and forms for her to sign, claiming that she had removed the clothing illegally! She refused.

The W.A.A.F.s' morale recovered immediately. Now that they had new uniforms, clean underwear and sound shoes the enemy could do his worst – no one was going to upset their enjoyment of life:

Evening time, down they came – tunics pressed, buttons shining, their dear little mugs made up in full war paint. And out they sallied, gay and expectant, into the night. Heaven help those who ignored the risks of trying to prevent them from keeping their dates. They usually 'hunted' in couples, those kids, but I must confess there were times when even I, who knew them so well, was sometimes anxious until, with a scurry and bump at the door, back they came, full of triumph, their minds dwelling not on the trials and tribulations of the morrow, but on the success of their evening out.[1]

Inexplicably, 4th September was a quiet day and the Spitfires remained docilely idle at the dispersals. Next day, however, the *Luftwaffe* returned. Shortly before 11 a.m. a formation of Do. 215s, escorted by the usual large number of Me. 109s, was reported over Maidstone, clearly bound for Biggin Hill. 'B' Flight of 79 Squadron was ordered up at once and met the enemy at 15,000 feet – six against nearly a hundred, but the odds were far from hopeless. The sheer fury of their attack split the bomber pack wide open – the Messerschmitt pilots cold-bloodedly deserting their wards – so that the bombs fell wide and only destroyed a line of telegraph poles. 79 Squadron claimed no certain 'kills', but damaged some of the Dorniers so badly that their crews chose capture rather than risk drowning in the Channel.

One pilot, who had ripped his parachute as he jumped, landed by a miracle on a haystack near the road from Westerham to Sevenoaks. The driver of a passing bus pulled up sharply. 'He came down – quick!' he exclaimed, flabbergasted, as he and his conductor armed themselves with suitable spanners before tackling the parachutist.

The German, seeing two men approaching in what he thought were military uniforms, sprang to attention, gave a smart Nazi salute and sneered, *'Biggin Hill ist kaputt.'*

This so infuriated the bus driver that he brought his heaviest spanner crashing down on the unfortunate pilot's skull, knocking him out cold. Such was the spirit in Kent that autumn.

Immediately after the raid Group Captain Grice went up in a 'Maggie' to inspect his station from the point of view of an enemy bomb-aimer. He had become obsessed with the notion that the attacks would continue just as long as any of Biggin Hill's buildings apeared to be intact and serviceable. From 10,000 feet one hangar did look quite undamaged and the enemy could hardly be blamed for thinking otherwise

[1]Related by Flight Sergeant H. E. Turner, M.M., W.A.A.F.

though, as Grice knew, it was a mere burnt-out shell.

He decided that, to save further loss of life, the hangar must be reduced to wreckage. With the connivance of his Engineer Officer, Flight Lieutenant Jackson, and some Royal Engineers, charges of gun-cotton were laid and wired up ready for detonating. Gleefully, Grice planned this to take place during the 6 p.m. blitz, which had practically become a daily routine, but the *Luftwaffe* perversely held off that evening. He waited no longer.

'This is your Station Commander speaking. All personnel in the vicinity of the triple-bay hangar are to take cover at once. This is not a warning of enemy action.'

With one of the loudest explosions yet heard on the 'Bump' the hangar disintegrated into a mushrooming cloud of dust and flying debris. When all had settled down again, Grice surveyed the result with satisfaction: the destruction of Biggin Hill was complete. As he had predicted, the attacks by large formations during hours of daylight ceased though, for some months to come, the station was plagued by the odd hit-and-run raider who dropped out of the sheltering clouds.

Later, the Group Captain was subjected to a Court of Enquiry which censured his unorthodox action in destroying a hangar which everyone knew was past saving. In the opinion of all at Biggin Hill he should, instead, have been rewarded for his foresight and wisdom.

Whether this did, in fact, influence the *Luftwaffe* was never determined, for two days later, on 7th September, the Battle of Britain entered a new phase. Infuriated by Bomber Command's unexpected attack on Berlin, Hitler called off the offensive against the sector airfields and launched the full might of his air force against London. The Blitz proper had begun.

CHAPTER FIFTEEN

THE END OF THE BATTLE

ONCE again, a 'changing of the guard' took place, and another team, 92 Squadron, came into the history of Biggin Hill, arriving in place of 79 Squadron, posted away to Pembrey on 8th September for a spell of rest and maintenance. The new squadron, the 'Ninety-second Foot-and-Mouth', was soon to become one of the most renowned in Fighter Command and, during its time in the Biggin Hill Sector, even outstripped the total victories of the incomparable '32nd Pursuit'.

Formed after the outbreak of war with personnel from the Auxiliary Air Force and the Volunteer Reserve, 92's pilots delighted in giving an impression of being a bunch of long-haired playboys, but appearances are deceptive. They dressed in silk shirts, sported polka-dot cravats and had their tunics lined with red silk. They drove fast racing cars, cultivated glamorous models from London and were famous for their high party spirit – but they also shot down Huns. Their first squadron leader had been Roger Bushell, himself an old Biggin Hill officer who flew with the Auxiliary Squadron, No. 601, in the carefree days of peace. A South African, a practising barrister and champion skier, Bushell instilled into the squadron his own terrific spirit of gaiety and verve. Had he still been with them, he would have rejoiced in their light-hearted, but deadly, way of waging war, but he was now a prisoner in Germany,[1] shot down over the beaches of Dunkirk. The squadron, however, remained fiercely loyal to his inspiration, and woe betide any new C.O. who tried to change its ways.

[1] Roger Bushell eventually became 'O.C. Escaping' in the notorious *Stalag Luft III* and was murdered by the Gestapo after a mass break-out in March, 1944.

On its arrival at Biggin Hill 92 was commanded by Squadron Leader P. J. Sanders who was in hospital within three weeks, having lit a cigarette while wearing a petrol-soaked uniform. He was quickly followed by his successor, Squadron Leader A. M. McLachlan, with the tendons of one hand severed in forcing his way out of a cockpit with a jammed canopy.

In combat Flight Lieutenant Brian Kingcome, commander of 'A' Flight, usually led. Tall and square-jawed, his face scarred from an accident at Cranwell while driving a car too fast and slightly off-course, Kingcome was very much the moving spirit of 92 Squadron. Together with Pilot Officers Tony Bartley and Bob Holland, the latter a terrific swing pianist who could switch from 'In the Mood' to a Chopin prelude without a break, he set the pace in parties night after night – yet they were always ready to fly next dawn.

This trio apart, the squadron had a full quota of 'types': 'Wimpey' Wade, a great post-war test pilot, and Allan Wright, very much the quiet one of the bunch whose courage and self-control were an inspiration, who took the war calmly in his stride and never let it worry him. There was Roy Mottram; Howard Hill; Johnny Bryson, a burly Canadian ex-Mountie; and Tommy Thompson, former Public Schools heavyweight champion and so large that he could barely squeeze into a Spitfire's cockpit. Flight Sergeant 'Titch' Havercroft, on the other hand, needed to sit on two cushions to see over the engine cowling. Another sergeant pilot was Don Kingaby, the mild, soft-eyed, vicar's son who became the top-scoring sergeant in Fighter Command with three D.F.M.s. Later, he accepted a commission and won the D.S.O. with an official score of twenty-one enemy aircraft destroyed. During four years' fighting, on more than three hundred sorties, Kingaby's only wound was a finger shattered by a stray bullet from a Messerschmitt strafing Manston aerodrome as he was walking away from his Spitfire.

Finally, there was Zeke, Kingcome's bulldog, very much liked by all, fat, bleary-eyed and boozy. He would drink his

189

pint of beer and enjoy it. Zeke was intelligent too, and quickly mastered the nuances of the air raid warning system. When the general alarm went, like everyone else he took little notice but, at the first sound of the bugle, he would stagger to the top step of the nearest shelter and squat there, ready to tumble inside if the bombing came too close.

About to leave the squadron was Flight Lieutenant Robert Stanford Tuck, posted to command No. 257 (Burma) Squadron. Slim and fastidiously elegant, with a gay buccaneering spirit, Bob Tuck was the epitome of the fighter pilot as popularly imagined, calculating and merciless. With his record of fourteen confirmed victories and a phenomenal luck in surviving collisions and crashes, he was fast becoming a legend in Fighter Command. 92 Squadron was sorry to see him go, but he was never far away, often dropping in at Biggin Hill for a drink and, on occasions, flying with his old friends.

The move to Biggin Hill was very welcome. After the rough-and-tumble of Dunkirk the squadron had been relegated to Pembrey in south-west Wales. While others were in the thick of the fighting, 92 frittered away the hours of daylight in maddening, often futile, pursuits of reconnaissance machines over the Bristol Channel and Irish Sea and was rarely caught up in the fringe of the battle to the east. The days of frustration were now over.

The squadron swung vigorously into action, bagging a 'certain' He. 111 and two 'probable' Me. 109s within its first twenty-four hours on the 'Bump'. For three days 92 flew alone. Biggin Hill was still too much a battle casualty to support two operational units, so 72 Squadron remained temporarily at Croydon. On 12th September it returned home and thereafter the two squadrons fought together, destroying sixty Huns by the month's end, with another thirty 'probables' and 'damaged'.

There was no shortage of targets as the *Luftwaffe* strove to inflict one final, decisive blow on Britain in readiness for 'Operation Sealion', now retimed for 21st September. Misled by his own pilots' reports into believing that Fighter Command was down to its last hundred aircraft, Goering argued that repeated daylight attacks on London would draw out Dowding's final reserves. These would be speedily eliminated and the way would be clear for the invasion armada already assembling in the occupied Channel ports.

The Battle of London began late in the afternoon of Saturday, 7th September. From Biggin Hill the smoke rising above the ravaged docks was clearly visible, black against a cloudless sky. As the Blitz continued and more and more Londoners suffered, the attitude of civilians living on the 'Bump' towards their R.A.F. neighbours changed abruptly. If London could 'take it', then Biggin Hill village could 'take it', too. Gone were the intransigence and self-pity of a month ago; householders could not do enough for the station. At night the older inhabitants stared at the lurid glow to the north and recalled the Gothas which had once bumbled overhead; now they heard the ceaseless desynchronised drone of Dorniers, Heinkels and Junkers.

Every so often a lone marauder would serve notice that Biggin Hill was still rated a worthwhile target. These attacks had more nuisance value than destructive effect:

A large number of incendiaries dropped by a single enemy raider. No damage was caused to buildings.

Four H.E. bombs, presumed weight of each – 50 lbs., dropped on S.E. corner of aerodrome, slightly damaging a runway only.

The W.A.A.F.s were now billeted in a large house, the 'Cedars', in Keston village. One evening, as the girls were carrying their bedding down to the entrance hall where they slept for quietness and safety, they heard the familiar, ominous whistle of a falling bomb. Instinctively they tumbled to the floor breathlessly waiting for the explosion. It was strangely muffled. The bomb had penetrated deep into the trunk of the magnificent cedar which stood sentinel outside. The old tree, however, stoutly withstood the shock and no damage was done.

A few evenings later there was a sequel, when the Mess

was crowded with W.A.A.F.s during an 'Alert'. In one of those sudden, unpredictable silences they heard a peculiar slithering noise outside, much too close for comfort. As one they flung themselves down, only to scramble up a few seconds later with sheepish grins. The great cedar had at last heeled over, brushing the windows with its boughs.

This incident, trivial as it was, made Group Captain Grice realise that a single direct hit could kill all his pilots at once, and he sensibly decided that the two squadrons should live apart and as far away from the airfield and each other as possible. The arrangement suited 92 Squadron admirably, whose Adjutant thereupon requisitioned a lovely manor house, 'Southwood', two miles from Biggin Hill. Once the owner, Captain McNair Scott, had stored his precious furnishings and pictures in safety, the squadron moved in complete with jazz band (the batmen had been selected for their skills with saxophone, trumpet and trombone) and cellarful of liquor.

Lit by oil lamps and candles, with casual, cigarette-scarred furniture, 92 Squadron's new home carelessly achieved the effect of a sophisticated night club, occasionally the scene of parties which lasted until dawn warned the roisterers that it was time to prepare for another day of battle.

15th September, 1940, for ever celebrated as Battle of Britain Day, was, as we now know, the turning point in Nazi Germany's bid for the subjection of Britain and her Empire, though at Biggin Hill it seemed little different from any other day of action in that warm and sunlit month. Like the Battle of Waterloo it fell on a Sunday, but there was no sybaritic enjoyment of a late morning in bed for the pilots of 92 Squadron.

They were called at 4 a.m. Swearing at the hideously early business-hours, they staggered downstairs and grabbed a quick cup of cocoa and a biscuit.

'Time we were moving,' said Brian Kingcome, and they crept out into the cool, still dawn where Ginger, the driver, was patiently waiting with a truck.

In the dispersal hut there was a large fire blazing. The majority just threw themselves on to camp beds and tried to sleep. A few sat around and fiddled with their helmets and oxygen masks. Each had their own thoughts and they kept them to themselves. The atmosphere was relaxed, the silence broken only by an occasional blasphemy or roar of a Merlin running-up.

'God! I hate this waiting,' grumbled 'Wimpey' Wade. 'Why don't the b——s come?'

'Take it easy, boy,' murmured Brian Kingcome, 'and let's get some sleep.'

The hours passed slowly. It was after 10.30 a.m. when the first wave of enemy aircraft crossed the coast.

That morning, at the Headquarters of No. 11 Group, the Prime Minister and Mrs Churchill stood in the Operations Room, deep underground, watching Air Vice Marshal Park and his staff direct the battle. For once Mr Churchill's cigar remained unlit as he followed the quick moves and countermoves on the plotting table. On the wall opposite him an indicator board with flashing lights gave the states of the squadrons: 'Stand by', 'Instant Readiness', 'Airborne' and 'In contact with the enemy'. Very quickly all 11 Group was engaged, the board showing that there was not a single squadron in reserve, and Park was urgently requesting reinforcements from 10 and 12 Groups. In Mr Churchill's own words: 'The odds were great; our margin small; the stakes infinite.'

Two of the red 'In Action' signals that he saw light up represented the squadrons of Biggin Hill.

At 11.03 a.m. the telephone at 92's dispersal rang with a harsh, ragged note. Everyone sprang expectantly to their feet. The Controller spoke to Brian Kingcome: 'Squadron patrol Maidstone . . . Angels 20 . . . Rendezvous with 72 Squadron over base.'

'Jump to it, chaps,' yelled Kingcome as they sprinted to their aircraft. 'Titch and Kingaby, you're weaving. Keep a good look out and give plenty of warning.'

Twelve Merlins coughed and roared into life; twelve pilots

leapt into their cockpits and buckled on their harness.

'All set, Red Station?' asked Kingcome's voice on the R/T.

'O.K. Let's go.'

His Section roared down the runway, gathering speed, followed by Blue and Green Sections. They joined 72 Squadron, already airborne, and started to climb.

There was silence on the R/T as the Spitfires circled, rising steadily into the blue.

Flying Red Two, close behind Kingcome, was Tony Bartley. He looked down at the earth three miles below. Under his port wing lay the Thames, winding through a city shrouded with mist and smoke from factory chimneys. The sun glinted on a myriad barrage balloons that sprawled up through the haze. Biggin Hill's runways were scarcely visible as the two squadrons swung south-east for Maidstone.

'Hullo, Gannic[1] Red Leader . . . Sapper calling . . . two hundred plus coming in over Red Queen . . . Vector 120 . . . Angels 22.'

Quietly, the Biggin Hill Controller digested, condensed and relayed the information that poured into the little emergency Operations Room.

'Hullo, Gannic . . . Look out for snappers[2] above, many snappers above . . . is that understood?'

'O.K. Sapper.'

In a tight, compact formation the two squadrons flew on – all eyes straining ahead, and above, and to the sides.

'Ack-Ack on the right!' someone yelled.

'Keep your hair on,' soothed Kingcome, 'I can see them.'

Bartley looked over his starboard wing and away in the distance saw little black puffs of cotton wool blossoming in the wake of a great gaggle of bombers in Vic formation with escorting fighters, oddly enough, below.

'Jeepers!' he muttered, 'where the hell do we start on this lot?'

Out of the corner of his eye he glimpsed six squadrons of

[1]Code name for 92 Squadron.
[2]Enemy fighters.

Hurricanes climbing up to port and felt less lonely.

'Hard at 'em, boys. Let's go,' snapped Kingcome, half-rolling to starboard and tearing into the leading formation from the quarter with flames from his eight Brownings blasting through the canvas covers of the gun ports.

Swinging tight after his leader, Bartley lowered his seat and thrust his face close to the windscreen – this always gave him confidence. He lined up on a Dornier and pressed the firing button, seeing his tracers stab home. The Hun jettisoned its bombs and started to burn. Tracers from behind flickered round Bartley's cockpit and he heard the dull thud of cannon shells exploding in the fuselage. He switched his aim to the leading bomber and knocked pieces flying from its tail. Wheeling after another, he caught sight of a Spitfire hammering a Junkers. He noticed its letters – QJR. 'Johnny Bryson's,' he thought. 'Too close, Johnny!' he shouted, his warning unheeded as the Spitfire was caught by the bomber's slipstream and flung aside. Bartley half-rolled nimbly after the Junkers, now beating it home. He pressed the 'tit', but there was only a brief response. 'Hell! Out of ammunition and what a peach of a target!' Four Me. 109s, propeller-bosses gleaming yellow, dived after him and shredded his port aileron with their fire. Slamming his boost control forward to 'maximum emergency power', Bartley screamed down through a squadron of Hurricanes for the safety of lower altitudes.

Others in 72 and 92 Squadrons had an equally confused but effective battle. Their reports are eloquent:

'Sighted large enemy formation of bombers and fighters, dodged fighters and climbed into sun, attacked Dorniers head-on . . . ' ' . . . I dived and attacked a Do. 17 in the middle of the formation. I did not have time to observe results as there were 109s above . . . ' ' . . . I gave it a burst from above and behind, and it spun into the Thames Estuary . . . ' ' . . . Enemy aircraft continued diving steeply and did not seem able to straighten up again . . . ' ' . . . And in my mirror I saw another 109 coming down on me. I evaded it and could not get round to fire at it because it climbed away and, as

195

there were twenty more above, I decided to leave it . . . '
' . . . He burst into flames. I then spun down to get away
from more 109s . . . ' ' . . . No time to observe effect as I was
hit by seven bullets . . . ' ' . . . Received a cannon shell
through my main plane which forced me to return to
base . . . '

By noon the sky was silent and empty but for the fading
plumes of vapour trails. Both Biggin Hill squadrons returned
to base without loss.

At 92's dispersal Tom Weise, the squadron's Norwegian
Intelligence Officer, was patiently trying to extract a coherent
report from the excited pilots. No one paid much attention
to him. Kingcome stalked into the hut and resumed the book
he had been reading before the scramble. He had little
interest in confirming his own victories; the personal satisfaction that came from doing a good, professional job was
sufficient reward. He believed that a pilot who broke off a
dog fight to confirm a victim was not doing his duty – unless
he had used up all his ammunition.

'I fired everything I had at a couple of them,' said Allan
Wright, adding judicially: 'They certainly looked a bit depressed, but I couldn't confirm them.'

'I saw one of yours hit the deck,' interposed 'Wimpey'
Wade.

Bob Holland stood on a chair and gave a spirited render-
ing of a bomber's death throes. 'I followed a Heinkel down
that I had plastered, and then got pushed out of the way by
five bloody Hurris who shot at it until it crashed at Malling.
Sheer sadism, I call it. I bet they all claim it – the sods!'

'I want all your combat reports before lunch,' Weise per-
sisted stubbornly. 'There's good boys.'

'O.K. Tom. Anything for peace,' they chorused in unison,
hating the anticlimax of cold-bloodedly analysing and
writing down their experiences.

Both squadrons were in action again that afternoon, along
with nineteen others, harrying and repulsing the *Luftwaffe*'s
second attempt to thrust through to the heart of London.

They gave a good account of themselves and were justifiably happy with the day's 'bag' of nine 'confirmed destroyed' plus a score of 'damaged', many of which undoubtedly failed to reach home. Only one Spitfire was lost, Bob Holland's, and he was safe in East Grinstead hospital, slightly injured in the knee.

15th September ended in overwhelming victory for the Royal Air Force.[1] Two days later, Hitler and his commanders met to debate the projected invasion of Britain. His decision is recorded in the War Diary of the German Naval Staff: 'The enemy air force is by no means defeated, on the contrary it shows increasing activity. The weather situation as a whole does not permit us to expect a period of calm. The Fuhrer has therefore decided to postpone Operation Sealion indefinitely.'

Then, for three days only, Biggin Hill reverted to its role of 1918 as a night-fighter station keyed to the defence of London. Appropriately enough, the squadron posted-in was No. 141, the original 'Cock' Squadron, which had latterly and briefly returned to its birthplace. Following its inauspicious début in July as a day fighter unit with Defiants, the squadron withdrew to Scotland to work up for night operations. Now it was ready, and 'B' Flight came down from Turnhouse, still with Defiants, arriving late in the afternoon of 15th September – just as the Spitfire boys were off to celebrate with a 'gynormous' party.

Several patrols were flown that night, all without incident. Next night, however, the Defiant crews earned the right to a celebration of their own. It was exceptionally clear, a harvest moon giving a visibility of twenty miles at 10,000 feet. Pilot Officer J. Waddingham, with Sergeant A. B. Cumbers as gunner, was patrolling a line from Maidstone to Tonbridge when, five miles away, he caught sight of an enemy bomber, unmistakably a Heinkel 111, pinpointed by the unwavering beams of searchlights.

[1]The destruction of 183 enemy aircraft was claimed, a figure amended after the war to 56, against the R.A.F.'s loss of 26.

'Don't lose him. For Christ's sake hold him,' prayed Waddingham as the Heinkel zig-zagged wildly to evade the merciless cone of light, then swore as the Ack-Ack gunners chose that moment to open up. Dazzled and exasperated by the barrage, Waddingham flashed the recognition letter of the day at the guns. It made no difference; the gunners continued firing, their shells bursting a thousand yards behind and below the bomber whose crew never noticed the Defiant, now closing in relentlessly.

Pulling his boost cut-out control, Waddingham turned in on the Heinkel's beam, edging up to it delicately, cautiously, a killer about to strike. Although the range was now only forty yards, the Defiant was still unsuspected by the Germans until Cumbers opened fire, red tracers raking the Heinkel from nose to tail. Over six hundred rounds poured from the four guns of the Defiant's turret. A giant shudder shook the bomber's fabric, then it reared up convulsively and heeled over, almost ramming the Defiant as it plunged headlong to earth. Its destruction was confirmed next day.

This, however, was not the end of Waddingham and Cumber's activities that night:

Still carrying on with my patrol, I caught sight of another enemy aircraft approximately 3,000 feet above me and about 5 miles away. I climbed to intercept . . . when within 1,000 yards of it I saw another aircraft, which I presumed to be enemy, 300 yards to the rear of my originally-sighted plane . . . At this juncture I saw the following aircraft open fire on the leading one . . . I identified the pursuer as a friendly Blenheim fighter . . . During this engagement I was rapidly closing in and, after five seconds during which the two aircraft were firing at each other, I had closed in to within 400 yards of the enemy aircraft, still on his starboard side. Then the Blenheim appeared to cease fire and broke away. I decided to engage the enemy aircraft which was rapidly going away and got to within 30 yards when my gunner opened fire with a short burst of barely one second. This burst, on account of our close proximity, went right over the enemy aircraft, my gunner then corrected his aim and let him have a long burst of eight seconds which set his engine on fire and the plane appeared to dive down.

The aircraft was seen by coastguards to be on fire, and R.D.F. ceased plotting it 8 miles from the French coast, where it obviously fell into the sea. Although, until confirmation has been received, the enemy aircraft was only claimed as 'probable', as it had only one engine on fire, I respectfully beg to apply for a 'destroyed' verdict, as well as for the first action result.

Next night 'B' Flight scored again when Sergeant G. L. Laurence and his gunner shot-down a Junkers 88 over Bexley. On this occasion the weather was atrocious, the clouds too dense for searchlights to penetrate, but brilliant work by the Biggin Hill Controller guided Laurence to within 150 yards of his quarry.

While the chase was on, the C.-in-C. Fighter Command himself, 'Stuffy' Dowding, dropped in unheralded at the emergency Operations Room in Biggin Hill village. He was startled to find the controllers and plotters nonchalantly working with a school blackboard and chalks, and said so, crisply. It was futile for them to protest that their system worked – witness Laurence's news of his 'kill' crackling over the R/T. Next day, however, they forgot their pique when they observed the redoubled efforts of the labourers converting 'Towerfields' into the new Operations Block. The C.-in-C., evidently, had taken action.

It was soon found impracticable to operate both day- and night-fighter units from Biggin Hill so the Defiants were moved to Gatwick to continue night patrols. From then until the end of the war Biggin Hill remained a base for daylight operations, though the Operations Room continued to control the night-fighter squadrons in the Sector.

After 15th September the days became more cloudy and the enemy was restricted to attacks on a reduced scale against fringe targets – oil-storage depots, aircraft factories and the like – though Bristol and Southampton were both heavily blitzed. Then, on Friday, 27th September, came the last of the great daytime assaults by big bomber formations on London.

The weather was fine with high clouds, ideal for fighters. Shortly before 9 a.m. both of Biggin Hill's squadrons were ordered up, No. 92 taking the lead, Brian Kingcome was 'driving the train' – leading the formation – as usual when they intercepted twenty Dorniers boxed in by a swarm of fighters. The Spitfires went in together, tearing the heart out of the bomber pack in a reckless head-on charge. No time to observe results or confirm victories; break away quickly, climb, re-form and slice into the 109s while surprise was on your side. The battle exploded over Kent. Trails of dark smoke, curving gracefully against a backdrop of high white cirrus, were ephemeral pointers to the fate of some raiders and Spitfires, too, their blazing wrecks scattered from Sheppey to Dungeness.

'Wimpey' Wade, alone, encountered a dozen Dorniers over Brighton. As he dived hard to attack, they whipped into a tight defensive circle. Nipping in smartly behind the last one's tail Wade set his starboard engine smoking before he was caught by the other Dornier's cross-fire. Glycol streamed back from his shattered Merlin and he crash-landed with a somersault on Lewes race-course. Rushing to the nearest police station, he wheedled and blustered his way into getting a fast car to take him back to Biggin Hill and was in action again that afternoon.

Sergeant Glew of 72 Squadron had forced a Dornier down to within fifty feet of the Channel shore when he ran out of ammunition. 'So I proceeded to dive steeply on him. This had some effect as, after one dive, he seemed to panic and went straight into the water three miles out. Three men jumped out but I could see no dinghy.'

Glew flew back to the coast and attracted the attention of a trawler, using up his slender reserve of petrol in guiding it to where the Dornier's crew was struggling to keep afloat.

A certain ten of the enemy were destroyed, but four Spit-fires failed to return.

One pilot, Acting Flight Lieutenant Paterson of 92 Squadron, had already been shot-down during his first week at Biggin Hill and had jumped for it with his clothes on fire. Terribly burnt about the face, he insisted on flying again before he could properly see. Even 'Group' Grice could not dissuade him from taking off on this, his last sortie. Brother pilots saw his Spitfire, a blazing torch, fall spinning before three Me. 109s with Paterson inside, struggling blindly to escape from the flame-choked cockpit.

Both squadrons were airborne again at 11.45 a.m., this time to head-off a force of seventy 'bandits' reported over Maidstone.

92 Squadron's greatest hour came during the third major assault of the day; ordered up at 3 p.m. in partnership with West Malling's 66 Squadron, Brian Kingcome and the others were feeling stiff, sweaty and very tired until his staccato 'Tally ho, chaps. Here they are!' sent fresh adrenalin flowing in their blood.

We attacked the bombers head-on. I gave a Ju. 88 a two-second burst and saw it drop back out of the formation. I climbed back and attacked another Ju. 88 from ahead and the machine also dropped back losing height. I then noticed another 88 which turned away from the formation and headed south and, as it appeared to be damaged, I attacked it. Two more Spitfires turned up and also attacked it, the machine crashing in flames in a wood. I afterwards found the remainder of the enemy formation returning south over the coast and made one final burst from the beam but without any apparent effect.

Kingcome was not the only pilot who was busy – Tony Bartley sent a Junkers crashing down near Redhill and 'Wimpey' Wade a Heinkel 111 which he chased to tree-top height and saw plough through a hedge near Lympne. Three of the crew scrambled out and dragged the fourth to safety. They waved a good-natured valediction to Wade as he

201

circled and climbed back to the fight.

The slaughter continued until thirteen of the bombers had been destroyed. Significantly, many of their escorting Me. 109s made little attempt to interfere.

It was as well that 72 Squadron was held in reserve. Shortly after Kingcome and his party had left, fifteen He. 111s flew insolently over Biggin Hill. 72's Spitfires were waiting, airborne in readiness, and drove the marauders back to the Channel, downing two. Sergeant Lee found himself in the predicament of Glew earlier in the day, with a juicy target and empty magazines. 'I made mock attacks on the enemy aircraft in the hope of forcing it down. In the end the bomber came down in the sea off Brighton. Three of the crew escaped in their life-jackets.'

*　　　*　　　*

October was Messerschmitt month. As the clouds of the coming winter gathered in the skies and the first frosts touched the woods round Biggin Hill with russet and gold, the pattern of battle changed. After the crushing losses of past weeks the German bombers struck only by night, leaving the hours of daylight to fighters and fighter-bombers flying at a great height, or skimming the Channel at wave-crest level. It was a vicious, snarling battle of attrition, an attempt to wear down our fighter strength with frequent small-scale attacks by Me. 109s and 110s.

Life at Biggin Hill became less hectic, more orderly. Rather than wait for the Hun to appear and then try to gain his altitude when it was often too late, standing patrols at regular intervals were introduced and 'Tonbridge, Angels 20' was no longer necessarily a portent of 'bandits'. Often the squadrons would patrol four or five times a day without firing a round.

07.41: Spits went on patrol over Dover, landed 09.00. No enemy aircraft.
10.29: 7 Spits patrolled base at 25,000 feet and were vectored to Ramsgate and Rochester without en-

countering the enemy. They all landed back at
11.50 hrs.

13.44: 7 Spits patrolled Maidstone and landed 14.30 without result.

15.40: 7 Spits patrolled Maidstone and landed 16.40
without result.[1]

Quite often, too, the deteriorating weather would allow the
squadrons to be held at 'reduced state' with only half the
pilots at 'readiness', one eye open to windward for a break
in the clouds. They came to hate the sun, for sunshine and
blue, open skies brought Messerschmitts and sharp, ferocious
dog fights at altitudes ranging on the limits of endurance.
Although Biggin Hill's squadrons more than held their own,
the flight-serviceability boards increasingly tagged grounded
aircraft with the melancholy description: '109 trouble'.

The Roll of Honour grew distressingly large. A month at
Biggin Hill had made veterans of 92 Squadron, but many of
those who had flown down so blithely from Pembrey were
missing: Johnny Bryson, the Canadian . . . Peter Eyles, a
little girl stumbled across his wreck in the middle of a wood
. . . Eddie Edwards, his body driven seven feet under plough-
land by the impact of the crash . . . Hargreaves . . . Paterson
. . . Oldfield . . . Sydney . . . and Howard Hill. They found his
body a month later, strapped in the cockpit of his Spitfire
in the tree-tops with the top of his head sliced off by a cannon
shell.

Just as the lost Spitfires were replaced by new aircraft from
the factories, so were fresh pilots posted-in to fill dead men's
shoes. Many only lasted a few days – some arrived in the
morning and were casualties by noon. There was only time
to teach them the golden rule: 'stick to your leader and watch
your tail'. A few had big ideas of their own on how to kill
Huns. They were rarely seen again. Others were more
sensible, but there was no escaping the strain of survival.

They found themselves subconsciously studying each
other's faces wondering who would be the next to get the

[1]Report by 72 Squadron, 7.10.40.

'chop'. Many of them sought relief in the philosophy of 'Let's eat, drink and be merry . . . ' to which the team of individualists that was 92 Squadron wholeheartedly subscribed. Each evening, released from operations, they piled into a battered Humber shooting brake and clattered off to the station bawling:

> High ranks, low ranks, everybody come,
> To the pilots' locker-room and have a tot of rum
> I know, you know, we can chase the blues,
> So let us introduce you to the fighting 92s.

Sometimes they visited the half-empty cinemas of Bromley to sit, bulky in flying-jackets, alone in the circle, hearing the crash of bombs outside and the crackle of shrapnel on the roof. Westerns were their favourites: the gun-play of Hopalong Cassidy, the 'Frisco Kid and others a refreshing thrill after a life-and-death scrap with a Messerschmitt.

But it was the 'White Hart', seven miles away in Brasted, that was 92 Squadron's favourite haunt. Of all the pubs in the district this had best claim to being Biggin Hill's 'local'. Since the early thirties pilots had been in the habit of dropping in here for a noggin of beer and the friendly hospitality of landlord Teddy Preston and his wife Kath. During the war they scrawled their names in chalk on one of the blackout screens; it is still there today, framed and glazed in a place of honour, and bears the autographs of nearly all the fighter 'aces'.

92 Squadron adopted the 'White Hart' for its own, enjoying the classic country-pub charm and the low ceiling'd bar with oak beams from the timbers of old sailing ships, its sporting prints and gleaming brasses. Here they could relax in the company of placid and conventional civilians, whose life was so very different from theirs, and forget their frustration and tensions in light-hearted banter with the squadron's 'Godmothers', the O'Neill twins, Moira and Sheila.

However tolerant the local constabulary was of lax closing hours, and they were very wise, there inevitably came the cry of 'Time, Ladies and Gentlemen, if you please!' Everyone fumbled their way out into the night, but this did not always mean the end of the party. A pause to stare at the sky over London lit up by flares and the unearthly glow of incendiaries reflected from the clouds, then they were off at breakneck speed to the squadron's billet where swing music would outplay the gunfire for another hour or so.

The medicos advised 92's pilots to go easy, but true relaxation was impossible to achieve; only in complete exhaustion could some of them find peace. No man could achieve normal sleep, lying in bed listening to the thunderous barrage outside and thinking about the next day, which might well be his last. Some were secretly taking benzedrine but every time Group Captain Grice suggested they should take a rest, they denied their weariness.

Those hectic, unrelenting four weeks of battle inevitably took their toll, however; the accumulated strain of continual flying probably contributed its factor to the tragic incident of 10th October.

Ironically, it was 92's birthday: exactly a year before the squadron had been formed at Tangmere. Just after dawn a section was scrambled to intercept a solitary Dornier 17 reported over the South Coast. No one thought much about it. It was routine: six Spitfires could take care of one Hun.

The rest of the squadron relaxed in the dispersal hut, noisy and cheerful. Brian Kingcome was reading and affectionately cursing his dog Zeke.

'The boys should be back soon,' remarked someone after half an hour.

In the distance they heard a Spitfire coming in to land. Some minutes later 'Wimpey' Wade walked in. His face was white and drawn. He stared round at the others belligerently.

'What a frightful black!'

Everyone looked up, puzzled by his tone.

'Bill Williams has gone,' he told them, throwing himself down exhausted. 'I saw him go down in flames. They blew his wing off, I think. And I saw two more go down, too. I don't know who they were.'

'What was it?' asked Kingcome.

There was misery in Wade's eyes. He spat the words out savagely: 'Just one bloody snooper all by himself.'

'Did you get it?'

'I don't think so. That's what's so bloody. I think the bastard got back.'

For a few seconds no one spoke. Kingcome returned to his book.

'We did our best,' Wade's voice split the silence, 'and we got the rear gunner.'

Just then two others landed, Bob Holland and Johnny Mansell-Lewis, and from their stories Tom Weise was able to piece together what had occurred. The Spitfires had found the Dornier without difficulty, Pilot Officer Williams and Flying Officer Drummond were the first to attack, but an unaccountable, and disastrous mistake was made. They collided in mid-air. Sergeant Ellis then dived on the Dornier and was shot-down. The others attacked again and again until their ammunition was exhausted, but only managed to damage one engine and silence the rear gunner before the Dornier escaped into cloud.

Later, they learnt that Williams had crashed near a church on Romney Marsh. A priest was able to administer the last sacrament before the young pilot died in his arms.

This episode left 92 Squadron in the depths of depression and just to make matters worse, Lord Haw-Haw had to broadcast their disgrace. A single reconnaissance aircraft, he crowed, returning from photographing the holocaust of London had been attacked by six Spitfires. Its gallant crew had shown great courage in destroying three and had reached France where their aircraft had crashed, but the photographs were saved.

Two days later 92 Squadron was back on top of the world. That morning Squadron Leader Tuck had flown over from Martlesham to visit his former comrades. They found him unchanged: the same old Bobby Tuck, full of dash and confidence, with his spotless cravat and monogram'd handkerchief dangling from his sleeve. While they were reminiscing over the old days at Pembrey, a scramble came through and it was only natural that Tuck should borrow a Spitfire and join in, delighting everyone by downing an Me. 109. During the afternoon they destroyed three more 109s and were bucked to get a signal from 'Stuffy' Dowding himself congratulating 92 Squadron on being back in form.

As Commander-in-Chief, Fighter Command, Dowding's biggest problem was not shortage of aircraft, now forthcoming from the factories in ever-increasing numbers, but pilots. The casualty rate of trained, experienced men had become so desperate that, had the Germans only known of Dowding's plight and been able to turn it to their advantage, we might well have lost the victory that was the Battle of Britain. It took many weeks to train a pilot to operational efficiency, by mid-September there were no fresh squadrons to replace battle-weary units, some of which Dowding was even forced to withdraw to bring on trainee-pilots from the flying schools.

After six weeks at Biggin Hill 72 Squadron's turn to leave came on 13th October when it was ordered, distressingly reduced to seven pilots of experience, to Leconfield for operational training duties. It was replaced on the 'Bump' by the redoubtable 74 (Tiger) Squadron.

The 'Tigers' were commanded at the time by Squadron Leader A. G. Malan, D.F.C. and bar – known throughout Fighter Command as 'Sailor'. Born in South Africa in 1910, Adolph Gysbert Malan went to sea at the age of fifteen to serve, first as a cadet and later as an officer, with the Union Castle line. Then, tiring of life afloat, he came to England to try his hand at flying and joined the Royal Air Force in 1936. When he passed out as a qualified pilot, he opted for Fighter Command because, as he put it, 'he wanted something to throw about', and it was the 'Sailor' who was nominated to collect the first production Spitfire from Vickers-Supermarine. The 'Spit' was Malan's first love; flying it as to the manner born and with uncanny marksmanship, he was fast becoming the outstanding fighter pilot of the war. On the ground he was noted for his monosyllables, a granite charm and an ability to carry strong liquor better than most.

The 'Sailor's' two henchmen were J. C. Mungo-Park and H. M. Stephen, D.F.C., who together ran a private sweepstake on who could kill the most Huns. By the time they were posted to Biggin Hill Mungo-Park, a gay and gallant Liverpudlian, and Stephen, the stubborn Scot who started life as a copy boy in a newspaper office, had accounted for over twenty of the enemy.

Malan, Mungo-Park and Stephen: this triumvirate ran 74 Squadron with an iron discipline. 'Kick their arses once a day,' said Malan, 'and I have the toughest bunch in Fighter Command.' The 'Tigers' were the very antithesis of the easy-going pilots of 92 Squadron who argued that as long as they were good in the air, it did not much matter how they conducted themselves on the ground.

'Should now get back into our stride again': despite the reduced opportunities for combat in mid-October, this prediction in 74's diary on the day the squadron moved to Biggin Hill was quickly fulfilled.

Two days later, during the afternoon of 17th October, the 'Tigers' were pitching into a formation of Me. 109s above the Thames Estuary. Malan's methodical, businesslike attitude to the war in the air is reflected in his combat report:

I was leading Dysoe[1] Squadron from B/Hill and took-off at 15.10 hrs. to intercept fighter raids approaching London.

I climbed mostly on an up-sun course to 26,000 feet and flew towards A.A. bursts over the Thames Estuary.

At approx. 15.30 hrs. we suddenly saw two yellow noses (109s) crossing our bows and surprised them from the sun.

I gave the righthand one a two-second burst with quarter-deflection from 200 yards and closed to 150 yards astern, and delivered another two-second burst. I closed to 100 yards and delivered a four-second burst which appeared to damage elevator controls as his nose went vertically downwards very suddenly instead of the usual

[1]Code name for 74 Squadron.

half-roll. My engine naturally stopped when I followed suit, but it picked up again and I closed to 150 yards on half-roll and gave another four-second burst.

I found myself doing an aileron turn to keep direction and delivered another four-second burst. He then started to smoke, but I blacked-out completely and lost consciousness for a couple of seconds, and eventually pulled out at 9,000 feet above 10/10ths cloud.

My port guns failed to fire during the whole engagement.

92 Squadron jokingly accused Malan of keeping his boys in order at the point of a pistol; he replied that, given the disciplining of the material in 92, he could lick both Mölders and Galland's *Gruppen* together. Nevertheless, the two squadrons made a fighting partnership which gave Biggin Hill the distinction of becoming the first station to score 600 'kills'.

30th October, 1940, has been officially designated the end of the Battle of Britain, but there was no clear-cut, decisive finish. The pattern of fighting continued on into November, albeit on a diminishing scale as the fogs and storms of winter clamped down on airfields on both sides of the Channel and the *Luftwaffe* conserved its bombers for the night-time Blitz. It had been no easy victory. Almost a year had passed since the day when Flying Officer Davies and Sergeant Brown shot-down a 'flying pencil' over the Channel and now Biggin Hill's tally stood a score short of six hundred. Surveying the ruins of what had become 'the most bombed station in Fighter Command', Group Captain Grice could justifiably boast, like a certain London theatre beloved by fighter pilots: 'We never closed!'

CHAPTER SIXTEEN

SIX HUNDRED STATION

BIGGIN HILL was still a battlefield. The North Camp was completely devastated without a building intact and many too badly blitzed even for repair. By the beginning of November nothing had been done and the camp itself was deserted: Station Headquarters, the Operations Block, the Transport, Equipment and W.A.A.F. Sections were all in requisitioned premises in the Keston area. The pilots of 74 and 92 Squadrons, now joined by No. 66 from waterlogged West Malling, were sleeping in country houses in the district. The majority of airmen, about a thousand, lived in huts in the South Camp vacated by the Army, while three hundred more were billeted out in the villages of Biggin Hill and Downe.

This dispersal made the normal running of the station out of the question; without proper offices, transport, or even telephones that worked, the handful of administrative officers and N.C.O.'s just could not cope with the mass of paperwork thrust upon them from on high now that the emergency was over. For many weeks there was no nominal roll. After the raids no one knew to a man who was stationed on Biggin Hill, or who had been killed. When the rebuilding began, an airman was found living unconcernedly in a disused Decontam. Centre. He had sheltered there during the bombing and had not ventured forth since, getting food and the bare essentials of life from friends. Questioned as to his motives, he replied quite correctly that it seemed the safest place on Biggin Hill. The Station Commander was forced to agree!

This state of affairs was not allowed to continue for long. A visit by Air Chief Marshal Sir Edgar Ludlow-Hewitt during November produced rapid results: adequate transport and a small army of workmen for the reconstruction of the station.

The first building to be pronounced ready was Station Headquarters, but its reoccupation was hardly popular. It took place on a dull, cold day and the vista of ruins beyond the partially-glazed windows reduced the W.A.A.F. typists to tears. Their office ceiling lacked plaster, it leaked copiously and they had to trek a mile through mud for meals. To complete the joys of home-coming, six delayed-action bombs were dropped across the road and went off at intervals during the day.

There was an acute shortage of administrative staff: the C.O.'s Adjutant was away sick, the Station Adjutant was fully occupied with the problems of reconstruction and Group Captain Grice was forced to place the routine running of his station in the inexperienced but willing hands of his Assistant Adjutant, Pilot Officer H. B. Leeming. To help him out, Warrant Officer Gill was posted in from 11 Group. Though well over age – he had been Trenchard's Flight Sergeant in the first world war – 'Half-pint' Gill was never ruffled or upset, even when blown from his bicycle by blast. His knowledge of King's Regulations was encyclopedic, so much so that the girls in his office swore that the blood in his veins was Air Force blue.

That winter strict orders were given for Station Headquarters to be closed at 4.30 p.m., only one member of the staff being permitted to remain during the hours of black-out. This meant an intolerable rush for Leeming and Gill to get through the work which had to be done if Biggin Hill was to function efficiently. Their day started with a priority report to 11 Group Headquarters on the readiness-state of all aircraft; then the overnight signals had to be dealt with, the registered and secret mail; flying orders had to be dispatched to Biggin Hill's squadrons and those at West Malling, Gravesend and Hawkinge; then came Daily Routine Orders, Standing Orders, Courts of Inquiry, leave passes, ration books, petrol coupons and claims on the R.A.F. and station benevolent funds. Any form of cohesion and discipline would have been impossible had it not been for the truly fantastic *espirit de corps* of the station. No one grumbled when leave passes were late in forthcoming, on the contrary, the Operations staff volunteered to take some of the load off the 'Admin. types' by appointing their own Orderly and Duty Officers and looking after all men in the Keston area.

The emergency past, Group Captain Grice insisted on a return to peacetime standards of smartness and general behaviour. Airmen who had to move around the airfield were required to march correctly in parties, and at night flying-clothes were taboo in the Mess. The W.A.A.F.s were startled to learn that daily P.T. drill was to be reinstated. In protest they privily dumped their gym shoes in one of the Keston ponds and pleaded that they could not possibly take exercise without them. Sergeant Freeman of the Sports and Welfare Section unsympathetically held his first class barefoot. That discipline was lax was obvious and 'Muscles' Freeman had to request the W.A.A.F. Section Officer to see that her airwomen were properly clothed at all future classes.

Nor were the squadrons exempt from the general tightening-up. After weeks without a C.O., 92 Squadron, now adopted by the East India Fund and known as the 92 (East India) Squadron, was shaken by the arrival of Squadron Leader J. A. Kent, D.F.C., A.F.C., in the last week of October. His reception was typical: walking into the Mess for the first time, Johnny Kent was accosted by 'Wimpey' Wade with an impudent: 'Good morning, and what the hell do you want?'

Kent replied that he was the new C.O. of 92 Squadron.

'That's fine,' commented Wade, quite unabashed. 'Stick around and we'll show you the form.'

For three weeks Kent bided his time, getting the measure of his squadron. He led it in battle and reopened the C.O.'s office where correspondence had lain untouched for a month.

Tall and lean-faced with an engaging sardonic smile, John Alexander Kent was born in Winnipeg in 1914 and held a pilot's licence when he was sixteen. After joining the Royal Air Force in 1935, he was posted to Farnborough as a test pilot where he flew ninety-two different types of aircraft: heavy and medium bombers, trainers and fighters were all put through their paces by this young Canadian. He was given the task of finding out just what happened when an aircraft hit various kinds of barrage-balloon cables – cables designed specifically to cripple and destroy. His solution was characteristically straightforward. Fly at the cables and observe the results while the incident was filmed from another aircraft a safe distance away. War was declared and Kent joined 303 Squadron, the famed Polish fighters, as a Flight Lieutenant, often leading them in battle. For his cool, ruthless courage he was awarded the *Virtuti Militari*, Poland's equivalent of the V.C. Then promotion to Squadron Leader brought him the task of disciplining the rampageous pilots of 92 Squadron.

They were not kept wondering about the new C.O. for long. Summoning all the officers and N.C.O.s together in his office, Kent delivered a monumental dressing-down, such as had never been heard on Biggin Hill.

'I have been C.O. of this squadron exactly a month and have several comments to pass on to you all. My N.C.O.s are slack and slipshod. They have allowed the men to get lazy and out of hand. The Station Warrant Officer has complained to me that they are blatantly arrogant and so conceited that they refuse to take orders from anyone but their own officers. This will stop immediately or I will be forced to take drastic action.'

He paused to dismiss the N.C.O.s, then turned to the officers.

'I have studied my officers' behaviour with concern and frankly I think it stinks. You are the most conceited and insubordinate lot I have ever had the misfortune to come up against.

'Admittedly you have worked hard and got a damn good score in the air – in fact a better score than any other squadron in Fighter Command – but your casualties have been appalling. These losses I attribute to the fact that your discipline is slack; you never by any chance get some sleep;

you drink like fishes, and you've got a damn sight too good an opinion of yourselves.

'My second-in-command puts up the biggest black I have ever experienced in my air force career, and none of you have the decency to inform me. When one of my flight commanders comes out of hospital, hobbles down to dispersal, throws down his crutches, uses his authority to demand an aircraft and takes off on a mission, I have no further use for him in my squadron.

'On his own admission he was feeling weak and giddy, and his only excuse was that he wanted to prove to himself he had not lost his nerve.

'Now, your billets. It appears that you have turned the living quarters which were allotted to you to provide a certain amount of security and rest into a night club. It also appears that you ask your various lady friends down to spend weekends with you whenever you please.

'This will cease. All women will be out of the house by 23.00 hours sharp.

'Your clothes – I can scarcely call them uniform. I will not tolerate check shirts, old school ties, or suede shoes. While you are on duty you will wear the regulation dress. Neither will I tolerate pink pyjamas under your tunics.

'You all seem to possess high-powered automobiles. None of these appear to be taxed and insured, but I hear from the Adjutant that you have an understanding with the local police. Well, that may be, but how do you explain where you get your petrol from? Your cars reek of 100-octane, and I can assure you you're not fooling the Station Commander.

'Finally, I want to see an immediate all-round improvement. At the moment I think you're a lot of skunks!'

White-faced and sullen, hardly bothering to conceal their fury, the East India boys filed out of Kent's office. No outsider was going to attack 92 Squadron and get away with it. They swore to break him if it was the last thing they did, but in their hearts they knew his words rang true. Common-sense prevailed and when Johnny Kent shot down the squadron's hundredth Hun, he was enthusiastically and ungrudgingly accepted as 'one of the boys'. Months later, when he was posted away to command an operational flying training unit, the squadron nearly mutinied and sent off a unanimous protest to the C.-in-C. Fighter Command.

Throughout November operations were at a low level. The weather was atrocious and the *Luftwaffe* was flying higher, faster and further. Opportunities for combat were few, but there was always the hunt for the daily weather roconnaissance machine, counterpart of our own 'Jim Crow' flights. This was an exhilarating game of hide-and-seek at dawn, searching out the single bomber that dodged in and out of the clouds collecting meteorological data.

At 6.30 a.m. one day early in November, 92 Squadron was settling down to catch up on sleep in the dispersal hut when the telephone orderly poked his head round the door and shouted: 'One section patrol Beachy at 10,000 feet.'

Ignoring the chorus of 'You'll be sorry!', Pilot Officer Lund and Sergeant Fokes grabbed their kit and ran outside. Four minutes later they were airborne, climbing steadily at three-quarter throttle. They swung due south, Fokes leading, and slanted up towards a ravine in the clouds, creamy white with the vaporous crests touched with gold. Lund scarcely noticed the beauty around him. 'Would there by any escorting 109s?' he wondered, ' . . . probably not with this cloud cover . . . one bomber would only find them embarrassing . . . he would be a good pilot, though, not the usual *Luftwaffe* "stooge" whose only virtue was his discipline.' Tunnelling upwards through the mist, Lund recalled the masses of bombers that looked for all the world like a fleet of buses driving on steadily, being picked at by fighters, losing one every ten seconds, and closing ranks and carrying on. It was admirable in its way. This weather pilot, though, would be a man of different calibre; he would know his machine and himself and his gunner.

The clouds hemming in the two Spitfires thinned out. All at once they burst into the wonder of a blue, cloudless sky.

'Vector 090 degrees,' the Controller's voice crackled, 'and buster!'

215

Fokes and Lund slammed their throttles open. The clouds below were thick and without end, reaching the horizon. Through ragged gaps they glimpsed the Channel shore running parallel to their course.

'Bandit ahead. Two o'clock, see him?'

Lund crouched forward and switched on his gun-sight, searching the cloudscape below for the Hun that Fokes had spotted. Ahead and slightly to starboard, half a mile away, was a Dornier.

Without warning, Fokes swung over on his right side, applying bottom rudder, Lund followed him down, flying in line astern.

The Hun reefed round in a tight turn and dropped for the safety of the clouds. Twisting to starboard, to port and back to starboard to avoid cutting-out their Merlins in the dive, Fokes and Lund gave chase. The Hun was wily, throttling back in a steep turn to port as Fokes opened fire. His Spitfire overshot. It was up to Lund. The Dornier was well below him, reaching for the cloud-bank with a faint white stream spewing from one engine. 'Good show, glycol!' thought Lund as he came in dead astern and fired a burst. His target swung to starboard. Carefully, Lund lined up for the correct deflection and pressed the 'tit', and found himself immersed in an opaque world of vapour. His eyes flicked down to the Sperry panel, seeking guidance from his instruments. He pulled up with the idea of coming out on the right flank of the cloud and looking left for the Hun. Breaking cloud, he climbed to see all around it. There was no sign of Fokes, but a mile to port was the Dornier. It was now streaming black smoke. Lund drew nearer, diving hard, but the Hun vanished once again.

'Hell's bells; I shan't find him again, but anyway, I've hit the bastard.'

With the cloud cover as it was, Fokes and Lund could do no more. They were credited with 'half a Dornier destroyed' between them.

Rarely was the weather bright and clear, then the Messerschmitts would scamper over the Channel in droves, often carrying light bombs which they dropped at random before streaking nose-down for home. The 'Tigers' and 92 Squadron enjoyed several good scraps, honours being roughly equal, as on 15th November when ten Me. 109s were destroyed, no fewer than four being claimed by Don Kingaby: a record 'bag' for a pilot in one day.

He was persuaded to describe this feat in a broadcast, introduced, in accordance with Air Ministry regulations, anonymously: ' . . . a sergeant pilot who is only just twenty-one. He was born in London, joined the R.A.F. Volunteer Reserve in April, 1939, and was called up on the first day of war. His total of enemy planes up to the present is ten, all Me. 109s. In his own words: "The 109 is my favourite meat".'

Explained Kingaby: 'The reason I've got so many Messerschmitts may be that it's just my luck to have run into more of these enemy machines than of any other kind.

'But during the day I am going to tell you about Messerschmitts in formation of fifty or more were being tackled and broken up and shot-down by a dozen Spitfires. On this particular occasion our squadron was sent out in the morning and intercepted one of these formations of 109s coming in over the Channel. There were fifty of them. When our leader, a Canadian, gave the order to attack, I got on the tail of four 109s at about 17,000 feet and attacked the outside one. After I had given him two bursts of fire, he crashed near Gravesend. When I looked round again the sky was full of Messerschmitts scattering in all directions. We chased them back to France and returned to our station for lunch. It seemed to me a pretty good morning's work.

'In the afternoon we were sent up again and told that there were 109s off Selsey Bill. We saw them when we were at 20,000 feet. There were forty of them about 500 feet above us. As they outnumbered us by more than three to one, I suppose they thought they were on to a good thing. At all events, they started to dive on us.

'We evaded their first attack and then turned on them. I picked on three. They made off towards France, one strag-

217

gling a bit behind. I concentrated my fire on him and he went down in flames.

'The other two Messerschmitts had not seen me come up so I closed up behind the leader and gave him a burst. As I did so, the other one on my right came up on my tail. But I held on to the fellow I'd got. He must have been carrying a bomb for, after another burst from my guns, he blew up before the one behind could protect him. There was nothing of him left in the sky that you could recognise as part of a plane. Just a flash and a puff of smoke and bits of debris hurtling all over the place.

'I must give that third Jerry pilot his due – he could have got away but he stayed to fight. But my Spitfire's eight machine-guns were too much for him and after a couple of turns he went down in flames. Then I turned, found the squadron and came home, and that's about all there was to it.'

Such an invitation to broadcast about their own experiences was seldom welcomed by pilots; besides being an embarrassing 'line-shoot', the Air Ministry took a commission from the fee paid by the B.B.C.

By sunset on 29th November Biggin Hill's tally of enemy aircraft destroyed totalled 599. The half-thousand had slipped by unnoticed in the welter of fighting towards the end of September, but now that things were quieter, a special significance was given to the 600th Hun. No other station in Fighter Command came within reach of this figure. For days past all Biggin Hill had been speculating: who would take the score to 600? Odds were freely quoted and bets taken, while the station staff, ground crews and W.A.A.F.s all chipped in to make a sizeable kitty for the lucky pilot.

The last day of the month dawned cold and forbidding. Cloud-base was barely 1,000 feet and a white ground-mist blanketed the airfield. Hardly the weather for flying, so most pilots thought, but not so 'Tiger' Squadron's two flight commanders, Mungo-Park and H. M. Stephen. Tired of hanging about their dispersal doing nothing, they mutually decided to go and hunt down the 600th Hun. The roar of their two

Spitfires taking-off brought the whole station running out to see who was crazy enough to fly in this weather.

'Of all the bloody cheek!' remarked the Station Commander when he learnt who the two pilots were.

Led by 'Sailor' Malan, a stream of cars and motor bicycles converged on the Operations Room to follow the chase by R/T. His two flight commanders had already called up to tell the Controller that they were out on a voluntary patrol. The news was flashed to 11 Group which sportingly advised: 'Vector those two idiots to Deal. There's a convoy moving up-Channel which might tempt Jerry – even in this weather!'

Sure enough, as they dodged the burst of Ack-Ack fire from Deal's guns firing blind through the overcast, Mungo-Park and Stephen spotted eight Messerschmitts coming in from the South at 30,000 feet. Their simultaneous cries of 'Tally ho!' resounded through the Operations Room. 'Sailor' Malan grinned in anticipation: 'Any minute now.'

They stalked the 109s with care, picking the 'weaver' as their target. First to open fire was Mungo-Park but the Messerschmitt pilot glimpsed him in his mirror and dived, and he overshot. Stephen then attacked with a two-second burst on deflection. The other Messerschmitts fled, leaving their comrade to face the two Spitfires alone. He half-rolled into Mungo-Park's gun-sight. A long burst sent his hood flying off, then Stephen came in from dead astern and closed to twenty yards for the *coup de grace*. The Hun dived sickeningly, well past the vertical, and sliced through the clouds to crash near Dungeness. *Oberleutnant* Schmidt, Biggin Hill's 600th victim, died fifteen hours later and was buried with full military honours.

It was typical of the 'Tigers' wholly serious attitude towards the air war that Mungo-Park did not immediately join in the celebration awaiting him and Stephen at the base; instead, he spent some time reporting on the efficacy of a new windscreen material, 'No-mist', fitted as an experiment to his Spitfire.

The apotheosis of Biggin Hill as the first '600-station' was a triumphant vindication of Air Chief Marshal Sir Hugh

219

Dowding's conduct of the air defence of Britain to which the interception experiments carried out at Biggin Hill from 1936 onwards contributed in no small measure. But Dowding, alas, was no longer at Fighter Command to enjoy this triumph, though he sent Group Captain Grice his personal congratulations. One phase of the air war had ended, and a fresh offensive spirit was animating the conferences of the Air Staff whose Deputy Chief, Air Marshal Sir Sholto Douglas, succeeded Dowding at Bentley Priory on 25th November. At the same time bluff, forceful Air Vice Marshal Trafford Leigh-Mallory, formerly A.O.C. 12 Group, took over the command of the all-important 11 Group.

December opened with an event which was ultimately of far greater significance than the 'bagging' of the 600th Hun when Flight Lieutenant 'Pancho' Villa of 92 Squadron shot down an enemy aircraft by cannon fire. For some time past a controversy had been raging in Fighter Command over the new 20 mm. cannon: should they be adopted, or should our fighters keep to the .303 Browning machine-guns which had served them so well in the Battle of Britain? Some pilots, like Douglas Bader, were dead set against a change: the Hurricane's eight Brownings were good enough for him. Others, notably Stanford Tuck and Malan, were all for trying the new cannon, although unproved, and instanced the enemy's increasing use of armour.

It was 92 Squadron that received the first of the new Spitfire Vs, mounting two cannon and four Brownings. There were teething troubles, as with all new weapons, but dogged trial-and-error work by the squadron's armourer, Warrant Officer Jimmy Stewart, eliminated these.

'Pancho' Villa's demonstration of the devastating effects of cannon fire was greatly enjoyed by the Operations Room staff who received a blow-by-blow commentary on the R/T.

It took place during a routine convoy patrol off the South Foreland. Villa was almost due to return to base when he encountered a solitary Me. 109 'stooging' above the clouds. He told the Controller he was going to attack.

'O.K.,' drawled the voice in his earphones. 'Get cracking!'

The Hun was diving at full throttle for the clouds. For a moment Villa thought he could not catch him in time, then he knew the other had left it too late.

'I'm after him now . . . I'm opening fire in a second . . . ' then exultantly, 'Watch out!' as he pressed the firing button and felt his Spitfire shudder with the tremendous backlash of the 20 mms.

Cannon shells tore through the wings and fuselage of the 109, disintegrating metal showered on to Villa's Spitfire. He ducked his head instinctively.

'Christ Almighty!' he yelled, forgetting his R/T was transmitting. 'The ——'s blown to pieces, do you hear me? Into bloody little pieces!'

'Take it easy, Pancho boy,' the Controller sounded quite unconcerned, 'and come back before you run out of fuel. Nice work, and we'll have a drink lined up for you when you get home.'

Otherwise, December was a quiet month: bad weather – snow, rain, low cloud – limited operations for friend and foe alike. For the five thousand civilian inhabitants of the district winter brought great hardship. Despite repeated representations by their M.P. the road through the aerodrome remained closed to all, and those who had to travel to work rose an hour earlier to make a lengthy detour via Cudham and Downe, hardly pleasant in the black-out on a bitter December morning.

Awards and recognitions were showered on the squadrons for their work during October and November. 'Sailor' Malan received the D.S.O. for 'commanding his squadron with outstanding success over an extensive period of air operations' and H. M. Stephen was honoured by being the first recipient of a D.S.O. awarded in the field in Great Britain. For his share in the 600th victory Mungo-Park got the D.F.C., while nine more D.F.C.s and D.F.M.s went to others in both 74 and 92 Squadrons.

The spate of parties celebrating these awards failed to dispel the general depression engendered by news of the Station Commander's posting. For two years 'Groupy' Grice had led and inspired Biggin Hill, guiding the station through the frenzied months of preparation for war to its present proud status. His first concern was always for the welfare of his pilots; almost his final act as C.O. was to persuade a rebellious Malan to take seven days' leave when he thought the 'Sailor' looked done in.

Pride mingled with embarrassment as the squadrons toasted Grice on his departure. 'Worst squadrons I ever knew,' he berated them. 'Couldn't get them into the air. Lazy lot of devils.' But a look of unwillingness to quit was in his eyes, tired from watching the skies for the return of his 'boys'. His final take-off was conducted in style with six hefty pilots carrying him shoulder-high through the Mess.

The new Station Commander was another veteran of the Royal Flying Corps, Group Captain F. O. Soden, D.F.C., nicknamed 'Mongoose'. He was very quickly initiated into the state of affairs at his new Command. Entering Station Headquarters for the first time, he found two 'erks' digging deep outside the entrance and asked them what they were doing.

'We're after one of them 500-pounders, sir.'

'Oh, and have you much further to go?'

One of the men straightened up and gave his new C.O. a beaming smile. 'We're quite near now, sir. Can't you hear it?' he asked, tapping the bomb none too gently with his pick-axe.

The Group Captain gave him some hasty words of advice and departed quickly.

Progress in building and repairing the bomb-damage had become distressingly slow, the Works and Buildings 'types' seemingly powerless to keep their men on the job, many pushing off after one look at what was left of Biggin Hill.

After repeated complaints to higher officialdom, Group Captain Soden invited the Parliamentary Secretary to the Air Ministry to come and see for himself. His visitor was not amused by a prominent notice in Station Headquarters: 'Even more in this war than the last, have we to fight not with the enemy, but with the dull-witted at home'. Nor did he take kindly to a note which Soden addressed to the Secretary of State which read in part: 'I have just taken over here and the chaps are living under conditions of unnecessary filth and squalor; in fact: seldom, if ever, has so little been done for those few who have done so much for so many!'

The Station Commander's forthright tactics were rewarded with a gratifying quick response and the reconstruction of Biggin Hill was carried on apace.

More serious, though, was the creeping deterioration of the pilots' morale. This was only to be expected, living as they were wretchedly on a half-ruined station and spending, not hours, but days of idle frustration on the ground. The weather was wholly to blame: in the month of December no flying was possible on fifteen days and on others all three squadrons were only able to chalk up a meagre nineteen enemy aircraft destroyed. It was a malaise common to all Fighter Command. To take the offensive was the cure, to strike out and fly over occupied territory, to carry the war into the enemy camp.

On Christmas Day 92 Squadron remained on 'readiness' all morning. A deep intrusive sweep over France had been carefully planned and rehearsed. The sight of Spitfires flying over France for the first time in six months would be a fine present for the French spending Christmas under Nazi occupation. The hours slipped by but the weather remained dull, with low cloud and thick mist, forcing 11 Group regretfully to cancel the operation at noon.

Christmas was celebrated in traditional style, the officers serving the airmen their dinner before repairing to their own Mess. The bar stayed open all day and all the following night, and the party only broke up to watch a show put on by E.N.S.A. Afterwards the girls were taken to 'Southward', 92 Squadron's country home. Here they danced and drank until the early hours of the morning, when one of the prettiest turned to an elderly 'Admin. type' and said in all candour: 'Well, I'm tired. Let's go to bed.'

'Do you think we should?' expostulated the officer of her choice, caught off-balance. He had been summoning up

223

courage all evening to pop the same question.

'Why not? It's my war work and, besides, you might be dead tomorrow.'

This was going too far for a young pilot officer who over-heard this exchange and he felt compelled to explain to the girl that such 'types' never flew and the only risk of death they ran was suffocation amongst their files.

'Golly! His life must be dull,' she said sadly, then brightened up. 'In that case, he'll need me all the more!'

On 27th December an operation took place which, though small in itself, was an indication of bigger things to come. Cheated out of their Christmas Day sweep over France by the weather, two pilots of 92 Squadron, Allan Wright and Roy Mottram, were briefed for an offensive patrol. It had been a long time since Fighter Command had penetrated the enemy sky.

They slipped over the Channel, flying well-concealed in low cloud, and let down over Abbeville to seek a target. For Wright it was a bitter anticlimax; it was cheering to see the French labourers in the fields wave in friendly greeting, but there was not a sign of the Hun. He flew back to Biggin Hill without firing a round. Storming over the countryside at tree-top level, Mottram spotted a German staff car guiding a small motor convoy down a road. Shouting with glee, he reefed his Spitfire round in a tight turn and flew back recklessly following the winding road, his eight Brownings spitting flame. All ammunition spent, he pulled up into the sheltering clouds, leaving two lorries blazing and some very startled Germans cowering in a ditch.

December merged into the New Year; the squadrons moved around the Sector in turn, to Manston for a spell, then to Gravesend and back again to Biggin Hill. There was little doing in the air. Towards the end of February 66 Squadron was posted to Exeter to join 10 Group after a singularly inactive stay on the 'Bump'. Its place was taken by 609 (West Riding of Yorkshire) Squadron which flew in from Warmwell, thankful to hand over its Spitfire Is in exchange for 66's Spitfire IIs.

It was a fatigued and somewhat apprehensive crowd of pilots which made its way to the bar that evening. The non-arrival of their luggage only emphasised the bleakness of the huts in which they were temporarily installed. One pilot, inspecting his sleeping quarters, saw a row of machine-gun bullet holes immediately above his bed and in his locker was a tunic, similarly perforated. The fact that they had not flown on operations for three months contributed to their lack of ease. Their gloom was not dispelled by Group Captain Soden's suggestion that on the morrow they should take part in an offensive sweep over France. It was a notion about which Squadron Leader Michael Robinson, in his own words, felt 'keenly doubtful'.

CHAPTER SEVENTEEN

TAKING THE OFFENSIVE

THE Station Commander's suggestion reflected the aggressive spirit of Fighter Command under Air Chief Marshal Sholto Douglas. Within forty-eight hours of its arrival, 609 Squadron's Intelligence Officer 'Spy' Ziegler, was able to report:

> The squadron was stunned to learn at 11 a.m. that its first operational flight from Biggin was to take place in an hour in the shape of a Circus patrol over Calais – i.e. it was to form the top guard of three squadrons, which were to be one of several wings escorting twelve Blenheims bombing Calais. Pale but determined they duly set off, while an apprehensive intelligence officer awaited their return. But they need not have worried; though they stooged over Calais at 26,000 feet, and were shot at by not-too-accurate flak, all that they saw were three Me. 109s

high above and a few unidentified speedboats. Though something was left to be desired in the matter of formation, the venture was a splendid thing for morale, all agreed that the feeling that scores of other British fighters were in the vicinity was a heartening factor, as was the fact of having actually been over enemy territory.[1]

At the briefing conferences of the Station Intelligence Officer, Squadron Leader de la Torre, 609's pilots learnt the jargon of offense: 'Rhubarb' to designate a low-level sortie by a few fighters against any opportune targets – locomotives, bridges, flak-sites, road convoys and barges were all desirable game; 'Circus' signified a large fighter escort, often a hundred or more, accompanying bombers as bait to lure up the *Luftwaffe*; 'Ramrod', on the other hand, was a straight-forward escort for bombers; 'Roadstead', an attack against the enemy's coastal shipping; and, finally, 'Rodeo', a sweep by fighters only.

The newcomers were fortunate in participating in a 'Circus' so soon for, in general, the first offensive efforts of Biggin Hill were puny, the weather restricting operations to a few 'Rhubarbs' and 'Roadsteads', and inspiring 92 Squadron to a new song expressing everyone's feelings of frustration:

> The legion of the lost they call us,
> The legion of the lost are we,
> Legionnaires, outcasts, 'Beau Gestes' – and fini.
> Marching on to Hell with the flags swaying,
> Marching on to Hell with the drums playing,
> Listen to the drums, what are the drums saying?
> 'Scum, scum', every tap of the drum
> Says 'Scum of the earth, scum of the earth' – still we come
> To fight and die for *la belle France*,
> The legion of the lost are we!

When operations over France did take place, the squadrons were frequently united into a wing formation, fighting

[1] 26.2.41.

226

and flying as one, led by a Wing Commander. The first two to be appointed were Malan, who relinquished his beloved 'Tiger' Squadron in order to command the Biggin Wing, and the 'Sailor's' friend and rival in fame, Douglas Bader, who led the Tangmere Wing.

Malan commanded three squadrons in his Wing: Nos. 92 and 609 from Biggin Hill and his old unit, No. 74, now at Gravesend.

92 was still a squadron of unrepentant individualists, slightly subdued, perhaps, in consequence of Johnny Kent's admonishment, but still proudly jealous of being the top-scoring unit in Fighter Command. Kent was gone, posted away at the end of February, and the new C.O. was a twenty-eight-year-old Scot, Jamie Rankin, rugger-player and golfer. This was his first operational command, which provoked some angry, but premature, comments from 92's veterans, for he quickly proved himself to be a first-class pilot and outstanding shot, destroying 109s with such regularity that he was justly dubbed 'One-a-day Rankin'.

At the same time two of the first wartime-trained pilots to join an operational unit, nineteen-year-old Neville Duke and Gordon Brettell, were posted to 92 Squadron. Duke's first exploit, tipping his Spitfire on to its nose when Mr Churchill was paying a visit to Biggin Hill, gave little promise of his later fame as a test pilot, but he quickly made amends for this *faux pas* on operations.

It was Brettell, however, who set all Biggin Hill chuckling over an escapade unique in the annals of Fighter Command: flying a Spitfire with a W.A.A.F. in his lap and having the misfortune to be found out. A party was being thrown one evening and Brettell flew over to Tangmere to collect his girl friend. Returning to Biggin Hill, he touched down just in front of the Station Commander who watched flabbergasted as the hood of Brettell's Spitfire slid back and a blonde and very feminine head appeared. There was nothing in King's Regulations stating specifically that a passenger could not be carried in a single-seater fighter and at the ensuing court martial Brettell was charged with endangering one of His

Majesty's aircraft. He refuted this and offered to repeat the feat with the same girl. The Presiding Officer hastily vetoed this as being unduly risky.

'In that case, sir, I beg permission to do it with a dummy W.A.A.F.!'

This enterprising offer too, was refused. In Brettell's defence Tony Bartley then volunteered the statement that he, too, had flown a Spitfire with a passenger and had demonstrably lived to tell the tale, furthermore he was prepared to do it again. The charge against Brettell was quashed.

609 was a gay and cosmopolitan squadron, by 1941 'West Riding' in name only, for few of the original Auxiliaries remained. Its mascot was Wing Commander William B. Goat, a gentle and whimsical creature with an appetite for cigarette butts, who was presented to 609 by the landlady of the 'Old Jail'. The legend grew that Billy had been with the squadron ever since he was an A.C./2, and no pilot would dare chance his luck by failing to salute the 'Wingco' each morning.

'C' Flight was entirely Belgian, pilots who had made the perilous pilgrimage to fight on in the hospitable ranks of the Royal Air Force. They brought a refreshing Continental touch to Biggin Hill, their voluble French obscenities on the R/T being jealously admired by their English-speaking colleagues whose own foul language had earned a special letter from the A.O.C. in the interests of listening W.A.A.F.s.

One of the Belgians, Pilot Officer Comte Rodolphe de Grunne, was no stranger to the 'Bump'. He had flown with 32 Squadron during the heroic summer days of 1940 until shot-down in flames over the Channel. Now he was back, suspiciously sunburnt at the tail-end of winter, from a secret mission to Portugal. As an ex-pilot of Franco's air force in the Spanish civil war he had been able to fraternise freely with the Nazi agents swarming in Lisbon, capital of neutrality, finding them rewardingly loquacious after a couple of bottles of wine.

609 Squadron became joint tenants of 'Southwood' with No. 92 where the Belgians, at first, seemed ill at ease with

such squirearchal pursuits as tree-felling, rabbit shooting, vegetable-growing and the consumption of much beer when released from duty – until the night of the house-warming. Champagne, brandy and Cointreau flowed freely; with Wilmet at the piano and Vicky Ortmans gyrating on the lid, their *gaucherie* was swept away in a wild war-dance, jackets off and shirt-tails flying, round a bonfire in the centre of the dining-room.

The Blitz, meanwhile, continued and on the night of 14th April Bromley and Keston suffered their worst raid to date, many incendiaries showering on to Biggin Hill, fortunately without effect. At 11 p.m. the telephones in 'Southwood' rang with orders for a patrol over London. Two Canadians, newly-posted to 609, were nominated for this unprecedented operation. They waited gloomily in the dark at dispersal, hopefully trying to recollect the little they knew about night flying. To their utter relief they were released soon after midnight.

In the morning a signal arrived from Leigh-Mallory instructing 609 Squadron to fly patrols over London during the next phase of good moonlight, operating from West Malling. No one had any experience of night-fighting and a very apprehensive squadron listened sceptically to the announcement of the C.O., Michael Robinson, that in the last major night raid our fighters had accounted for a record thirty-one of the enemy.

On the first of the 'fighter nights' the whole station turned out in sympathy to watch the squadron take-off for West Malling. 'Spy' Ziegler had sweated to produce 'A Stranger's Guide to Night-Flying' which he thrust into the hands of each flight commander at the last minute. Anticipation, however, proved worse than reality and the first spell of full moonlight turned out a three-day holiday, the Hun remaining at home. The routine was pleasant: 'release' all day, fly to West Malling in the evening, sleep and return to Biggin Hill for breakfast. During the day pilots, bewildered by so much free time, were observed strolling about discussing the relative merits of Newmarket, a trip to Town, or the local 'flicks'.

'Keep your eyes skinned and stick together,' the voice of 'Sailor' Malan echoed from the R/T relay speaker in the Operations Room. 'Red Two, if you don't keep up, you'll have had it!'

'O.K., Leader.'

It was a warm humid day in May with thick cumulus building up over Biggin Hill. The cloud-base was lowering rapidly, but over the Channel and Northern France it was still clear. The air in the Operations Room was stifling. Sweat soaked the shirt of the Controller, Bill Igoe, the fiery little Irishman who had reported back to the station on the eve of war. He lit a cigarette irritably and watched the movements of his plotters. 'Circus' 10 was under way, a raid on an oil refinery at Bethune by 18 Blenheims with an escort of 180 fighters. The Biggin Wing, led by Malan, was patrolling from the North Foreland to Gravelines, covering the raiders' withdrawal. Igoe glanced at the clock: the raid should be over by now, the oil refinery an inferno of flame – if all had gone according to plan. In a few minutes the Blenheims and their escort would be passing under the umbrella of the Biggin Wing.

'Hullo, Sailor. Jamie here. Bandits ahead and behind, 109s I think.' 92 Squadron, led by Rankin, was providing top cover that morning.

'Got them. Keep together everybody. Open your eyes and prepare to break.'

'Look out behind you,' a voice shouted, high-pitched and excited. 'Behind you!'

'Wait for it,' the 'Sailor' sounded cool, unflurried. A pause, seconds seeming minutes to taut nerves, then decisively: 'Beauty,[1] break port!'

'Gannic, down! Jamie here.'

The R/T channel was a sudden babel of shouts.

'Blue Three, break immediately. Break!'

'Watch your tail, Yellow Two.'

'*Alors, merde!*' this from a Belgian.

'Got one!'

[1]Code name for 609 Squadron.

230

Then, sadly and quietly: 'My engine's had it. I'm baling out. Ta-ta for now.'

'Take it easy, boy, and good luck.'

'Jamie here. More of them ahead.'

'Bounce the bastards good and hard. Sailor speaking.'

The Operations Room staff followed the battle as best they could from the crackling R/T. Any moment now there would be crippled aircraft to guide back to safety and pilots to be rescued from the sea.

'Sailor calling. That's all for today. Watch your petrol. Land forward if in trouble.'

The whirling *mêlée* of battle was over. The Blenheims, less one, were back at base. The Biggin Wing, low in fuel and with its ammunition used up, broke off from the fleeing 109s and headed home. Five Messerschmitts were claimed 'destroyed', but two Spitfires were missing. They returned in twos and threes, some landing at Hawkinge or Manston to refuel, others flying straight to Biggin Hill. The clouds were thick and low, and Sergeant Chestnut, a Canadian new to 609, had difficulty in finding the airfield. The Controller brought him within a mile, then told the look-out on the Officers' Mess to listen for the engine.

'There'e is . . . Ah, lost 'im again . . . now I can 'ear 'im . . . 'e's getting near . . . 'e's coming in . . . 'e's just over the 'edge . . . Nah, 'e's gorn round again . . .'

The Controller and his assistants listened spellbound. This little 'erk' was far better than the B.B.C.

' 'E's coming in . . . I think 'e'll make it this time . . . 'e's 'olding off . . . 'olding off . . .'

There was a long silence then, with profound satisfaction: ' 'E's crashed. I knew 'e —— well would!'

The pilot, however, was unhurt.

One of the two missing Spitfires had been flown by Rodolphe de Grunne. Two of his fellow Belgians saw him jump and circled his parachute as he descended into the sea. A rescue Lysander searched the area, but he was never found, only a spreading patch of yellow dye to mark his grave. De Grunne's last act before taking off had been to jump from his cockpit and dash over to 'Spy' Ziegler for his wallet from which he extracted the miniature horseshoe he had so nearly forgotten.

Later in May 609 Squadron magnificently avenged de Grunne with its greatest victory since the Battle of Britain. It all happened by chance, starting with a rubber dinghy floating in mid-Channel with a German airman on board. Judging by the battle waged over his rescue, he was a man of some importance, Werner Mölders perhaps, but his identity remained a mystery. A patrolling Lysander spotted and reported the dinghy and in due course an air/sea rescue launch put out to investigate. As the R.A.F. seamen were helping the German on board two Me. 109s streaked down and attacked, their cannon shells and bullets lashing the sea into a white fury. Whoever he was, the man in the dinghy was evidently better dead than a British prisoner. The Messerschmitt pilots must have radioed for assistance, and an E-boat put out from Boulogne with a cover of 109s from Abbeville, lair of the crack Fighter *Geschwader* 26.

Meanwhile, 609 Squadron was flying a 'stooge' patrol over Maidstone. After two early morning convoy patrols and a hectic party the night before with the prospect of another that evening to celebrate the C.O.s birthday, the pilots were hardly in the mood for a wild-goose chase.

'Mayday from air/sea rescue launch nine miles south of Dungeness. Investigate and report.' It was just a routine call from the Biggin Control.

Within five minutes they were staring down at the David-and-Goliath struggle below. It was odd: the rescue launches were usually inviolate on both sides.

'Blue Section, circle and cover. Red Section, Yellow Section, attack. Line astern. Down we go.'

One glimpse of the eight Spitfires hurtling down out of the sun was enough, the two Messerschmitts turned like lightning and fled.

The covering Section, led by Flight Lieutenant Paul Richey, was orbiting at 12,000 feet when the 109s from Abbeville were sighted.

232

'Beauty Leader, gaggle of 20-plus at twelve o'clock above.'

'O.K. Yellow and Red Section re-form. Climb like hell!'

It was a dirty, ragged fight with 609 Squadron caught split into two, four above, and eight below. A cannon shell smashed through Sergeant Mercer's windscreen like a deafening clap of thunder. It missed his head by a hair's breadth and passed on without exploding. Breaking hard to port, he dived on one of two yellow-nosed Messerschmitts that flashed past. It spun down over Kent, trailing smoke. Michael Robinson sent another crashing into the Channel. Red Two, Flight Lieutenant Churchin, yet another and damaged a third before a shell ripped off one of his ailerons and smashed his oil tank. He landed safely at Hawkinge.

Far below the maelstrom of battle and within sight of the shore an act of piracy was taking place as the E-boat came alongside the air/sea rescue launch and a boarding party, brandishing revolvers, took off the German pilot who was the focus of the operation.

The E-boat wheeled away, reaching for the safety of Boulogne harbour with the remaining 109s dutifully overhead, harried and mauled by 609's Spitfires.

Belgian Sergeant Rigler, this his first combat, shot-down two 109s at point-blank range in quick succession. Blue Two, Sergeant Palmer, chased another pair all the way to Calais and only broke off when he heard his C.O.'s plaintive cry: 'Beauty Leader being fired on.'

Robinson had just shot-down his second 109 of the day into the surf off France when he was jumped on by nine others. He plunged for the waves and looked back. The Huns were after him like a pack of wolves. He had no ammunition left, only his skill as a pilot. Breaking in towards each Messerschmitt as it fired, he held his course unwaveringly until the German's nerve cracked. Palmer loyally covered his C.O., thriftily attacking each attacker with short bursts and only firing his last round when he saw Robinson's Spitfire safe over Romney Marsh.

The 'grapevine' carried news of 609's engagement all over Biggin Hill. As Robinson jubilantly performed a double victory-roll over the airfield, Group Captain Soden and Wing Commander Malan drove up, their shining cars contrasting vividly with the drab, battle-scarred Spitfires, gun-canvasses all shot away. A little procession moved towards each pilot as he left his cockpit, the Intelligence Officer busily sifting claims and pestered with 'How many do you make it now?' In the end he made it six 'destroyed' and two 'probables' against Churchin's damaged Spitfire.

Next afternoon Sergeant Mercer, who had escaped death so narrowly, was killed when he made a forced-landing on a landmine buried in the beach at St Margaret's Bay.

The status of 'Britain's premier fighter station' entailed certain disadvantages and embarrassments besides the glamour. During 1941 hardly a week passed without an official visit of some kind, all requiring 'bags of bull'. The squadrons were besieged by journalists, photographers and script-writers who wanted to enjoy the air war vicariously from a safe distance. In quick succession came Dorothy Thompson, Quentin Reynolds doing a profile of 'Sailor' Malan, and reporters from Australia, Canada, New Zealand and the West Indies. The Archduke Felix of Austria paid a visit to collect stories for broadcasts in the United States, while Leslie Howard came frequently to gather material for his film biography of R. J. Mitchell, designer of the Spitfire, which was released under the title 'The First of the Few'. Most amusing of all were the representatives of the Philippine Free Press: *'Extrémement gentils, extrémements philippins, extrémement journalistes,'* commented a Belgian.

But there was one visitor who was always welcome, the Prime Minister, who delighted in dropping in on his way to and from Chartwell. He was an inspiration to all, and the station felt proud to have him as a friend and neighbour.

In all, Biggin Hill summed up its unwonted fame as being a 'bit of a bind' but there were some pleasant compensations, for the station was very popular with stage and screen stars anxious to entertain the troops: Laurence Olivier and Vivien Leigh, Bea Lillie, Carroll Gibbons, the Gang Show, Jack

Warner and Noël Coward, who awed his audience with a log of 42,000 miles flying in less than a year. Duty Pilot Officer of Biggin Hill was Flight Lieutenant C. D. Stephenson, 'Stevie' to all. Born an American, a volunteer of the Royal Flying Corps, 'Stevie' was both fond and proud of his airfield, and kept the Watch Office and its surroundings immaculate. His wife was Jeanne de Casalis, and 'Mrs Feather' of radio fame was a most welcome visitor and entertainer. It was 'Stevie' who organised the exclusive 'P.Y.F.O.' (Pull Your Finger Out) Club, whose membership was only accorded to those Biggin Hill liked.

One entertainment nearly ended in disaster. A lecture on 'Art Appreciation' by Sir Kenneth Clark only attracted an audience of six. An emergency call by 'Stevie' to the W.A.A.F. Section Officer saved the day, and three truck-loads of girls were hastily dispatched from the 'Waafery' with instructions at least to appear interested. More welcome were the many visits of the Windmill Theatre troupe, and it is said that it was at a Biggin Hill show that the statuesque nudes first moved!

Some entertainers, regrettably, never ventured beyond the Officers' Mess, not so Joe Davis who always insisted on playing snooker in the N.A.A.F.I. 'Don't bother, I've played on worse tables than this,' he told the Manageress, who was trying vainly to remove grease-spots from the cloth, and blithely proceeded to give an exhibition of dazzling virtuosity. One evening he challenged 'Sailor' Malan, giving him twelve blacks for a start. Joe Davis was off-form that night and, much to his own surprise, the 'Sailor' won, receiving the champion's cue as a memento of his victory.

For a few days Biggin Hill was the object of a fierce literary battle. It started when Flight Sergeant 'Muscles' Freeman wrote to James Agate, book critic of the *Daily Express*, asking his advice on titles for the station's new library. Agate quoted a number of classics, all unimpeachable, and concluded by suggesting an English translation of *Das Niebelungenlied*, supporting his remarkable choice by saying: 'When these people were tired of slaying dragons and

235

burning their womenfolk on funeral pyres, they got themselves slain on the battlefields whence they were picked up by semi-fabulous, more or less feminine creatures called Valkyries and borne aloft to Valhalla on horses borrowed from the nearest merry-go-round. It is this preposterous bosh which makes every German think he is a demi-god. It should give the Mess a good laugh.'

As a result Agate was inundated with correspondence accusing him of disseminating pro-German propaganda; at Biggin Hill *No Orchids for Miss Blandish* remained a firm favourite.

The squadrons' night-time forays into London were planned with as much care and attention to detail as an operation. At dusk telephones between Biggin Hill and other sector stations in 11 Group hummed with the appropriate orders in operational style: 'Defensive circle at Prunier's, rendezvous 20.00 hours', 'Target for tonight is Shepherd's', 'Maximum effort to be launched against the Suivi and Kimmul Clubs', both haunts of fighter pilots when in town. And next morning casualties were duly reported: '92 Squadron grounded by lack of taxis', and '609s Humber pranged in Lewisham High Street'.

These nocturnal excursions fostered a sentimental partnership between the pilots of Biggin Hill and London's cabbies. One spring evening a group of taxi-drivers were deep in unending political argument in their West End hang-out, Soho's Beaufort Club, when in burst Billy Bird, known to all as the 'Cabbies' fighter', though he had never won a bout.

' 'Ere, there's a mob of Air Force blokes at Grosvenor 'Ouse as wants a ride' ome,' he announced, adding with withering sarcasm: 'Instead of sitting there and jawing yer 'eads off, why the 'ell don't you go and take 'em?'

The taxi-drivers, all veterans of the Blitz, had a soft spot for the Air Force and very soon some eighty-odd cabs were rattling through the black-out to Grosvenor House where the 'taxi-types' offered to take any pilot and his girl friend home – free of charge.

In return, they were invited down to Biggin Hill for a

party. They arrived bearing two gifts: a grandfather clock and the steering wheel of a cab tagged with their names. After a tour of the airfield, they all trooped to the bar and drank eternal friendship to their hosts.

'Any time you want a taxi in London, chums, just ring up the Beaufort and say you're from Biggin.'

This was a promise that held good until the end of the war.

May, on the whole, was a disappointing month. Although the Biggin Wing had flown a number of 'Circuses', 'Rhubarbs' and 'Roadsteads', the results were far from satisfactory to the station's amateur statisticians who recorded the war as a game of cricket: 17 enemy aircraft destroyed and 7 damaged. The cost was high: 12 Spitfires written-off and 5 pilots killed.

June opened with 'pea-soup' weather, curtailing operations to a handful of attacks on German coastal shipping. Biggin Hill was now commanded by Group Captain Philip Barwell, who had succeeded 'Mongoose' Soden. Short in stature, always cheerful and with a phenomenal memory for faces and names, Dickie Barwell was the ideal Station Commander who realised that his place was on the ground and not in the air. Nightly, he made a round on the station, talking with his N.C.O.s and airmen: 'Who are you? . . . Where do you work? . . . Like it?' If the answer was negative, the man concerned could be confident that action would be taken, not tomorrow but now. On occasion Barwell would sneak out of Station Headquarters and fly with the Wing, hugely enjoying this change from tedious routine. Once, when taking-off, his Spitfire's engine cut out and he fell in the valley to the west of Biggin Hill. He was dragged out from the wreckage with a broken vertebra. Two weeks later he was back at work and flying again, proudly collecting autographs on his plaster strait-jacket. It was a very sad day when he was shot-down flying a new mark of Spitfire over the Channel, tragically mistaken for a Hun by two pilots of Fighter Command.

The last half of June, however, blazed forth with a six-week heat-wave of clear, sunlit days, ideal for intensive, large-scale operations over France. Offices on the 'Bump'

237

became sweltering ovens and their occupants were thankful when sunset brought a cooling breeze. The squadrons' dispersal huts were unbearable and pilots slept on deck-chairs outside, several going down with sunburn and sunstroke. They discarded their tunics and flew in shirt-sleeves, ignoring an official warning that such undress could make them spies to the enemy.

The fighter offensive mounted in fury and not a day passed without the Biggin Wing crossing the coast of France at least once. There was more to these operations than the mere bombing of ground-targets and destruction of Messerschmitts; on 22nd June Hitler launched 'Operation Barbarossa' against the Soviet Union, and overnight it became the utmost importance to pin down every German aircraft in the West. On 'Circus' operations our new four-engined Stirling bombers were used, each carrying fourteen times the bomb-load of a Blenheim; time and again the Biggin Wing admired their steadfast progress, usually in threes, undaunted by flak or swarming 109s. It was magnificent; less pleasant was the spectacle of one of these giants turning over on its back and plunging earthwards in flames. 'Those Stirlings don't look British,' remarked one pilot, seeing them in action for the first time, 'but like some Russian monster. Well, anyway, Russia is our ally now.'

An average day was 7th July, as reported by 609 Squadron:

A busy day with two 'Circuses': the first, No. 37, was the farthest south that 609 had been. Target was the Potez repair works near Albert. The Biggin Wing gave escort cover to four Stirlings at 13,000 feet. Considerable criticism voiced of the bombers arriving six minutes late, causing fighters to waste precious petrol. The operation, however, seems to have taken the Jerries by surprise, the bombers bombed and the fighters met no opposition until they approached the coast on the way back. P/O Offenberg then spied a German convoy patrolled by a couple of low-flying 109s. These sheered off, but his section was

238

attacked by others just off Le Touquet. Offenberg chased one in a steep dive then, fearing he might hit the water, turned left and blacked-out. Coming to, he noticed a large splash right amongst the boats and thus joins the select society of those who have destroyed an enemy aircraft without firing a shot. This enemy aircraft, however, had first attacked Sgt Evans and, though he missed, another aircraft scored and Sgt Evans became aware his engine was on fire. He baled out at 10,000 feet. During his descent his dinghy became detached from its cover and blew away, and he entered the sea only two miles from the convoy which made no attempt to pick him up. He began to swim manfully towards the French coast four miles away, under the impression it was England. After 1½ hours he was spotted by some Spitfires, and a Lysander dropped a dinghy which he had only just reached when he was picked up.

'Circus' 38 took the squadron back to the Kuhlmann works at Béthune. A considerable number of enemy aircraft were seen, but not contacted. F/Lt Bisdee reported Le Touquet aerodrome as camouflaged with black blobs to resemble bushes. These did not deceive F/Lt Bisdee. F/Lt Churchin had the misfortune to suffer his engine cutting-out in mid-Channel owing to lack of petrol. He glided in to Hawkinge but had to make a forced-landing as several Hurricanes were coming in at the same time.

On returning, pilots were honoured by the visit of the Prime Minister and the C.-in-C., Air Marshal Sholto Douglas. The former looked more cheerful than on his last visit and asked the apposite question: 'What would you do if this drome were attacked now?'

22.30 hrs. Pilots assembled at dispersal for a briefing conference prior to an early take-off next day. They were somewhat distracted, however, by the antics of Wing Commander William B. Goat who, after drinking pints of beer from his baby's bottle, made three unsuccessful attempts to climb the steps into the dispersal hut. Pilots were more successful and there they slept, or failed to sleep owing to the heat, till dawn.

During these six heat-stricken weeks of June and July northern France became as well known to the Biggin Wing as Kent and Sussex: in place of Maidstone or Brighton there were Abbeville and Lille, the power-stations of Béthune and Gosnay were familiar landmarks, and they dreamt of the marshalling-yards at Hazebrouck.

In these weeks the Wing claimed the destruction of 50 enemy aircraft with 35 more 'probables' and 'damaged'. 'Sailor' Malan added another six to his already impressive score, and Jamie Rankin won the sweepstake for his squadron's 150th Hun. Most satisfactory was the realisation that now it was the Hun who remained at instant readiness throughout the day, while two of the three squadrons in the Biggin Wing were always released once operations were over.

These figures, however, like those of the Battle of Britain, were unavoidably exaggerated. From mid-June to the end of July Fighter Command claimed the destruction of 322 enemy aircraft in operations over Northern France; German records have revealed the true figure as being 81. Now that the crazy merry-go-round of combat was over alien soil, it was more difficult than ever to assess results from pilots' fragmentary reports without the corroboration of observers on the ground.

Once a 'Circus' had started, the Intelligence Officers had little to do but 'sweat it out', waiting for the Spitfires to return. The first home were those who turned back with a faulty oil-gauge, perhaps a leaking oxygen-supply. Thirty minutes, an hour, later, others started coming in, their gun-port covers hanging in shreds. A squadron leader climbs down from his cockpit sweating. He has fought for ten minutes, he says, and is obviously very tired. 'Yes, I fire,' laughs a Belgian, 'but the Jerry, he go on.' 'Had a crack at one,' reports another pilot, 'three other Spits were after him, too.' ' . . . Blew up with a great explosion . . . ' 'One Stirling went down like a torch. The poor blokes inside never had a chance . . . ' ' . . . can't be sure, we were milling around like peas in a colander . . . '

Some aircraft were missing. Everyone is certain they saw one Spitfire collide with a Messerschmitt and go down. 'Thank God for that!' exclaims an Intelligence Officer, unintentionally callous, only amazed that there is any unanimity. Hawkinge reports that two of the Wing have landed there to refuel. West Malling has another two. There is a rumour that Manston has one. For a moment there is hope, then Manston rings through to apologise: it is a Spitfire from Kenley.

'Come on chaps,' calls the Wing Leader. 'Who's buying me a beer?'

Only of our own losses could there be any certainty. Now that the battle was over the Channel and enemy territory, the casualty-rate was high. Most grieved of all was Mungo-Park, C.O. of 'Tiger' Squadron after 'Sailor Malan, who disappeared over St Omer and was never heard of again. There were many others; in June 609 Squadron lost its 'heavenly twins', Flight Lieutenant Churchin, shot down off Le Touquet, and his partner, wayward, mischievous Pilot Officer Hill, killed a week later. 'No time for sentiment,' said Michael Robinson, 'there's a war on,' and wisely ordained an immediate celebration for Jean Offenberg's D.F.C., the first Belgian so honoured. The party was held, naturally, but Offenberg had to wait for a month before his award was confirmed. Diplomatic protocol had apparently been ignored, Fighter Command having omitted to obtain formal permission of the Belgian Government-in-exile, and there was a flurry of minutes to be initialled before he could sew on the coveted purple and white ribbon.

Some were fortunate, like Pilot Officer Malengrau who had his engine knocked out by cannon-fire off Gravelines. The rest of 609 Squadron heard his 'M'aidez, m'aidez' and circled round the stricken Spitfire while he glided twenty miles back across the Channel, over the English coast at 2,000 feet and crash-landed down-wind in a hayfield. In the Mess that evening, Malengrau claimed the world's long-distance gliding record for single-seater fighters! Some days later Sergeant Chestnut, one of 609's Canadians, lost his life trying to beat it. His Spitfire badly mauled by some 109s, he chose deliberately not to hear Michael Robinson's 'Jump for it, you clot. That's an order,' and tried to glide home. He crashed into the cliffs at Ramsgate – another fifteen feet of altitude and he would have survived.

A dozen pilots owed their lives that summer to the bumbling Lysanders of the R.A.F.'s Air/Sea Rescue Service and the high-speed launches that darted out almost before their parachutes had opened. One Belgian, Vicky Ortmans, survived five duckings, four times rescued by the same launch.

'What, *you* again?'

'*Oui, justement.* I am cold and would like some rum, if you please,' demanded the indestructible Ortmans.

A compatriot, de Spirlet, was less enamoured of the rescue service. Baling out over the South Foreland, he landed in the Channel and inflated his dinghy, not forgetting to tip the yellow marker dye into the water. Three Spitfires circled overhead. De Spirlet stood up to wave, overbalanced and flopped headlong into the yellow sea. He scrambled back into his dinghy, smoking and waiting philosophically until he saw a naval corvette and an R.A.F. launch bearing down on him from opposite directions. They arrived simultaneously, their skippers loudly disputing the kudos of rescue. Tired of being argued over, de Spirlet opted for his own Service only to find that all the 'medicinal' rum had been consumed. Then, adding insult to injury, he was confined to hospital for a week as a suspect case of jaundice – thanks to the life-saving dye!

At the end of July the long-heralded and oft-postponed move of 609 Squadron to Gravesend took place. No one knew the reason, for the squadron remained in the Biggin Hill Wing, but there was no disputing the edicts of Fighter Command. It was all most frustrating and confusing to pilots who had come to regard the 'Bump' as home. Their new quarters were in Cobham Hall, a lovely mansion belonging to the Earl of Darnley, whose amenities included a bed reputedly slept in by Queen Elizabeth, massive oaken furniture and florally-decorated lavatory basins but, to everyone's disappointment, no ghost.

Back to Biggin Hill came No. 72 (Basutoland) Squadron, returning after nine months' absence. Its first operation of importance was 'Circus' 81, the Wings of Biggin Hill and Tangmere combining to escort some Blenheims over to Gosnay power-station. During this raid a long, yellow-painted wooden box was dropped by parachute over St Omer airfield. Its label read: *'Dieser Kasten enhält Beinprothese für Wing Commander Douglas Bader, R.A.F., Kriegsgefangener.'*

On 9th August all Fighter Command had been shocked to hear that Bader, the legendary and immortal 'Tinlegs', who had become an inspiration and symbol of courage to all fighter pilots was missing from a sweep over France. It seemed incredible, but this was the bitter truth. In an unusually fierce dog fight south of Le Touquet an Me. 109 had collided with his Spitfire, shearing away the tail and part of the fuselage. As he struggled out from the cockpit, Bader's right artificial leg became caught up and he was left dangling, hurtling earthwards with his Spitfire until the leather harness of the limb snapped and he fell free to use his parachute. His subsequent adventures – capture, escape and recapture – are too well-known to be retold. It was *Obersleutnant* Adolf Galland, commanding the Fighter *Geschwader* at St Omer, who arranged for a small R.A.F. aircraft to fly to France with Bader's spare set of artificial limbs. This sporting gesture was repudiated, and rightly so, as being gratuitous propaganda for Goebbels, though no one questioned the sincerity of Galland's offer. Aerial warfare was no longer a game of chivalry, the Blitz had taught us that, and Sholto Douglas ordered the legs to be delivered in the course of a routine 'Circus'. Every pilot in the two Wings knew what the box aboard one of the Blenheims contained and were delighted to hear that it had been picked up and delivered to Bader in hospital – with their own added gift of eleven Huns shot down.

During August the Biggin Wing enjoyed some welcome

inactivity, not on account of the weather which admittedly had deteriorated, but because intelligence reports were revealing that our offensive was not effectively forcing the *Luftwaffe* to withdraw its fighter squadrons from the Russian Front.

The lull brought changes: Malan had finished his tour of operations as Wing Commander and was now sent on a mission to the United States. Lately, the 'Sailor' had shown signs of tiredness, not surprising since he had been fighting without respite since the Battle of Britain, and the Wing had increasingly been led by Michael Robinson, now promoted Wing Commander. The whole station was sorry to see him go. More than anyone, Malan had made the Biggin Wing what it was, and now pilots would no longer gather courage from his calm, authoritative 'Sailor, here' on the R/T. Owners of bitches in the village, however, were pleased to see the last of his bull terrier, Peter, the father of many mongrel pups.

Jamie Rankin now became Wing Commander Flying, handing over 92 Squadron to Dickie Milne, a young Scot who had recently replaced Brian Kingcome as 'A' Flight's commander. This double change took place on the eve of 92 Squadron's anniversary at Biggin Hill, but, unhappily, 92's days in the Sector were numbered. At the end of September another inexplicable shuffle took place: 92 moving to Gravesend, where 609 gladly handed over the Elizabethan comforts of Cobham Hall and hastened home to the 'Bump', then was ordered north to Digby in Lincolnshire, never to return. 72 Squadron took its place at Gravesend so that an entirely fresh unit, No. 401 Squadron of the Royal Canadian Air Force, could gain experience as junior partner to 609 at Biggin Hill.

Autumn brought no startling changes and such operations as were flown by the Biggin Wing had more nuisance value than real destruction.

19.9.41. Rhubarb by P/O Bocock and Sgt. Falkiner.
The French coast was crossed midway between Berck-sur-

mer and Le Touquet. North towards Etaples an army lorry with cables was shot up by Sgt. Falkiner; strikes were observed. Coming out at the coast, P/O Bocock shot up a Bofors gun. Two of the crew were seen to fall.

20.9.41. Circus 100: Abbeville marshalling-yards.

12 aircraft including W/Cdr. Rankin leading the Wing. The bombers were met over Rye, and the French coast crossed without incident. A few 109s were seen but not near enough to attack. The weather was perfect and visibility 10 miles.[1]

27th September was a day to remember: the début, as far as Biggin Hill was concerned, of Germany's new fighter, the Focke-Wulf 190. The Secretary of State for Air, Sir Archibald Sinclair, happened to be visiting the station that morning and a 'Circus' was laid on which he followed from the Operations Room. Jamie Rankin led the Wing, providing high cover to twelve Blenheims out to raid Mazingarbe.

After encountering some stiff opposition which cost the *Luftwaffe* three 109s, the Wing turned for home. It was then that Squadron Leader Gilroy, O.C. 609 Squadron, spotted the two strange fighters.

'Bogeys at ten o'clock below.'

'O.K. Beauty Yellow Section investigate.'

Four Spitfires, obedient to the Wing Leader, broke and dived to meet the Huns. They appeared to have an amazing rate of climb. Their outline was unfamiliar: squarer wing-tips and a more tapering fuselage than the Me. 109. Pilot Officer Dieu thought they had radial engines, but was not sure; this was not the occasion for precise observation. They streamed tracer like a fire-engine; four cannon apiece, estimated Gilroy. After making several half-hearted passes at the Spitfires, they sheered off, their pilots possibly not fully confident with their new fighters.

At Biggin Hill no one doubted that these were the much-rumoured Focke-Wulfs, though Fighter Command was oddly unresponsive to Gilroy's report and suggested that the

[1]Reports by 72 Squadron.

'bogeys' were obsolete French fighters. The Air Ministry expressed interest, but declined to comment and congratulated the Wing on its three 109s. Only one Spitfire was lost, flown by Vicky Ortmans.

'Where's Vicky?'

'In the drink.'

'What, again?'

'Yes, and for the fifth time, too! Apparently he ran out of juice.'

October was depressingly quiet. 'Thus the winter bull-season may be considered to have begun', wrote a disgruntled Canadian on learning that everyone was expected to appear at dispersal at 9.30 a.m. whether there was any flying, or not. Without operations, high authority began to seek other ways for the squadrons to employ their time usefully. Under a new scheme all but one squadron of the sector were to be released one day a week for training in the morning and organised games in the afternoon. The training was necessary, many pilots of experience had been posted to the Middle East and their replacements lacked combat-discipline. As for the organised games: five officers of 609 went riding, two played squash, the sergeants played cards and Flight Lieutenant Jean Offenberg played the gramophone – still others went to Town.

609 was now the senior squadron at Biggin Hill, but on 21st October it suffered the loss of two of its best pilots, Vicky Ortmans and Sergeant Palmer. The weather for once in that dismal month was perfect, and a mammoth sweep, a 'Rodeo', was mounted in the Boulogne area, the Biggin Wing provided rear support. By a coincidence it was the first operational sortie of Ortmans' younger brother, Christian, with the squadron.

Approaching the French coast, they were jumped by twenty 109s diving out of the sun and only the wary eyes of the Wing Leader saved them.

'Beauty Squadron, down! Break immediately. 109s on your tail.'

Blue Section, Squadron Leader Gilroy flying Blue One,

failed to hear Rankin's warning. A fluky deflection shot from extreme range caught Sergeant Palmer and sent his Spitfire spinning down. Gilroy and Christian Ortmans, Blue Four, dived after him. They did not notice that Blue Three Christian's brother, was not with them.

'Bale out, Palmer. For Christ's sake jump, man!'

There was no answer. He was either dead or unconscious. The Spitfire seemed to make a recovery and landed well, then slowly heeled over and sank beneath the waves.

'Beauty Leader calling Blue Three . . . do you receive me?'

Silence.

'*Allo, Vicky. Répondez . . . répondez . . . c'est moi, Christian.*'

No one in 609 had seen what had happened to him or heard a '*M'aidez.*'

Refuelled and re-armed, the squadron took-off to search Everyone felt certain they would see the Belgian pilot[1] waving to them from a dinghy somewhere in the Channel, enjoying his sixth ducking. With tanks almost empty they were forced to give up and return to Biggin Hill.

The dreaded departure of 609 was scheduled for mid-November. It left reluctantly, not as a tired squadron with declining morale, but at the top of its form after a great run of success.

Coming from Castletown, the most northerly airfield in Scotland, the replacement squadron, No. 124, was delighted with the move south. Commanded by Squadron Leader Duke-Wooley, it was even more of an international assembly than 609, with pilots from Belgium, Czechoslovakia, France, Norway, Australia and Canada, as well as Britain.

Unfortunately for their enthusiasm the weather that December was as arctic as it had been up north and when they did fly, it was usually to encounter Focke-Wulf 190s for which they developed a cautious respect. More and more F.W. 190s were appearing over France, stiffening the Messer-

[1]He had, in fact, been wounded and had baled out. After three days at sea his dinghy was beached near Dieppe and he was taken prisoner.

schmitt formations in twos and threes, and outclassing our Spitfire Vs in equal combat.

One afternoon the station was visited by the Minister of Aircraft Production accompanied by Sholto Douglas, A.O.C. Fighter Command. The pilots were all assembled in Biggin Hill's new cinema theatre to hear the Minister discuss the manifold problems of the British aircraft industry. Afterwards, in general debate, the Minister requested suggestions as to the types of aircraft they would like to fly and any improvements to their Spitfire Vs. An Australian, McDonald, replied with great feeling that he considered it an excellent thing if they were all re-equipped with Focke-Wulf 190s. This brought the discussion to a hasty end and the visitors departed, visibly disconcerted. The occasion was not improved by 'Hen', 72 Squadron's cockerel mascot, who marched out ahead of the Minister and stood, feathers bristling stiffly, until he had entered his car and driven off.

CHAPTER EIGHTEEN

OPERATIONS CONTINUE

12TH FEBRUARY, 1942; it was drizzling at Northolt and the tarmac gleamed wetly under the grey, misty overcast. The men drawn up on parade shivered inside their greatcoats and eyed the sky knowingly: there would be no flying display this day. They prayed that the V.I.P.s would not be too late. It was a special occasion, the presentation of the Colours of the Belgian Air Force, smuggled out clandestinely and brought to Britain, to Fighter Command for safe-keeping. In addition, Belgian *Croix-de-Guerre* were to be presented to certain R.A.F. officers, notably Wing Commanders Jamie Rankin and Michael Robinson, who, as Leader of the Biggin Wing and O.C. 609 Squadron, had done much to keep the spirit of the Belgian Air Force alive. Attending the ceremony were the A.O.C. 11 Group, Leigh-Mallory, Prince Bernhard of the Netherlands and the Belgian Minister for National Defence, M. Gutt.

The parade snapped to attention, the band played the three national anthems and then there followed the traditional inspection of the Guard of Honour, rather perfunctorily in view of the weather. Without warning, a Tannoy interrupted raucously: 'Will Air Vice Marshal Leigh-Mallory please report to Station Headquarters at once.'

Even before the A.O.C. had time to move, his personal assistant had dashed undecorously across the parade ground and spoken to him. Onlookers noticed the urgency of his gestures and Leigh-Mallory's sudden change of expression. Minutes later he was in his car, speeding down Western Avenue to 11 Group Headquarters at Uxbridge.

The ceremony at Northolt faltered on, no one knew for certain what the 'flap' was about but a rumour spread quickly from the officers on parade down to the humblest W.A.A.F. typist: the German battle-cruisers *Scharnhorst* and *Gneisenau* with the cruiser *Prinz Eugen* had broken out of Brest and were at that moment hazarding the passage of the Channel.

For months past our reconnaissance aircraft had kept patient watch over Brest, while crews of Bomber Command had hammered the ships by day and night, but without crippling results. Sooner or later they would be forced to make a break and try to reach sanctuary in the Fatherland's home ports. The Admiralty anticipated correctly that the attempt would come in February, but expected the Straits of Dover to be passed at night and not boldly by day as Vice Admiral Ciliax chose to do.

The weather on the night of 11th February was as bad as the Germans could possibly hope for: it was now or never. After an abortive raid by sixteen Wellingtons of Bomber Command, the *Scharnhorst, Gneisenau* and *Prinz Eugen* slipped moorings shortly before 11 p.m. and put to sea to join their escort of destroyers, E-boats and mine-sweepers. That night Hudsons of Coastal Command were patrolling the

Channel but through sheer ill-luck and foul weather failed to detect the German fleet.

At first light the battle-cruisers and their escorts were well up Channel, screened, in relays, by every available fighter in northern France. They flew low to deceive our radar stations and under strict R/T silence. At the same time General Martini, head of the German radar service, started systematically jamming our stations with new and hitherto-unsuspected equipment, but not before we had plotted the slow movement of the fighter 'umbrella' off the coast of France. At Biggin Hill it was erroneously tagged an 'air/sea rescue operation'.

By a sheer mischance the enemy's daring ruse was given away. At 10.10 a.m. Group Captain Victor Beamish, the genial Irish station commander of Kenley, took-off on a 'Rhubarb' with Wing Commander Boyd, Leader of the Kenley Wing. Their only thought was to find a spot of excitement after some days of boring idleness. Slipping over the Channel through swirling mist and clouds, they throttled back and eased down over the French coast. At once they spotted two Me. 109s and gave chase, suddenly finding themselves right over the German battle-cruiser fleet. It was unbelievable: there were the *Scharnhorst, Gneisenau* and *Prinz Eugen*, which everyone thought were snugly tucked away in Brest, steaming steadily up 'our own bloody Channel' with a whole armada of destroyers and E-boats weaving around. As for the Messerschmitts – the sky was full of them. Beamish and Boyd did not stop to fight, their one thought was to get back alive with the news. They dived down through the terrific curtain of flak that arched up almost lazily from every ship and emerged unscathed to tear back over the wave-crests to Kenley. They landed at 11.10 a.m. Within fifteen minutes the hunt was up.

The loading-up of 250 aircraft of Bomber Command commenced. At noon the ships were within range of the Dover 'heavies', and the first M.T.B.s put to sea. At Manston six torpedo-carrying Swordfish of Fleet Air Arm, there for just this eventuality, were taxied-out. From 11 Group Headquarters Leigh-Mallory ordered Biggin Hill and Hornchurch to provide maximum escort for the Swordfish: rendezvous over Manston at 12.25 p.m.

Biggin Hill was caught unawares. No one had anticipated any flying with the weather as it was and neither the Canadians nor 124 Squadron were at 'readiness'. It was the same at Gravesend where Brian Kingcome, now Squadron Leader, was hustling to get 72 Squadron airborne.

By 12.15 p.m. the Swordfish at Manston, led by Lieutenant Commander Esmonde, were ready. Biggin Hill then reported that both 124 and 401 Squadrons would be late. Esmonde decided not to wait; with each minute lost, his prey slipped further from the torpedo-carriers' limited reach, and at 12.20 p.m. the Swordfish took-off. As they orbited Manston, ten Spitfires of 72 Squadron arrived. The 'stringbags' would not be entirely unaccompanied on their rendezvous with the German Fleet.

The two squadrons at Biggin Hill, meanwhile, were airborne at 12.25 p.m. Realising that they were late, Squadron Leader Douglas headed straight for the open sea, hoping to overtake the Swordfish. He missed them, doubled back to Manston, found they had already left, and flew to sea again, losing vital minutes in confusion.

At 12.30 p.m. the Swordfish and 72's ten Spitfires sighted the two battle-cruisers and their escort, Me. 109s and F.W. 190s swarming around like angry bees. Esmonde never faltered. Ignoring the fiercely attacking fighters, he led his section of three Swordfish straight for the big ships. 72 Squadron turned away to fight off further waves of Messerschmitts and Focke-Wulfs that materialised from the swirling mist and rain. Every ship in the fleet was firing now, but the Swordfish kept on through the deadly curtain of flak. Esmonde was the first to fall; the two remaining crews managed to launch their torpedoes before they, too, were shot down. The second section of three were all destroyed. Not a single Swordfish escaped, and only five of their crews were rescued. For this bravery Esmonde was awarded a posthumous V.C.

By now 124 and 401 Squadrons had joined 72 in the bitter and confused battle. The Canadians scored at once: Pilot Officer Ormston sent a 109 crashing on to a destroyer's deck with a blinding, thunderous explosion before finishing off another already crippled by Pilot Officer Harley and Sergeant Morrison. Two other 109s were damaged, and 124 claimed two more and a F.W. 190 before they were recalled.

It was pointless to attack the enemy fighters alone, the ships were what mattered. And these the Spitfires were powerless to hurt.

The assault was carried on by torpedo-laden Beauforts, M.T.B.s and destroyers before our heavy bombers took to the air. At 2.45 p.m. both of Biggin Hill's squadrons were airborne once again, this time to escort the first wave of Wellingtons. Cloud-base was now down to 200 feet in places; none of the pilots made contact with the enemy fighters and all returned to base safe, but sad at this fiasco. Their depression increased when they heard that the German ships had all escaped apparently unscathed; not for a long time was it learnt that both the *Scharnhorst* and the *Gneisenau* had been severely damaged by our aerial-laid mines and rendered virtually *hors de combat*.

The Channel dash by the German ships came as a depressing climax to weeks of gloom for all at Biggin Hill. Since the New Year the squadrons had done little but training and radar-calibration flights with some cooperation flying at night for London's searchlights. There had been a few 'Rhubarbs' and 'Roadsteads', but even these proved exceptionally dull. It seemed that the *Luftwaffe*, like Biggin Hill, was preoccupied with the snow and frost that turned the runways into ice-rinks and made life unbearable for all who had the misfortune to be stationed on bleak, exposed airfields. Nor was it cheering to learn that the new Wing Commander Flying had been shot-down and was a prisoner-of-war after barely six weeks at Biggin Hill.

On 17th December, 1941, Jamie Rankin had left Biggin Hill to become Wing Commander Training at 11 Group; the formal dinner given in his honour was attended by Leigh-Mallory, 'Sailor' Malan and the new Wing Leader, Stanford Tuck, fresh back from a mission to the United States.

Commanding the crack Wing of Fighter Command was a job after Bobbie Tuck's own heart whose restless, zestful spirit demanded and thrived on action. Only the cursed weather was against him. The foggy, snow-bound days were infinitely irksome to a man longing to get back into his stride, to pit his wits and skill against the Hun.

They were hard months, too, for civilians who remained living on the 'Bump'. True, they had been repeatedly asked to leave, but, for many, home ties and associations were too strong. The road through the aerodrome was still forbidden them and, making matters worse, London Transport announced that the emergency bus service round the airfield via Downe and Keston could not be run during the hours of darkness. Unless they could travel to and from work during daylight, manifestly impossible in winter, they were marooned. All appeals to higher authority failed. Eventually the Station Commander, Dickie Barwell, applied the Nelson touch and allowed a bus with boarded-up windows and an armed guard to run through the camp, though the road remained 'closed under D.O.R.A.' for another two years.

The Biggin Wing had flown another barren sweep on the morning of 28th January. That afternoon Tuck, craving some excitement, planned a 'Rhubarb', taking with him a young Canadian, Pilot Officer Harley. De la Torre provided them with a juicy target: the alcohol distillery at Hesdin, inland from Le Touquet. They crossed the Channel, skimming the white horses, then rocketed up over the cliffs of France to sneak in low over the fields. A steep climb for altitude just short of the target, and the two Spitfires roared down in line abreast streaming cannon shells at the fat, tempting vats of alcohol. Tuck and Harley glimpsed erupting smoke and flame before they climbed back into the clouds. Both had shells aplenty left in their magazines, sufficient to shoot up a military transport and a high tension pylon. A stationary locomotive, peach of a target, then lured them into sight of

Boulogne and its flak defences. They dived together on the engine and saw it vanish in a geyser of scalding steam before Tuck's Spitfire was trapped in the merciless, unerring cross-fire of Bofors guns. Hit in the fuselage, the engine, the radiator, streaming black oil and glycol, he made a desperate forced-landing in a field.

Harley flew back alone to report that the 'immortal' Tuck of the newspaper headlines had fallen victim to the enemy's flak. Two days later the German radio announced that he was alive and a prisoner. His place at Biggin Hill was taken by Wing Commander Masterman.

On the last day of February the squadrons were somewhat intrigued by being called to 'readiness' at 8.25 a.m. There had been no previous briefing and, as far as anyone knew, no operation was in the offing; besides, a heavy ground mist reached up to 1,000 feet. Thirty minutes later they were released, still none the wiser, and were finishing breakfast when the pitiless Tannoys sent them back to the dispersals. It was no false alarm, and 124 and 401 Squadrons took-off under orders to escort two destroyers up the Channel. Even the Wing Leader was puzzled: twenty-four Spitfires were surely excessive protection for two small ships?

What Wing Commander Masterman and the others did not know was that on board the destroyers were the victorious survivors of a commando raid on the German radar station at Bruneval. During the night twelve Whitleys had pinpointed Bruneval and dropped a detachment of specially-trained paratroops with a party of Sappers and an R.A.F. radio mechanic whose task it was to photograph and dismantle the *Würzburg*, the enemy's top-secret radar used for controlling flak and searchlights with disconcerting accuracy. This hazardous mission was carried out, calmly and methodically, though under fire, while the paratroopers held the radar station's defenders at bay until all the secrets of the *Würzburg* had been secured and the party could withdraw to the beach where the two destroyers were waiting.

The Spitfires took-off in a blinding snow-storm, their pilots hoping for the best.

'Vector 210 degrees for 20 minutes at 200 m.p.h.' The Controller sounded cosily warm in his Operations Room.

Four of the Canadians lost sight of the others and returned to base, followed soon after by nine of 124 Squadron who meandered in a futile follow-my-leader game over the Channel. The remainder clung to the Wing Leader, flying wing-tip to wing-tip through the murk and, much to their surprise, met the destroyers on time to shepherd them back to Portsmouth. No enemy aircraft were seen. Had conditions been better, however, it might have been a very different story, for the *Luftwaffe* would most certainly have tried to prevent this rape of one of its most cherished secrets.

The Wing was again over the Channel that afternoon, flying as high cover to six Blenheims out to get a U-boat sheltering in Ostend and had a ragged, inconclusive fight with a large gaggle of enemy fighters, significantly more F.W. 190s than Me. 109s. It was like the high summer of 1941: the *Luftwaffe* was stirring into action and that was what counted. The Mess bar did a record business that night.

It was as if the Bruneval raid had touched off a new offensive policy. For Biggin Hill the winter doldrums were over; squadron leaders were actually observed out running with their pilots at the double round the perimeter track, while the Canadians went so far as to be initiated into the mysteries of rugger. Bomber Command shed its policy of conservation and released light and medium bombers for daylight assaults. Leigh-Mallory held regular conferences with the wing commanders and squadron leaders of 11 Group, inviting suggestions for hurting the *Luftwaffe* as hard and frequently as possible. The weather improved, only on seven days in March was there no flying, and the Biggin Wing swung enthusiastically into action escorting Blenheims, Stirlings and, increasingly, American-built Bostons, over France to strike at airfields, marshalling-yards, power-stations, factories and shipping, besides tempting the *Luftwaffe* to resist so that it, too, could be destroyed.

These operations grew increasingly complex, 200 fighters, or more, being involved. Nothing was left to chance, every detail was planned in advance. Biggin Hill's veterans remembered with nostalgia the days when it was every man for himself and the devil take the hindmost. Now they felt like cogs in some well-oiled machine, and only individuals when it came to combat. Typical was 'Circus' 119, a raid by 12 Bostons on the railway station at St Omer:

Escort wing:	Kenley	14-16,000 feet.
Escort cover:	Northolt	17-21,000 feet.
High cover:	Biggin Hill	22-25,000 feet.
Target support:	Hornchurch	20-22,000 feet.
Forward support:	North Weald	20-22,000 feet.

It was a policy that paid off well and the Biggin Wing's tally of 'kills' increased proportionately. More distressing, however, were the growing numbers of aircraft grounded with 'Focke-Wulf trouble' as the 190s rolled off the assembly lines in Germany. A new Spitfire, the Mark IX, was already in production, said to be more than the answer to the F.W. 190, but for the time being Biggin Hill had to make-do with its outclassed Spitfire Vs.

Even more disturbing were the stories in circulation of the Allied aircraft being shot-down by our own fighters; rumour having it as high as twenty-five that spring. This tragedy was bound to happen, of course, as new and unfamiliar types were being flown daily: Typhoons, Mosquitoes and later marks of Hurricane and Spitfire, as well as the American aircraft now flooding over the Atlantic – Bostons, Baltimores, Marylands and Tomahawks, and the Mustangs which looked so like Messerschmitts. In the welter of combat there was no time to consult a manual of aircraft identification. This became an absolute fetish with the Station Commander, Dickie Barwell; identification competitions were held, aircraft models festooned the dispersal huts and Messes, and attendance was made compulsory at film shows and lectures given by 'Spy' de la Torre who did not, however, confine his lessons to the Air Force.

Returning from a 'Roadstead' one morning, the Canadian Squadron, No. 401, saw a convoy of trucks drive up to its dispersal and debouch several companies of the Royal Warwicks. They advanced at the double and were only restrained from taking pot shots at 401's Spitfires by de la Torre who, mounted successively on a Spitfire II and V, a Hurricane II, a Mustang and a Blenheim, preached recognition in a loud, booming voice. The aircraft then formed a bastard procession across the sky with Sergeant de Nancrede upside down in line astern, a sight which amused the Army but piqued Dickie Barwell. The sergeant was condemned to attend the funeral at Detling of a pilot killed doing exactly that.

March passed smoothly into April, the mounting fury of our offensive marking the onset of warm, sunny spring days. Jamie Rankin was now back on the 'Bump' as Wing Commander Flying, while the Canadians changed places at Gravesend with the Basutoland Squadron. His Majesty King George VI visited the station with Queen Elizabeth and spent a pleasant hour chatting to the pilots at dispersal; King Haakon passed an afternoon with the Norwegians of 124 Squadron and, later, the Duke of Kent attended a dining-in night at the Mess. On 23rd April the Biggin Wing participated in London's Warships Week: the three squadrons making a rendezvous over the centre of Hyde Park. Few of the Londoners who stared up at the silvery Spitfires wheeling overhead with immaculate precision, realised that within the hour they would be in battle over St Omer. In April, too, the Army finally quit Biggin Hill, having been there in some capacity or other ever since 1918, the defence of the station now being entrusted to the newly-formed R.A.F. Regiment – Squadron Nos. 2709 and 2834 moving in from Henlow. The C.O. of the latter, Squadron Leader Cave, was soon to lose his life when he grabbed a live grenade, its pin accidentally released, and tried to throw it away to protect his men during a training session.

Even with his spine encased in plaster, Dickie Barwell ignored doctor's orders and flew whenever he could, his favourite position being Red Two to Squadron Leader Duke-Wooley. Knowing that he could not turn his head sideways or backwards, pilots of the Wing took especial care to watch over his Spitfire. He was with 72 Squadron when the Basutoland boys brought their total 'bag' up to 101 on a diversionary sweep over Abbeville while Bostons were raiding Ostend and Le Havre. Their tactics were to stay below 500 feet until half way across the Channel and then climb as fast as they could. This was highly successful: the Spitfires had height and speed on the Huns, as they raced up from their airfields, and accounted for four with the loss of two pilots. Sergeant Hughes was lucky to get back from this particular mission. Returning home after destroying one of the Me. 109s, his Spitfire was shot-up from the rear. The air pressure system was smashed, his radio, hydraulics and artificial horizon were all hit and his helmet neatly grooved. The sergeant landed at Biggin Hill without flaps or brakes. He ran along the entire length of the main runway, across the perimeter track, on to a new extension being built and out beyond that, finally pulling his wheels up and coming to rest within a stone's throw of the 'King's Arms' at Leaves Green. A pint of bitter was never more welcome!

72 Squadron became the acknowledged 'aces' at attacking shipping, adding quite a list of tankers, mine-sweepers and patrol vessels to its total of 100-plus aircraft destroyed. The shooting-up of fishing smacks, motor-boats and dinghies was strictly forbidden; life for the French was hard enough as it was without the intervention of our Spitfires.

Early in May Flight Lieutenant 'Timber' Woods of 72 Squadron was leading a section on a shipping patrol in the Havre area when he sighted a coaster of 200 tons, or more, placidly steaming up the coast.

'Just like a ruddy rowing-boat,' yelled Woods, forgetting his R/T transmitter was on, then: 'Going down to port . . . Attack! Attack! . . . Go!, and don't shoot until you see the rowlocks!'

The four Spitfires neatly slid into position and roared down in line astern, their cannons murderously raking the coaster from stem to stern, smashing into the bridge, through the deck plating and hull. They left the ship sinking, belching steam and black smoke as its crew hastily took to the life-boats.

Unfortunately, Woods' exuberant remarks were heard in the Operations Room at Biggin Hill where Dickie Barwell and de la Torre happened to be listening-in. They were furious, thinking that some unfortunate French rowing-boat had, in fact, been shot-up. The Spitfire pilots found an icy reception awaiting them on their return. It took a lot of talking to convince the Station Commander that they had attacked quite a large armed vessel. 'Next time we'll break both their bloody oars!' muttered the outraged Woods.

On occasions, pilots returning to base flew over a bomber ditched in the Channel. Once it was a Stirling, its tail sheared off by a damaged Wellington which collided with it, that 72 Squadron saw and reported. Next day they received a polite 'thank-you letter' with a pound note enclosed to pay for drinks from 'all the crew of T for Tommy'. It was little acts like this that made the war seem more human, more bearable after the strain of long hours over enemy territory.

Oh,   ***   ***   ***
***   ***   ***   ***
On me no mercy bestow!

W.A.A.F.s keeping R/T watch in the Operations Room smiled at each other with raised eyebrows, not so much at the words, but at the singer's lazy Texan drawl. During the coming months they were to grow very familiar with this battle-song of the Third 'Eagle' Squadron, No. 133.

It was on 3rd May, 1942, that 'Old Glory' was unfurled for the first time on Biggin Hill, waving proudly outside the dispersal hut vacated that morning by 124 Squadron. Inside, the decorations were quickly changed, the 'pin-ups' and Esquire Girls giving place to advertisements in mouth-watering colour of Virginia hams, California oranges and steaming, juicy steaks, for Britain's war-time rationing was a sore point with American volunteers in the Royal Air Force.

No. 133 was the youngest of the three 'Eagle' Squadrons;

the other two, 71 and 121, were already seasoned in combat. Its pilots, civilians who had been inspired to cross the 49th Parallel to join the Royal Air Force by a love of adventure, for experience, or from a hatred of Nazi Germany, came from thirteen of the States. The town of Visalra in California alone provided four, Middleton, Ahrends, Lambert and Eicher, inevitably dubbed the 'Four Horsemen of the Apocalypse', Beaty, Sperry, Gentile, Harp and Gudmansen had all spent a few hours puttering about on light aircraft before volunteering, that was all, but they could not wait for their own country to enter the conflict. There was Robertson of Oklahoma whose plaintive cry: 'They're shooting at me!' on his first mission over France set the whole Operations Room laughing, and there was Doyle, the Boston Irishman who reckoned that fighting Britain was Ireland's exclusive privilege, not Hitler's. Emmerson paid his own passage from the Argentine in order to volunteer, and Don Blakeslee, a veteran of the Canadian 401 Squadron, who promptly demanded a transfer when he heard his fellow-countrymen were coming to Biggin Hill. Always happy, a superb pilot and shot, better with a hangover than most men when sober, Blakeslee's only fear was that he would be taken off operations, consequently his combat-flying was carefully logged 'practice missions', just in case! The Flight Commanders at first were 'Cobey' King, a Hollywood stunt pilot who was shot down over Abbeville without having fired a shot, and 'Red' McColpin, a brilliant pilot and leader, who was voted the most dangerous poker player on the 'Bump'. Americans all, they were proud to wear their eagle shoulder-badges on the R.A.F. uniforms.

The squadron formed at Eglington shortly before Pearl Harbor, 7th December, 1941, that 'date which will live in infamy' of President Roosevelt. Events in the Pacific seemed very remote on a rain-swept airfield in Ulster where the Third 'Eagles' were learning to handle Hurricanes, rebelliously knuckling under to R.A.F. discipline and making several highly pleasurable raids into neutral Eire. Their Squadron Leader was E. H. Thomas, an officer who, in the words of one 'Eagle' pilot, was 'a quiet, reserved Englishman who through sheer quality of leadership was able to make a cohesive unit out of a bunch of individualistic Yanks.'

From Eglington they moved to Kirton Lindsey for training on Spitfires, and thence to Biggin Hill. The 'Eagles' spirits soared: Biggin Hill was the 'big time', it was in the heart of the 'big flap country' with the Abbeville *Geschwader* as dependable playmates. They had heard others 'bitching' that the Biggin Wing was given the rough, dangerous missions, but 133 Squadron ignored them and begged: 'Give us the operations that are too tough for anyone else to handle!'

The Americans quickly made themselves at home on the 'Bump' and adopted the 'Queen's Head' at Downe as their own, becoming expert at darts and shove-halfpenny. In all humility they revered Dickie Barwell. 'Jesus! To be beaten by a Groupie with a broken back!' explained one pilot after a strenuous game of squash. They were eager, even anxious, to meet the Hun in combat but Tommy Thomas wisely ordained four days' intensive training to get used to wing tactics, R/T procedures and the geography of south-east England. It was galling to have to wait and watch 72 Squadron take-off, sometimes twice a day, and eavesdrop on the R/T: 'Twenty-five bandits over Abbeville, climbing . . . Attack, attack, go! . . . ' punctuated by the staccato crackle of guns.

'Attention all pilots. Will 72 and 133 Squadrons please report for briefing.'

This was it at last. On 7th May the Third 'Eagle' Squadron joined the Biggin Wing in escorting six Bostons out to bomb shipping in Ostend harbour. No enemy aircraft were met, but the flak at 20,000 feet was unpleasant.

Pilot Officer Dooley lit a cigarette to calm his jangled nerves. A black mushroom materialised, as if by magic, in front of his Spitfire and he heard for the first time the sharp ping of steel fragments on his windscreen. He flinched and dropped his cigarette. After some hectic evasive action he calmed down and found his cockpit full of smoke. He had forgotten the cigarette. Convinced his Spitfire was blazing he 'sweated it out' all the way home, unable to decide whether to bale out, or not. He landed wet through, and at least ten pounds lighter!

Two more uneventful operations and then, on 17th May, the 'Eagles' drew blood over Abbeville when 'Red' Mc-Colpin shot down one Me. 109, the others claiming two 'probables'.

Once they had got over their qualms at flying over enemy territory, the Americans' aggressive spirit amazed everyone. Suffering a bad attack of dysentery, Pilot Officer Offspring blandly ignored doctors' orders to stay in bed and joined the squadron over Abbeville. At 30,000 feet he was embarrassingly beset by the 'G.I.s'. His only comment on the R/T was a succint '———!'

Pilot Officer Cook, Jnr, experienced the frightening sensation of being caught in a whirling maelstrom of aircraft at one minute, and then finding himself suddenly, terrifyingly, alone. Searching for the rest of 133, he ran into a whole squadron of Me. 109s.

'Come over here,' he yelled, forgetting all R/T drill in his excitement. 'I've got 'em cornered like rats.'

'How many?' inquired Pilot Officer Taylor, the only man to hear 'Cooksie'.

'Eight or ten of the —.'

There was utter silence from Taylor, who later claimed radio failure. Cook returned to Biggin Hill badly shot-up and furious.

'Hell,' commented Taylor. 'You had them covered. I reckoned you could take care of yourself.'

News of McColpin's victory reached Station Headquarters long before the Spitfires were back. In a flash Dickie Barwell was sending his congratulations by R/T and chuckling at 133's exultant:

Give me a love that is lewd and lascivious,
To the best things in life I am completely oblivious.

Very soon the advance guard of the U.S. Eighth Army Air Force was to arrive in Britain and was quickly in action, making its daylight raids on Occupied Europe with the mighty B-17s, the Flying Fortress. On the first of these forays, to Rouen, pride of place in the fighter escort was accorded 133 Squadron. No enemy aircraft were seen, but the Third 'Eagles' were incensed at being used for target-practice, happily inaccurate, by the B-17s' trigger-quick gunners.

'Why no claims?' asked de la Torre on their return. 'The bomber boys have claimed something phenomenal, at least ten destroyed and fifteen probables.'

The pilots ruefully regarded the holes in their Spitfires, but remained silent. Pride prevented them from blaming their fellow-countrymen's inexperience.

It required several more missions with the Fortresses to convince the Intelligence Staff that 133 Squadron was not 'turning chicken and goofing off' but that it was the B-17s' gunners who were 'off the beam, but good!'

The fine weather of June brought some really hot days and everyone made appreciative use of the swimming pool at Barfield. Only on the 12th did unexpected rain prevent flying; perhaps it was just as well, for, the previous night, the entire station had celebrated the anniversary of Dickie Barwell's command. Within a month he was reported: 'missing, believed killed.'

Every evening, for some weeks past, a solitary German reconnaissance aircraft had been plotted flying at a great height over the south-east coast. Its mere presence in his sector was an affront to Barwell. Biggin Hill then had a few Spitfire VIs, a high-altitude version with a pressurised cabin and extended wings. 'Just the job to get this blighter,' thought Barwell and, on the evening of 1st July, took-off in company with Squadron Leader Oxspring of 72 Squadron.

The lone Hun was clearly plotted in the Operations Room and the Controller vectored the two Spitfires to Beachy Head to intercept.

Unknown to Barwell, two others had also taken-off from

Tangmere, bound on the same mission. The Controller tried to tell him, but there was no acknowledgement. His Spitfire's R/T was out of order.

All four Spitfires met over the Channel. There was no sign of the German. The Tangmere pilots, seeing an unfamiliar, odd-looking fighter flash past below them, dived and opened fire. Two short bursts were sufficient and Dickie Barwell spiralled down in flames. The 'blip' that was his Spitfire VI faded and vanished from the cathode-ray tubes of the coastal radar stations. This fact was relayed to Biggin Hill. Sadly, the Controller passed on to Tangmere the only possible interpretation: 'I rather think your boys have shot down our station commander.'

His death unsettled the whole station and it was some time before it rallied under the command of Group Captain Hallings-Pott, A.F.C., D.F.C.

72 and 133 Squadrons had little time to brood over the tragedy; they were unexpectedly and secretly ordered to Lympne, while 19 and 234 Squadrons moved in to Biggin Hill. Pilots were told to fly below 500 feet and keep absolute R/T silence. At Lympne broad white stripes were painted on the cowlings and tail-planes of their Spitfires. Something big was clearly in the offing. Rumour and security-leaks provided the answer: they were being held in readiness to cover an impending assault on Dieppe. For several days they had little to do but rest and enjoy the sumptuous accommodation of Sir Philip Sassoon's country house with its marble halls and sunken baths, and the statues and temples, fountains and topiary of the lovely gardens. Originally, the Dieppe raid was planned for 4th July, bad weather forced a postponement to the 8th, and then four German aircraft attacked the assault ships lying in the Solent with the Canadian troops already embarked, and it was decided to cancel the operation altogether.

'So goodbye to Lympne – a visit with great expectations only to be doomed to disappointment,' noted 72 Squadron's Intelligence Officer.

A few days later the squadron's two Flight Commanders,

Hugo Armstrong and 'Timber' Woods, flew the first Spitfire IXs to reach Biggin Hill. Powered by the Rolls-Royce Merlin LXIII with a two-stage supercharger, the new Spitfire was vastly superior to the Mark Vs and more than equal to the Focke-Wulf 190. Armstrong and Woods were both impressed, and reported an indicated air-speed of 480 m.p.h. in a shallow dive at 25,000 feet! The whole squadron was quickly re-equipped, and then it was 133's turn.

The Basutoland Squadron had barely a week to enjoy its new fighters before handing them over to 401 Squadron, which returned to Biggin Hill from Gravesend when 72 Squadron was posted north to Morpeth to commence training for the impending invasion of North Africa. The move coincided with the departure of Jamie Rankin, the Wing now being led by Tommy Thomas, promoted Wing Commander.

Throughout August Biggin Hill echoed the varied accents of the New World as, in addition to the Third 'Eagle' Squadron and the Canadians of 401, the station now played host to one of the first two regular American fighter units to go into action in Europe, the 307th Pursuit. By August, 1942, the air echelons of the 31st and 52nd Fighter Groups, with a large part of the 1st Fighter Group, had reached the United Kingdom and were engaged in training. The 307th Pursuit (31st Fighter Group) had made the Atlantic crossing without its aircraft, P-39s, due to lack of shipping space, and was now flying borrowed Spitfires. After a short training spell at Atcham, the squadron moved to Biggin Hill to acquire operational experience.

Their olive-green uniforms a contrast to Air Force blue, the 307th Pursuit's pilots enjoyed the bicycle tours from pub to country pub, the beer was good and the landscape pleasantly green after the Arizona desert. The thought of drinking anything alcoholic before a mission, however, was sheer heresy according to their training, but they quickly made up for this abstinence in the evenings. Their 'Coffee-call' was introduced into station routine, everyone being of the opinion that this, added to afternoon tea, made a great combination. In one respect the Royal Air Force was voted superior, to be woken in the morning, not by a batboy, but by a friendly W.A.A.F. bearing a cup of tea.

The 'Magic 307th', to use its nickname, was closely supervised by Wing Commander Thomas who had a hard time teaching the American pilots the advantages of a loose, mobile combat formation rather than their tight, box formations they had always flown – 'pansy formations' as Thomas called them scornfully. The whole idea of a sweep was not well received. They had come to Britain to win the war, to chase the Hun around and shoot him down – not to play a game of sitting duck to lure him up and then, by clever manoeuvring which the British pilots had learnt so well, try to destroy him. They were delighted, however, with their Spitfires. One pilot, injudiciously talking to a reporter, so belittled the fighters the squadron had left behind in America, that he precipitated a Congressional hearing in Washington and the immediate appearance at Biggin Hill of General 'Hap' Arnold!

This American unit had arrived at Biggin Hill in good time for the 'Big Show'; six weeks after its cancellation 'Operation Jubilee', the Dieppe raid, was on again, timed for 19th August.

Once again 133 Squadron moved in advance to Lympne, partnered this time by 401 Squadron. The 'Eagles', benefiting from experience, took for themselves the best rooms of Sir Philip Sassoon's house, relegating the chilly Egyptian splendours of the halls and public rooms to the Canadians. They did not quibble. Many had friends and relatives who would be fighting, perhaps dying, on the beaches of Dieppe, and they would have endured purgatory itself to ensure being airborne that day. Two fresh squadrons, Nos. 222 and 602, flew in to Biggin Hill to add their strength to the Wing. The C.O. of 602, Squadron Leader Peter Brothers, was happy to return to the station where he had been for so many years with the gay, buccaneering 32 Squadron, and appropriately celebrated the home-coming by shooting-down an F.W. 190 the day before Dieppe.

On the eve the 307th Pursuit learnt that it was not to participate in the next morning's show. A delegation of furious pilots, some crying with chagrin, saw the Station Commander and implored him to have this decision reversed. 'Christ Almighty, sir, we didn't come all this way just to sit in the bleachers!' Captain Davis adding that he would not be responsible for his boys' actions if they remained on the ground whilst the Wing was fighting it out over Dieppe. Group Captain Hallings-Pott passed the request on to Leigh-Mallory who was delighted to say 'O.K.'

Briefing took place behind locked doors with armed sentries on guard as Hallings-Pott and de la Torre expounded the plan and purpose of 'Operation Jubilee'; even as they spoke the armada of assault was putting to sea. Biggin Hill was made *incommunicado* with the world outside, and it required the express permission of the Station Commander for every telephone call. It was a scene repeated at Lympne, and at Kenley, Manston, Tangmere – all the fighter stations in the south.

Shortly before dawn some 6,000 troops, the majority Canadian, would fight their way ashore at Dieppe with the intention of achieving the maximum destruction of all military objectives and installations. They would be screened with smoke laid by R.A.F. Bostons. Tanks would be landed; Hurricanes and Hurri-bombers would reinforce the naval bombardment of the Germans' coastal defences, while American Flying Fortresses would paralyse Abbeville aerodrome with saturation bombing. Command of all air operations was entrusted to Leigh-Mallory who had fifty-six fighter squadrons at his disposal – Hurricanes, Spitfires and the new Typhoons. He thought, and indeed hoped, that the *Luftwaffe* might throw 500 aircraft into the sky over Dieppe, in which event Fighter Command would be ready. The role of the Biggin Wing, Squadrons Nos. 133, 222, 401 and 602 with the 307th Pursuit, was straightforward: to help maintain a fighter 'umbrella' over Dieppe until the last soldier was re-embarked and on his way home, and destroy the maximum number of Huns.

There was little time to sleep, barely six hours before reveille at 3 a.m. Many pilots dressed in their best uniforms and took just that little extra care in shaving and brushing their hair. A quick breakfast, then out to the dispersals, shivering in a chill wind and looking up at the stars, wondering what the day would bring. Already the first waves of commandos were ashore at Dieppe, protected by fighter squadrons who would be relieved in turn by the Biggin Wing.

At 5.50 a.m. a green Very light arched up into a sky bright with the dawn, and twelve Spitfires of 602 Squadron took-off. Three minutes later 222 Squadron was airborne, with the 307th Pursuit close behind. Led by Wing Commander Tommy Thomas they orbited once, sliding like well-drilled marionettes into wing formation, then headed south to join 133 and 401 Squadrons over Lympne.

The Biggin Wing, five squadrons strong, swept out over the Channel, the Spitfires' slipstreams ruffling its glassy, tranquil surface, then climbed steeply off Dieppe. Others were already winging home to refuel, a few to re-arm, too. Below, through the early morning haze, the pilots glimpsed the muzzle-flashes of destroyers exchanging salvoes with batteries ashore. As they watched, a large transport received a direct hit and blew up. A pall of smoke hung over the town, thick and heavy, and hid the fighting on the ground from the anxious eyes of 401's Canadians. To the east the defenders' flak was firing with a wild inaccuracy. Over the Wing, and to the north, flew the twenty-four Flying Fortresses bound for Abbeville. The 307th Pursuit, stirred by kinship with the bombers' crew, felt tempted to break away and escort them, but the Wing Leader's quiet, crisp: 'Look out, chaps. 109s at nine o'clock,' snapped them back to duty.

The *Luftwaffe* had been taken by surprise and, at first, could only muster a handful of fighters to stab ineffectually at our 'umbrella' over the beach-head. 602 Squadron had a fleeting brush with some F.W. 190s: Pilot Officer Samson destroying one, the C.O. damaging another. The 307th Pursuit, hot to kill, caught one and sent it crashing down on to the roof tops of Dieppe, its first blood of the second World War, but lost Lieutenant Ed. Tovrea who baled out and remained a prisoner for the duration.

By 7.35 a.m. all the Spitfires, save Tovrea's, were back at Biggin Hill. The day gave promise of being really hot and almost cloudless.

The Wing was airborne again at 10.15 a.m. The scene over Dieppe was vastly changed. The *Luftwaffe* was fighting back savagely and swarms of Messerschmitts and Focke-Wulfs were mixing-it with our Spitfires and Typhoons while the bombers, Ju. 88s and Do. 217s, lurked on the fringe of the *mêlée*, awaiting a chance to slip in and catch our shipping off shore.

The wing seized its opportunity. Everyone had a target. 'Tally ho!' cried Pete Brothers at the head of 602 Squadron and charged for a bunched-up gaggle of Dorniers. Flight Lieutenant Bocok caught one with his cannon, then, hearing an urgent 'Blue One, break port, man!' turned sharply to damage an F.W. 190 in the act of attacking him. Sergeants Lund and Caldecott shared another Dornier, then Lund went after one of his own and saw it jettison its bombs as one engine burst into flames. Within ten minutes the squadron could confidently claim three 'destroyed' with nine 'damaged' and 'probable'. And so it went with the rest of the Wing, only 222 Squadron failing to kill.

There were sandwiches and lemonade waiting at Biggin Hill. 'Wonder what we'd do on oysters and beer?' asked 602's jubilant pilots.

The Wing's third sortie at 1 p.m. produced few results. The bloody, confused struggle for Dieppe was already over and the ships were returning with the pitifully few survivors. Outward bound, 222 Squadron saw one transport on fire, a chance hit by a German bomber perhaps, and, as the Spitfires circled in friendly encouragement, it exploded, disintegrating into a towering mushroom of smoke and debris reaching up to 3,000 feet.

The last patrol of the day took off at 5 p.m. Only one enemy aircraft was encountered, a Focke-Wulf, which audaciously attacked Sergeant Evans and forced him to crash near Hawkinge.

And so, back to Biggin Hill where everybody was 'released and had plenty of beer and, what was more important, sleep.'

The day's reckoning for the Biggin Wing was: five enemy aircraft destroyed, 7 'probables' and 29 'damaged', against a loss of 6 Spitfires. Good hunting, Biggin Hill! As was to be expected from such intensive, confused fighting our claims were overly optimistic and Fighter Command's total estimate of 91 destroyed and 151 damaged must be cut down to 48 and 24 respectively in the light of German records In all, we lost 106 aircraft; against this must be set the many lessons learnt – lessons taken to heart and put to good use in the Allied landings in North Africa, Italy and on D-Day.

After Dieppe all operations came as an anticlimax, though the Biggin Wing was logging more hours flying over enemy territory than ever. The American fighter squadron, the 307th Pursuit, was transferred to Merston in the Tangmere Sector, now an all-American station, and was replaced for a short while by the 2nd Fighter Squadron (52nd Fighter Group) sent to Biggin Hill to gain operational experience. The Spitfire IXs were now fitted with jettisonable fuel tanks which greatly increased their range. Escorting Flying Fortresses became the Biggin Wing's 'bread-and-butter' and with the extra petrol it could now reach to Rotterdam, Amiens, Courtrai, Le Havre and Rouen.

In mid-September the Third 'Eagle' Squadron, now under Squadron Leader 'Red' McColpin, heard rumours that all three 'Eagle' Squadrons were to be disbanded as such and their personnel transferred to the U.S. Army Air Force. Now that the Americans were in Britain in force it was clearly anomalous for Fighter Command to continue having the 'Eagles', though few of 133 Squadron could agree with this viewpoint and averred, vociferously and vehemently, that they would never exchange their R.A.F. uniforms for those of their country, despite the attraction of greater pay and more rapid promotion.

For twelve of 133's pilots the argument was wholly academic for their final mission from Biggin Hill ended in near-tragedy.

On 26th September a daylight raid by twenty-four Flying Fortresses on Brest was planned with a close escort of thirty-six Spitfire IXs drawn from 66, 133 and 401 Squadrons. At the briefing the Third 'Eagles' were assigned to 'target cover', and therefore flew down in advance to Bolt Head to refuel there for the maximum flying time over Brest itself.

They took-off from Bolt Head to rendezvous with the Fortresses and the remaining Spitfires over Start Point. Only fourteen of the B-17s arrived and they were seven minutes early; 133 Squadron 'being wise guys, were seven minutes early, too!' Bolt Head's Meteorological Officer forecast 8/10ths cloud over the target area and a wind of 100 m.p.h. from the south at 20,000 feet (this proved an unexplained but costly slip: the wind, in fact, was from due north).

The whole force left the coast of England behind and headed out across the Channel, the clouds thickening ominously to an unbroken blanket. The bombers' navigators had to work by dead-reckoning alone. Ten minutes passed and it was time for the Fortresses to let down through the overcast to seek their target, but they flew serenely on. The squadron leaders of 66 and 401 Squadrons watched their petrol gauges, anxiously calculating gallons in flying-time. All the while the 100 m.p.h. wind was carrying both bombers and fighters far off-course.

'Sorry, chums, got to leave you now. Good luck and good hunting.'

Twenty-four Spitfires swung away and headed home, leaving 133 Squadron alone with the Fortresses. They broke their box-formation and scattered, dipping down through the clouds to search for some familiar, identifiable landmark. None of the Americans had seen the coast of Brittany before. Back above the clouds, the Fortresses weaved and zig-zagged, wasting precious time and petrol in getting back on-course. 133 Squadron, with an unreasoning faith in the navigating skill of the bombers' crews, stayed with them until

271

the Spitfires' fast-emptying tanks forced them to turn back, too.

At the reckoned moment they dived down through the clouds, expecting to find themselves over the rocky promontory of Cornwall – they were over the heart of Brest. That head-wind from the north had cut their flying-speed by one-third and they were a full hundred miles out in their navigation. At once flak defences of the most-heavily protected port in Europe opened up with an inferno of tracer and flying steel, each Spitfire being ringed by black shell-bursts. Without petrol they were helpless, impotent to escape, and eleven were forced down to crash-land on fields and a *Luftwaffe* aerodrome. The twelfth man, some gallons of petrol still in hand, tried to make it back to Cornwall. He glided in with empty tanks and crashed on the cliffs of the Lizard.

Two days later, at Debden, was held the ceremony of handing over the 'Eagle' Squadrons to the U.S. Army Air Force. Squadrons Nos. 71 and 121 were on parade in strength, the small group that represented 133 was an eloquent testimony of the pilots' fate.

Addressing the parade the A.O.C. Fighter Command, Air Marshal Sholto Douglas, said: 'I would have wished that on this, my first opportunity of addressing all three Eagle Squadrons together on one station, that my words should have been other than words of farewell.

'We of Fighter Command deeply regret this parting, for in the course of the past eighteen months we have seen the stuff of which you are made, and we could not ask for better companions with which to see the fight through to the finish. But we realise – as you, too, must realise – that your present transfer to your own country's Air Force is in the long run in the best interest of our joint cause. The United States Army Air Force's gain is very much the Royal Air Force's loss. The loss to the *Luftwaffe* will no doubt continue as before.

'Goodbye and thank you Eagle Squadrons Nos. 71, 121,

272

and 133 of Fighter Command, and good hunting to you,
Squadrons of No. 4 Pursuit Group, Eighth United States
Army Air Force.'

CHAPTER NINETEEN

THE ONE-THOUSANDTH HUN

THOUGH many French pilots had fought from Biggin Hill,
340 Squadron, *le Groupe Ile-de-France*, was the first Free
French unit to be stationed there. Its personnel, led by
Commandant Bernard Dupérier, were sensible of the great
honour of being posted to Britain's premier fighter station.
They were pleased with the friendly reception accorded them
by Group Captain Hallings-Pott and were delighted with de
la Torre's impeccable French and his astonishing physical
resemblance to Don Quixote, besides admiring the smart
motor-bicycle combination he used for touring the dispersals
with 'Blitzie', his spaniel.

When at Hornchurch, their former station, the *Ile-de-
France* pilots had looked forward to their mid-September
move to the 'Bump' with some eagerness. At last they would
be flying Spitfire IXs in place of their Mark Vs. Alas, for their
hopes: the fighters they coveted were those which 133
Squadron had lost so disastrously over Brest. The French
were amazed by the R.A.F.'s attitude of fair play which so
often provided them with the latest and best equipment
before British squadrons, and they were confident it would
not be long before they got their Mark IXs. Meantime, they
continued to fly the Spitfire Vs, escorting Flying Fortresses on
daylight raids over France, Belgium and Holland. Like
others before them, they developed a healthy mistrust of the
B-17s' trigger-happy gunners.

'*Mon Dieu, gardez-moi de mes amis; mes ennemis, je m'en*

charge,' was Dupérier's daily prayer.

They were amazed, too, by the American's fantastic claims of victories. On one particular 'Circus' some 500 fighters escorted 100 Flying Fortresses, whose crews afterwards claimed 48 F.W. 190s 'destroyed', 25 'probables' and 32 'damaged'. During the entire operation the fighter pilots could only swear in all conscience to the destruction of 5 Huns! With fifty gunners, or more, blazing away at the same Focke-Wulf at one time, it was only natural that each individual should think himself responsible for its downfall. Far more important was the undisputed fact that the Fortresses were getting through to their targets and hitting them with destructive accuracy.

In partnership with the *Ile-de-France* Squadron at Biggin Hill was No. 611 (County of Lancashire) Squadron, which had long since lost all trace of its Auxiliary status. The C.O. was Australian-born Squadron Leader Hugo Throssell Armstrong, D.F.C., 'Sinker' to his many friends, who had been a Flight Commander with 72 Squadron during its long and highly successful sojourn on the 'Bump'.

Preparations for 'Operation Torch', the Allied invasion of French North Africa, were now proceeding apace and these, with the onset of winter, led to a falling-off in Fighter Command's offensive. For the Biggin Wing the rest of 1942 was fairly quiet, though Dupérier celebrated his hundredth trip over his homeland by shooting-down two F.W. 190s.

On 27th October the squadrons were enjoying a tranquil afternoon tea when they were torn from the snug warmth of the dispersal huts by a brusque command to take-off immediately for a 'Training operation for the benefit of new pilots'. Mystified and disgruntled, they grabbed their flying-kit and scurried out to the Spitfires already warming-up thunderously. Within seven minutes both squadrons were airborne, 340 flying its new Spitfire IXs.

'Vector 120 degrees. Angels six thousand.'

Over Romney Marsh the Controller ordered: 'Vector 105 degrees', but vouchsafed nothing further, merely reiterating that it was a 'training operation'.

Crossing the Channel the pilots jerked awake: the new course took them to Gris Nez and this could mean a squadron of F.W. 190s on their backs at any minute. For the next half hour they swept to and fro between Gravelines and Boulogne, the Channel ports hidden by cloud, then orbited to sea and returned again for another sweep, always obedient to that invisible puppet-master, the Controller, sitting before a microphone at far-off Biggin Hill.

'Focke-Wulfs à six heures!' cried Sergeant Bouguen, a phlegmatic Breton.

'Speak English, clot!'

Glancing round, Bouguen had seen a dozen F.W. 190s flash out of the clouds in front of 611 Squadron. By a miracle there were no collisions. The Huns were as surprised to see the Spitfires as the boys from Biggin Hill were to see them, and scattered at full throttle, but not before *Sous lieutenant* Boudier had knocked fragments flying from one 190 and Flight Lieutenant Compton had damaged another.

All returned safely to base where they angrily demanded the reason for this strange 'training operation'. It had been a Roman Holiday for Mrs Roosevelt who had been in the Operations Room that afternoon and wished to see how the control system worked!

Next day was a solemn occasion for the Free French Squadron, its third visit by General de Gaulle. A Guard of Honour was mounted by the R.A.F. Regiment, then the General, accompanied by Air Marshal Trafford Leigh-Mallory and Group Captain Hallings-Pott, inspected the pilots and ground crews of the *Ile-de-France* Squadron. He awarded the green-and-red *fourragère* to its Colours and *Croix-de-Guerre* to *Lieutenants* de Tedesco and Hélies and *Sous-lieutenant* Moynet. Lunch in the Officers' Mess followed, the General talking informally to the pilots, reassuring them that, although other Allied landings would necessarily take place before the longed-for liberation of France, preparations for this were already in hand. Some of the British officers present were impressed, and not a little startled, to observe the friendly and respectful, but also fearful, adulation the French men held for their leader.

The station had other visitors, too, a party of Brazilian journalists followed by Colonels Dragun and Borreneuko and Major Pozdoy. There was nothing unusual about a visit by these Allied army officers – except that they were Russian.

Dupérier and the *Ile-de-France* pilots recalled General de Gaulle's remarks at lunch that day when they heard, on 8th November, the first B.B.C. reports of the landing in French North Africa. Their instant reaction was bitter chagrin at not being present: their place was in the skies over Oran and Casablanca, not on fog-bound Biggin Hill. Their loyalties were further confused by news bulletins describing the military and political imbroglio that had flared up after the initial landings, and caused Dupérier, mischievously paradoxical, to remark that Darlan and Pétain would doubtless about face smartly and be made baronets by the King of England! A calm and dignified broadcast by de Gaulle, however, restored their equanimity of mind in time for the squadron's first anniversary on 11th November.

A whole year had passed since a number of French pilots serving in R.A.F. units scattered all over the British Isles had been summoned to chilly, mist-laden Turnhouse, near Edinburgh, to become the nucleus of the first of the Free French Squadrons, No. 340. Of the original twenty-four *Ile-de-France* members sixteen were absent from the anniversary celebration, killed or taken prisoner. It was a good party, beer and *pinard* flowed freely to the music of Kenley's dance band, while those in the squadron who came from Tahiti aroused a fierce nostalgia for sunnier, happier days with their own languorous rhythms.

'Fighter Command's top-scoring ace takes over Britain's No. 1 Fighter Station', was how the Press heralded the return of 'Sailor' Malan to Biggin Hill, the peak of his cap resplendent with gold and a fourth ring on his sleeve.

The New Year, 1943, brought several changes: Malan as Station Commander and Dickie Milne as Wing Commander Flying. 609 Squadron returned briefly to its old hunting ground, bringing the first Typhoons to operate from the 'Bump', and then departed for Manston. Dupérier had already said farewell to his *Ile-de-France* Squadron and left on a mission to America. He handed over to *Capitaine* Schloesing, nicknamed *'le Grand Chleuh'*, a group of pilots and mechanics, volunteers all, who, through sheer unity of purpose, had become one of the most esteemed squadrons in Fighter Command.

The 'Sailor's' return was timely. Pilots were spending more time in the cinema than in the air. The foul weather, the paucity of operations, had sapped the station's morale, but he quickly gave it new life. One of his first acts was to have posted up copies of his 'Ten Commandments':

Ten of my rules for air fighting

1. Wait until you see the white of his eyes. Fire short bursts of one to two seconds, and only when your sights are definitely 'on'.
2. Whilst shooting think of nothing else. Brace the whole of the body, have both hands on the stick, concentrate on your ring sight.
3. Always keep a sharp look-out. 'Keep your finger out.'
4. Height gives *you* the initiative.
5. Always turn and face the attack.
6. Make your decisions promptly. It is better to act quickly, even though your tactics are not of the best.
7. Never fly straight and level for more than thirty seconds in the combat area.
8. When diving to attack, always leave a proportion of your formation above to act as top guard.
9. INITIATIVE, AGGRESSION, AIR DISCIPLINE, and TEAM WORK are words that MEAN something in air fighting.
10. Go in quickly – Punch hard – Get out![1]

The pilots realised that here was a station commander not

[1] Copies of Malan's 'Bible' were in great demand by fighter stations all over the country. At least one has been reported seen posted up in the crew-room of an American fighter unit during the Korean war.

afraid to practise what he preached, as witness his own record, and their morale soared.

It seemed just as if the *Luftwaffe* had heard that the 'Sailor' was back for, on 20th January, the Abbeville *Geschwader* paid its first visit to Biggin Hill after an absence of two years.

Lunch was being served in the Mess when the Tannoy suddenly blared: 'All available aircraft scramble and protect base. Bandits approaching from south-east.'

There was a full minute's stunned silence.

'Of all the bloody cheek!' ejaculated Malan, then joined in the rush for the door, sending tables and crockery flying, as everyone raced to the dispersals. Outside, they saw some F.W. 190s streaking low over the northern end of the airfield. Within eight minutes of the warning, a dozen Spitfires were in the air, led by Malan and Milne.

While several squadrons staged diversions over the coast, twenty raiders, Focke-Wulfs carrying bombs, had swept in over Kent at zero feet bound for Biggin Hill. They overshot the airfield and dropped their bombs in Bromley, hitting a school and killing four teachers and forty-five children before they swung round over Croydon and made a hedge-hopping dash for the Channel and home.

'Height gives *you* the initiative'; rather than give chase at once, Malan took the Spitfires climbing to Beachy Head and was ready to pounce devastatingly when the Focke-Wulfs obligingly flew into his maw. In five blazing, hectic minutes of a dog fight Dickie Milne shot down a brace, 'Sinker' Armstrong two more and *Sous-lieutenant* Gouby yet another pair. Not a single Spitfire was lost or even damaged.

'Just like old times,' said Malan contentedly.

For many pilots and ground crews this had been their first experience of enemy aircraft over Britain in daylight. It was an experiment the *Luftwaffe* did not care to repeat.

'Rodeos', 'Rhubarbs' and 'Circuses' were mounted as often as the winter weather permitted. Inevitably, losses were suffered and, by a tragic quirk of fate, it was the most experienced pilots who failed to return.

278

Squadron Leader Hugo Armstrong took-off with two of his squadron, 611, for a routine practice flight on 5th February. While 'stooging around', he heard 340 Squadron being vectored to a flight across the Channel.

'Care to join the ladies?' he inquired of his two companions.

'O.K. Skipper. It's been a dull life lately.'

Flying 1,000 feet under the clouds the three Spitfires were 'bounced' by eight Huns off Boulogne. Armstrong's Blue Two and Blue Three were literally fighting for their lives when they heard his quiet: 'This is it, chaps. I'm baling out.'

They saw him diving from 500 feet towards the sea, black smoke pouring from his Merlin. Blue Two immediately sent out a 'May-day' giving his C.O.'s last position. Dickie Milne took off at once from Biggin Hill and led the rest of 611 Squadron in a fruitless search until rain cut visibility to nil.

Next to go was *'le Grand Chleuh'*, Schloesing of 340 Squadron, who failed to return from an attack on an armed merchant ship in Boulogne harbour. The French pilots watched him diving ferociously after four F.W. 190s, but he never saw the two close on his tail. Though shot-down, Schloesing survived and escaped to Switzerland. He was back again in England by August.

Then, in one day, the Biggin Wing lost two Wing Commanders and a Squadron Leader, a costly toll for the destruction of two F.W. 190s.

Leading the Wing on a 'Rodeo' towards Hardelot, Dickie Milne spotted eight Huns below, apparently unaware of the Spitfires overhead.

'Leader calling. Keep your eyes open chaps. Prepare to attack.'

A minute passed while Milne made certain this was no trap, then: 'Blue Section, Yellow Section, individual attack ... Go!'

This was his last order as Wing Commander Flying. He dived straight for the Focke-Wulfs, covered by his No. 2 who, without warning, developed engine trouble and broke away. Red Section, left aloft to provide cover, dropped to protect the crippled Spitfire. Milne was on his own. 'When diving to attack, always leave a proportion of your formation above to act as top guard,' but Malan's golden rule was now broken. Milne was shot-down and taken prisoner. At the same time Wing Commander Slater, a newcomer to Biggin Hill who had borrowed a Spitfire for this 'Rodeo', was 'bounced' off Le Touquet with *Commandant* Reilhac, 340's new C.O. Neither returned to base. A show by the Windmill Girls that evening was called off. No one felt like a party.

The post of Wing Commander Flying was now filled by a twenty-three-year-old New Zealander, Alan Christopher Deere. With some justification Al Deere was known throughout Fighter Command as 'The man the Germans couldn't kill'. One day at the height of the Dunkirk evacuation he had been flying for eight and a half hours and had bagged three Huns when he was himself shot down. Surviving a crash-landing on a beach near Ostend, he made his way to Dunkirk in a series of abandoned cars. After a two-hour wait in the hell of those beaches he scrambled aboard a destroyer and reached England. Six weeks later he had a head-on collision with an Me. 109. With his cockpit hood jammed and unable to bale out, he managed to keep his blazing Hurricane in the air for another five minutes then crashed, slithering along the ground until brought up by a tree, broke through the perspex with his bare hands and stepped out. He was back flying next day. During the Battle of Britain Deere took-off from Hornchurch just as a stick of bombs straddled the airfield. One exploded beneath the wheels of his Spitfire, tearing off a wing and the propeller. Momentum carried him on up to 100 feet, then his aircraft flopped over, fell and slid along the grass upside down with Deere inside. He was dragged out from the wreckage unhurt.

With Malan as Station Commander and Deere as Wing Commander Flying, the Biggin Hill squadrons anticipated an eventful, action-packed spring and summer.

No. 1 Squadron, however, which came for a brief stay of five weeks, found the journey down from Acklington more hectic than any 'Rodeo'. The ground party with the baggage

280

and squadron equipment was due to leave Newcastle Central at 5 a.m. 'An unmerciful, godless hour when we can expect "finger trouble",' prognosticated an N.C.O. For a start, the R.T.O. at the station was new to the job and prematurely signalled out the squadron's train, leaving twelve N.C.O.s behind. Arriving in London, the airmen found that the trucks containing the equipment and personal kit had all been uncoupled *en route* and diverted to Hull, Peterborough and Norwich. By driving all through the night and next day in commandeered lorries, they managed to round up everything and report to Biggin Hill a mere twenty-four hours late. No. 1 Squadron's pilots, meanwhile were having their troubles. Flying down from Acklington they ran into bad weather, broke formation and were scattered all over the Midlands and south-east England. One came down at Wittering, another at Southend. The latter's brakes and flaps failed, he overshot the runway, caught his undercarriage in a ditch and somersaulted, wrecking his Typhoon but escaped unscathed. Somewhere over Sussex Sergeant Hornall developed engine trouble. The ground below was over-run with troops on manoeuvres, he dared not jump and leave his Typhoon to crash amongst them unguided, and by a miracle he pulled off a dead-stick landing in a field the size of a tennis court – the only piece of ground unencumbered by the Army. Later, Hornall received a letter of thanks from the G.O.C. the 5th Canadian Division for saving the men's lives.

On 11th March No. 1 Squadron left for Lympne, its place being taken by the second of the Free French fighter units to be formed, No. 341, the *Groupe Alsace*. The squadron's record was phenomenal: raised on 1st February, after only six weeks' training it was posted to the Biggin Wing, the spearhead of Fighter Command's offensive. This was due entirely to its leader, 'René', *Commandant* Mouchotte, who, like so many of his compatriots with families left in German-occupied territory, dared only fight under a pseudonym for fear of reprisals. Mouchotte was a remarkable man and a compelling leader, described by one of his pilots[1] as being: 'a

[1] Pierre Clostermann in *The Big Show*.

281

tall, dark, slim man with piercing eyes and a voice that snapped and admitted of no argument, but was followed by a warming, friendly smile. The kind of man for whom you get yourself killed without discussion, almost with pleasure.'

He had but one ambition, to make the *Alsace* Squadron the most famous in Fighter Command. His pride, his love of the good name of France, had been hurt by the many criticisms of the R.A.F.'s French pilots: that they were openly defiant of discipline, held in utter contempt everything not directly connected with flying and were irresponsibly careless of their aircraft. When asked to form 341 Squadron 'René' drew up two lists, a golden one of pilots he was determined to have, and a black one of those he would under no circumstances admit, and then proceeded by letter, by telephone and by cajoling personal visits to batter down all official opposition to the transfer of the men he wanted.

There followed six weeks of strict training. A temptation to fight the *Boche* was subordinated to perfecting a new formation which Mouchotte had worked out. This depended on iron discipline in the air and tolerated no individual attack without the C.O.'s order. On the eve of 341 Squadron's move to Biggin Hill he was able to forecast: 'The day of the offensive which is fast approaching will find us a young force, terribly armed with a science of warfare and discipline. We shall put our whole soul into this holy war of liberation and the octopus shall perish, even if it costs us our lives . . .'[1]

Both Malan and Deere were impressed by the spirit of the *Alsace* Squadron, but queried the effectiveness of Mouchotte's tactics in combat. After twenty-odd 'Rodeos' and 'Circuses' they doubted no longer and admitted that no other squadron was so manoeuvrable or kept such good formation.

1st April, 1943, was the twenty-fifth anniversary of the founding of the Royal Air Force. In 1918 the diehards of 'Cock' Squadron, stationed at Biggin Hill, had viewed the advent of the new Service with some mistrust, fearing the loss of the traditions which they, as members of the Royal

[1] *The Mouchotte Diaries.*

Flying Corps, had founded. Had they been present at the ceremony held at Biggin Hill a quarter-century later and heard the Station Commander's address to all its personnel, they would have realised their fears were unfounded.

'You are members of the Sector Station which has produced the most outstanding achievements in the Battle of Britain and which, not being content with the standards set in 1940, has continued in the lead as the foremost sector in this Command.

'Today, as most of you know, the Biggin Hill Sector is very closely approaching its thousandth confirmed victory, not to mention the "probably confirmed" and "unconfirmed".

'I would like to say a few words in recognition of the magnificent support the pilots have always received from ground personnel, whether their duties have been concerned with the direct servicing of aircraft at dispersals, the dirty and arduous work in the workshops, or whether they have been concerned with the supply of equipment for pilots and aircraft, or whether they have been concerned with their payment, their clothing, their cooking, or their living conditions. You people who work in the background seldom get either official or public recognition. This is chiefly because your duties are not so glamorous and do not make "front page news". When you leave this parade today I want you to bear in mind that your duties, however boring and non-essential they may appear at times, are absolutely vital to the successful continuation and termination of this grim war. Whenever you feel bored, tired or dispirited I would like you to remember this. I want you to realise that you are honoured by being allowed to serve in a fighting machine that has performed wonders in the past and is playing a major part in the war effort. Every minute of every day you spend at your work you are performing a task which is making history and which will go down to posterity as the most glorious achievement by a magnificent Service at a time when its country and Empire needed it most.'

As Malan said, the tally of enemy aircraft destroyed by Biggin Hill was fast approaching one thousand, a figure unrivalled by any other station in Fighter Command. Everyone was gripped by a feverish expectancy: who would shoot-down the 1,000th Hun? It became a question of national interest. The B.B.C. sent down engineers to make recordings in advance of the great occasion, the interviewer was a Mr Gilbert Harding. A mammoth sweepstake was organised and whoever drew the winning ticket stood to collect over £150, while the fortunate pilot himself would get £300 which was, as Mouchotte said: 'Enough to make those least greedy for gain think twice . . .'

On 7th May the total stood at 995. Pilots due for leave stubbornly refused to go. Bad weather during the next five days cancelled all operations, then, on 13th May, Al Deere led the Wing on a 'Rodeo' over Triqueville – result: no score. The Huns wouldn't come up to play. Next day, however, while escorting Marauder bombers to Courtrai, the Wing fought off a savage attack by Messerschmitts. Squadron Leader Jack Charles, Canadian C.O. of 611 Squadron, was the first to score, then Sergeant Clark collided with a 109. Fatally interlocked, the two fighters tumbled earthwards and exploded in a searing thunderclap of flame – the tally was increased by another unit. Climbing up from the *mêlée* to join what he thought were three Spitfires, Martell of 341 Squadron glimpsed black crosses underneath their wings. His sight encircled one, a 109, and his cannon belched flame, thin pencils of smoke stabbing towards the 998th victim. This was the *Alsace* Squadron's first victory.

15th May was an exceptionally fine day but not until 4.20 p.m. did Deere announce: 'An easy one today, chaps. Just a quickie over Caen.'

The Wing made its rendezvous with a formation of Bostons over Selsey Bill, then crossed the Channel at zero feet, only climbing when Fécamp was reached. Bombers and fighters flew straight inland to avoid the flak at Le Havre and swept round in a great arc that reached to Caen aerodrome.

It was like a boxing arena in Biggin Hill's Operations Room with 'standing-room only' for the fans. Everyone had a hunch the 1,000 mark would be passed during this 'Circus'.

For a while they heard nothing, then came Deere's calmly cheerful: 'Brutus aircraft, look out! Bandits climbing at three o'clock.'

Before the first stick of bombs had fallen, a pack of Focke-Wulfs were in the air, climbing at an incredible rate to harry the bombers.

Mouchotte kept his *Alsace* pilots to give cover as Squadron Leader Charles took 611 down, diving almost vertically in line astern, to slice through the F.W. 190s. The Hun centred in Charles' gun-sight, wobbled comically under the impact of his cannon shells, then just disintegrated – the 999th victim. A quick half roll, a steep climbing turn and Charles had a second yellow belly transfixed in his sights. As he stabbed the firing button and felt his Spitfire judder in sympathy with the recoil, Mouchotte, 3,000 feet above, saw a lone 190 slide under his starboard wing. It was an opportunity not to miss, he was after it in a flash and saw it explode after a long, chancy burst from dead astern. Biggin Hill's total had reached 1,001.

But who had shot-down the 1,000th Hun? At the debriefing the Frenchman chivalrously claimed he had seen Charles' two fall first, the Canadian swearing that Mouchotte had bagged his 190 before, and not after, his second victim. Finally, Malan ruled that they should share the honour and the prize that went with it.

Biggin Hill was suddenly besieged by journalists, newsreel cameramen and radio reporters all demanding interviews with the two heroes. Both Charles and Mouchotte grew weary of shaking hands and repeating, 'Yes, let's share it. I think that would be fair,' for the benefit of cameras and microphones. '*Quelle autographe-manie anglaise!*' sighed Mouchotte after his hundredth letter requesting a signed photograph. He was more pleased at being made a Companion of the *Conseil de l'Ordre de la Libération*, a distinction rarely awarded.

The event was celebrated by the greatest party ever in the history of Biggin Hill, held at Grosvenor House. More than 1,000 guests were invited, including Air Chief Marshals Sir

Trafford Leigh-Mallory of Fighter Command and Sir Arthur Harris of Bomber Command, and the majority of pilots in 11 Group. Only the Biggin Hill Sector's night-fighter pilots were absent, at the height of the ball they were prowling the skies over the Home Counties, seeking intruders that had sneaked in under cover of darkness. The catering arrangements were lavish to a degree unknown in wartime Britain and featured a centrepiece of three outsize lobsters christened 'Hitler', 'Goebbels' and 'Mussolini'. The bar was free and three R.A.F. bands provided music for dancing. The cabaret was provided by a staunch friend of Biggin Hill, Vivian Van Damm of the Windmill Theatre.

For 'Sailor' Malan it was a double celebration. Only a few hours before the party commenced his wife Lynda had given birth to their second child, a sister to their son, Jonathan Winston, whose godfather was the Prime Minister.

After the final bars of 'Goodnight, Ladies' the pilots from Biggin Hill were faced with the problem of getting home in time for dawn readiness. Someone remembered the long-standing promise of London's taxi-drivers and sent an S.O.S. to the Beaufort Club. Fifteen minutes later a motley group of cabbies elbowed their way through the foyer packed with gold-braided officers and told an astonished flunkey: ' 'Ere, Cock, tell 'em inside the boys from the Beaufort 'as arrived.'

Thanks to their friends the pilots were all present and correct for 'Rodeo' No. 221 over St Omer.

In return Malan invited fifty cabbies to be his guests-of-honour at Biggin Hill. After a gloriously alcoholic evening they staggered out of the Mess on to the tarmac to serenade their host with a song composed by cabman Barney Dowling:

> Here's to the lads of Biggin Hill,
> Who gave us many a thrill,
> When things looked glum.
> Now we've got them on the run,
> When they fly from Biggin Hill,
> Led by Sailor Malan and
> His merry band . . .

As Malan and the pilots realised, the thousandth victory would never have been achieved without the tireless support of the ground crews. Since 1941 the increasing airmindedness of Britain's youth had been fostered by the Air Training Corps. The cadets' training was intensely practical and those living in North Kent were privileged to visit Biggin Hill regularly to absorb the atmosphere of a front-line fighter station. Pilots and airmen willingly instructed the lads who were, often enough, only a few years their juniors. Many came from Dulwich and Epsom Colleges. They were in their element wearing dungarees, smeared from head to foot with grease, and what they did not know about a Merlin engine was hardly worth knowing. Once, when the ground crews happened to be off-duty, some 150 cadets were scattered about the dispersals. An unexpected scramble came and immediately pilots started to rush for their aircraft on cycles, in jeeps and cars. They found the Spitfires with the engines warmed up for instant take-off. After they had gone the Station Commander broadcast a personal message of thanks to all ground crews for the speed with which they had put the Spitfires into the air. 'Sailor' Malan never realised that the job had been done largely by the A.T.C. cadets.

With high summer the Wing was in action almost daily. The pounding of the *Luftwaffe*'s airfields continued without respite and the announcement at briefing of yet another 'Circus' to Caen, Abbeville, Courtrai or even Rotterdam brought forth groans of 'What again?' The enemy was frequently 'conspicuous by his absence', or, when outnumbered, was content to shadow the Wing amicably, refusing the gage of battle, and successful dog fights became rare.

The strain of long hours over enemy territory with taut nerves and eyes unceasingly alert for Huns became unbearable. As in the Battle of Britain, squadrons had to be withdrawn from the front line for a spell of well-deserved rest. At the beginning of July, 611 Squadron left Biggin Hill after nine highly successful months. In its place came 485 Squadron of the Royal New Zealand Air Force under Squadron

Leader Johnny Checketts who quickly established a record for the fastest return from Occupied France. Shot down over Abbeville on a Friday, he was back at Biggin Hill the following Tuesday having crossed the Channel in a fishing smack with nineteen others who had been hidden by the French Resistance.

The *Alsace* Squadron stubbornly rejected any suggestion that it should take a rest. As long as there remained a *Boche* to be shot down, the French pilots were going to remain on the 'Bump'. 'And the sweeps go on, at a terrible pace,' wrote Mouchotte. 'I am at the record figure of 140. I feel a pitiless weariness from them. It is useless for me to go to bed at 9.30 each night; I feel my nerves wearing out, my temper deteriorating. The smallest effort gets me out of breath; I have a crying need for rest, were it even for forty-eight hours.'[1]

But he refused to take any leave when 'Sailor' Malan pressed him.

On 27th July Mouchotte had the satisfaction of leading the Wing in place of Al Deere on its most successful day since Dieppe, escorting Marauder bombers to Triqueville aerodrome, the base of the Richthofen *Geschwader* commanded by the redoubtable Major von Graff. It was hoped that, for once, the enemy fighters would join battle and give the Biggin Wing its chance to exterminate this nest of hornets.

The bombing was erratic, the majority of bombs exploding in the woods fringing the airfield. On leaving the target area Mouchotte was warned by Control: 'Hullo, Turban Leader. Bandits up to the south-east and climbing hard. Numbers unknown.'

'O.K. Grass-seed. Message received and understood.'

Mouchotte took the Wing climbing to port, manoeuvring between the sun and the reported Huns. Without warning the trap was sprung and three squadrons of Focke-Wulfs that had been lurking up-sun, unseen by the Biggin Hill pilots, tore down to meet the Spitfires head-on. Undismayed and held together by the Wing Leader's iron discipline, the

[1] *The Mouchotte Diaries.*

288

Frenchmen and New Zealanders climbed into them and knocked them over to the extent of nine destroyed for no losses – and this in the space of eight minutes!

That evening they heard the German radio announce that Major von Graff, Iron Cross with oak leaves and diamonds, had been wounded whilst in combat against overwhelming odds. In reality the Spitfires had been out-numbered two to one.

Next morning they received a telegram: 'Please convey my warmest congratulations to 341 and 485 Squadrons on yesterday's achievement. Nine for nought is an excellent score. Winston Churchill.'

One month later to the day Mouchotte was reported 'missing, believed killed.'

The Biggin Wing had formed part of the escort of a big formation of Flying Fortresses, 240 strong, raiding some marshalling-yards north of St Omer. The *Alsace* Squadron was shepherding the leading wave of bombers when it was attacked by a swarm of Focke-Wulfs diving out of the sun. To the out-numbered Frenchmen it seemed as if the whole *Luftwaffe* was airborne. Calmly, as if on a training flight, Mouchotte gave his orders, keeping his pilots together until the last second and then: 'Turban aircraft, break port! Attack!' In a flash the sky was patterned with a whirling mass of fighters, the Focke-Wulfs darting in to savage the big bombers – only to be hurled back by the Spitfires. It was chaos, each man for himself with all combat discipline ignored in the bitter life-and-death struggle. Mouchotte himself was isolated, and never seen again. His last words over the R/T were: 'I am alone with the bombers.'

It was dark when the Wing landed back at Biggin Hill. In the glow of the flarepath the pilots saw a knot of men anxiously waiting – 'Sailor' Malan, Al Deere and de la Torre. The last Spitfire was checked in, two were still missing. Calls were made to other airfields, to the Air/Sea Rescue Service and to the Observer Corps. There was no news. *Commandant* Mouchotte and *Sergeant-Chef* Magrot had both failed to return. It was the 'Sailor' who spoke 'René's' epitaph: 'He was a leader, a fighter and a gentleman. We shall all miss him.'

The name of René Mouchotte, together with the names of 453 other pilots, is emblazoned in gold on the reredos in the St George's Chapel of Remembrance at Biggin Hill, the inspiration of the station Padre, Squadron Leader Cecil King. After the celebration of destroying the 1,000th Hun he felt that it was timely to pay tribute to the many unrecognised pilots to whom the lion's share had fallen in raising the Sector's score to this figure and who had paid with their lives.

The Chapel[1] was housed in a disused army hut, the oaken reredos bearing the names of Biggin Hill's great engagements – Dunkirk, the Battle of Britain, Dieppe – the number of more than thirty squadrons which had, at one time or another, fought in the Sector together with the names of those who had paid the supreme sacrifice, pilots of eleven nations. The pulpit was executed by a woodworker of Biggin Hill village; a police constable in Sevenoaks carved the astral crown and the wings over the altar; the C.O. of the squadron of the R.A.F. Regiment stationed on the 'Bump' illuminated and lettered the pages of the Book of Remembrance.

The Memorial was dedicated on Sunday, 19th September, 1943. As Station Commander, 'Sailor' Malan unveiled the reredos. More than any other man he could represent those who had lost their lives, so many of whom had been known to him and numbered amongst his friends.

[1]This is not the Chapel the visitor to Biggin Hill sees today. The original one was burnt down and replaced by the present building in 1951.

CHAPTER TWENTY

FINAL VICTORY

FOR a station which had contributed so much during the Battle of Britain and was later the spearhead of Fighter Command's offensive over Western Europe, Biggin Hill had a pathetically small role in the final, decisive year of the war. For many months the airfield was completely bereft of aircraft and peewits uttered their melancholy calls in a sky once thunderous with the roar of Spitfires taking off. The irony lay in its geography: ideally situated for the defence of London, it was too far away for striking at the heart of Nazi Germany.

By autumn, 1943, plans and organisation for Operation 'Overlord', the Allies' invasion of Western Europe, were taking definite and final shape. General Eisenhower was appointed Supreme Commander with Marshal of the Royal Air Force Tedder as his Deputy, a reflection of the importance of air power in the coming assault. Air Marshal Sir Trafford Leigh-Mallory relinquished Fighter Command and assumed responsibility for the air forces covering the invasion. The fighter squadrons retained for wholly defensive purposes were renamed the Air Defence of Great Britain, an echo of the terminology of the inter-war years. Those to be used in support of 'Overlord' became the Second Tactical Air Force which, together with the United States Ninth Air Force, comprised the Allied Expeditionary Air Force.

Inevitably these dispositions, in the course of time, had their repercussions at Biggin Hill.

During September Al Deere had been taken ill and his post as Wing Commander Flying had been filled by *Commandant* Dupérier who had succeeded René Mouchotte as O.C. the *Alsace* Squadron. Then 'Sailor' Malan moved on to train a

Fighter Wing for the forthcoming invasion.

'It's the best fighter station I know,' he said, handing over Biggin Hill to Group Captain H. L. Maxwell, C.B.E., D.S.O. 'Its spirit and performance are due entirely to the team-work of the chaps on the ground and in the air.'

At the same time Biggin Hill lost its Intelligence Officer, 'Spy' de la Torre, who had served the Sector devotedly and brilliantly since the dark days of 1940. Many were the pilots who had occasion to be thankful for his lucid briefings and vivid description of how things would be on an operation – 'never as bad as the Battle of B.', to use his favourite expression.

The new station 'Spy' was Squadron Leader J. W. Hogben, a veteran of the Royal Flying Corps, who found to his dismay that one of his first tasks was to settle-up accounts for the Grosvenor House party. Its cost had been prodigious, a good £2,500, and Biggin Hill was faced with a deficit of over £1,000. This was covered by a levy on all other stations in 11 Group, a highly unpopular imposition with those who had not been invited to the celebration.

The Second Tactical Air Force, commanded by Air Marshal Sir Arthur Coningham, consisted of three Groups, one Light Bomber and two Fighter, and a Reconnaissance Wing. In October the *Alsace* Squadron and the New Zealanders were posted from Biggin Hill to start training for D-Day, and the identity of 'Biggin on the Bump' was concealed under the characterless designation of No. 126 Airfield of the 17 (Fighter) Wing of the Royal Canadian Air Force controlled by 83 Group of the Second Tactical Air Force. Three Canadian squadrons now moved in, Nos. 401, 411 and 412, equipped at first with Spitfire Vbs, but all flying Spitfire IXs before the year was out.

The American heavy bombers were now operating deep over in the heart of Germany in massive formations of 500-plus and it fell to the Biggin Wing, with its short-range Spitfires, to meet them on their return and shepherd them safely home. These withdrawal escorts were exceedingly unpopular with the Canadians, forced to fly to the limit of their Spitfire's endurance and often crash-landing or baling out through lack of fuel.

This type of operation is getting to be a terrific bind to all the pilots and ground crews. With the number of escort fighters provided to the bombers these days we can never expect to see a Hun come up and fight.[1]

At the very end of the year, on 30th December, the Wing did encounter the enemy. Whilst covering the withdrawal of some 700 Fortresses after a raid over South Germany, 10 enemy aircraft appeared from nowhere and rashly attacked the formation. In the fight that followed Flight Lieutenant 'Screwball' Buerling of 412 Squadron shot-down a F.W. 190 and brought his total score of enemy aircraft destroyed to 31.

To keep the squadrons occupied and prepare them for D-Day, all manner of exercises were laid-on that winter. Taken very seriously were the escaping-drills, for the pilots knew that, once the invasion had started, they might be forced down behind enemy lines. Dressed in 'civvies', they were driven in a covered van to 'somewhere in Kent' and dropped, with orders to report back to Biggin Hill without being picked up by the Home Guard or police, both on the alert for the 'escapees'.

No holds were barred and any means of getting back could be used. Two pilots once returned in a bus stolen from an army camp near Headcorn, three others helped themselves to some Spitfire IXs conveniently unguarded on Ashford aerodrome, and were followed by a fourth enterprising Canadian who took a Tiger Moth from the same airfield. To celebrate this feat, the 'derogatory finger' was painted on the borrowed aircraft, while the telephone wires hummed with orders for an immediate tightening-up of security at all R.A.F. airfields. In the event, the *Luftwaffe* would not be guilty of such laxness.

Training in glider-towing was also organised, the Spitfires acting as tugs to fully-loaded Hotspurs. Instruction on the gliders was heartily disliked, for without a throttle lever in

[1] 401 Squadron diary.

their left hands the pilots developed bad attacks of the 'twitch' and thought longingly of their Spitfires' Merlins.

Spring, 1944, brought little change. Sweeps and escorts to Marauders, Fortresses and Liberators continued but were comparatively few until April when the Canadian squadrons were posted from Biggin Hill. As D-Day approached, the fighter squadrons were concentrated on bases as far forward as possible. In mid-April Biggin Hill's role was taken over by Tangmere, and the station was relegated to that of sector station in No. 24 (Base Defence) Wing of No. 85 (Base) Group, Allied Expeditionary Forces. It made little difference, for there were no squadrons to fly from Biggin Hill. A month later brought another change of title when the station became part of the 100th Fighter Wing, in turn a unit of the XIXth Tactical Air Command – but there were still no aircraft. If there had been, they could not have flown, for Biggin Hill was now the heart of a balloon barrage, London's innermost line of defence against flying bombs.

On 3rd February, 1944, four months before the first 'doodle-bug' fell on Britain, Biggin Hill received a visit from Group Captain J. P. Hitchings, C.B.E., with twenty-four other officers and senior N.C.O.s. Their arrival caused quite a stir amongst the Canadian pilots who saw that the visitors all came from Balloon Command: no one could guess why the 'gasbag types' were interested in Biggin Hill. In two days they covered hundreds of miles along the crest of the North Downs, selecting the sites for over 200 balloon emplacements. Immediately, No. 5344 Airfield Construction Wing moved in and, by working day and night for a fortnight, built all the access roads, hard standings, central anchorages, hutted camps, and hydrogen depots required by a balloon barrage, as well as laid over 1,000 miles of telephone cable. Only the balloons were missing: everything else was ready, for no one could foretell if and when Hitler would commence using his *Vergeltungswaffe* 1, the V.1, flying bomb, or 'doodle-bug' of the Londoners who endured its terror.

That the Germans had such a weapon had been known for some time, thanks to the R.A.F.'s Photographic Reconnaissance squadrons and agents in the occupied countries and Germany. Many of the launching sites in the Pas de Calais and the Cherbourg peninsula had been identified and obliterated by Bomber Command and the Second Tactical Air Force, but others, cunningly camouflaged in woods and caverns, had escaped detection and destruction. They lay in a menacing arc inland from the coast of France whose focal point was the city of London. Across the track of the flying bombs directed on to the capital were the North Downs, a natural rampart whose keep was Biggin Hill. It was the logical situation for a balloon barrage, where the flying bombs would be converging thickly and the closely-packed balloons most effective.

The first flying bomb to be launched against London fell at Swanscombe, near Gravesend, at 4.18 a.m. on 13th June. Biggin Hill, now re-named No. 22 Balloon Centre, was once again a front-line station in the defence of London against enemy aircraft – this time the aircraft were pilotless and unseeing, and unable to take evasive action. There was a difference, too, in the spirit of the 519 airmen and 177 W.A.A.F.s living on the station. During the Battle of Britain they knew they were dealing with other human beings, a relationship of friend and foe was established, and they learnt to anticipate and brace themselves for the daily crises of danger. Now the danger was constant, a strain from which there was no escaping, and they had to learn to live with the threat of annihilation twenty-four hours a day.

Once it was certain that the enemy meant business with his V.1, counter-measures were swiftly put into action. The assault on the launching sites by our bombers was intensified, fighters started patrolling their allotted zones over the Channel and inland, while anti-aircraft batteries were deployed to cover the approaches to London. On 16th June the balloons of No. 945/7 Squadron arrived on Biggin Hill, the convoy of trucks having driven all night with a special police escort from Glasgow. Within twenty-four hours the fields and farms around the station were covered with winches and tents, and the sky was dotted with a rash of balloons that grew thicker each day as more squadrons, Nos. 953 and 958, moved in. By 19th June some 344 balloons were flying at 4,500 feet, a formidable barrier covering Brasted and Westerham, Tatsfield and Ide Hill. Next morning the Biggin Hill Balloon Centre 'chalked-up' its first 'doodle-bug' victory when a flying bomb severed the cable of site 108's balloon and crashed harmlessly in an orchard. Two more were quickly brought down and then, tragically, a Mosquito fighter whose pilot, intent on destroying his robot prey, had flown within reach of the balloons' lethal cables of steel.

The actual handling of the balloons was done by airmen, but the W.A.A.F.'s were magnificent. They managed all the transport, even to collecting the heavy cylinders of hydrogen delivered to Hayes station by special train from a gas works in Weston-super-Mare. Day and night they delivered the water supplies and food rations to the far-flung balloon sites, and drove the ambulances – always with one eye cocked on the sky for the first sign of a 'doodle-bug'. They grew inured to the snarling whine of the flying bomb, the silence followed by the explosion. If they heard it, they knew another built-up area was safe.

Once the balloons were securely aloft, life in the midst of a balloon barrage was unsually passive. To help pass the time the W.A.A.F.s took up knitting and embroidery. Each evening found the N.A.A.F.I. filled with girls hard at work on cushion covers, table-runners and bedspreads. Attendances at educational lectures rose to 'standing room only', there was an insatiable demand for serious books from the station library, as the girls, and airmen, too, started to think about their future life in 'Civvy Street'. When the teacher was wounded by a flying bomb, the announcement that 'Classes in German have been discontinued owing to enemy action' was greeted with sincere disappointment, not laughter.

Biggin Hill lay dangerously within 'Doodle-bug Alley' and many bombs fell on, or near to, the station. The married quarters were damaged for a second time in the war, the W.A.A.F.s' sick quarters at Keston were destroyed, and several of the balloon crews received injuries. Fatalities, fortunately, were few. On 1st July, at 5.30 a.m., a flying bomb glided down and exploded on top of a Nissen hut standing on the airfield. There was literally nothing left – just a raw, gaping hole in the ground. Despite the efforts of Flight Sergeant 'Muscles' Freeman and 100 airmen, all that could be found were six pound notes and some scraps of correspondence, barely sufficient to identify the three men who had been sleeping inside the hut.

The assault on London by flying bombs continued through July and August and on into September. In all, over 8,500 bombs were launched and of these barely 2,400 got through to their target. Some exploded prematurely shortly after launching, many more fell to our fighters and anti-aircraft guns, while the balloon barrage was credited with the destruction of 279 'doodle-bugs'. By 5th September the attack was virtually over and orders were given for the balloons to be grounded. Before the end of the month the whole barrage was deflated and the squadrons were on the move again, this time to Southend to counter flying bombs launched from aircraft over the North Sea.

During September the regular sections – Station Headquarters, Administration, Accounts, Welfare, Communications, Transport, etc. – that together comprise an R.A.F. station began to return to Biggin Hill and, by the middle of October, the airfield was once more in use. A Spitfire squadron, No. 340, moved in briefly but Biggin Hill was too far from the battlefront, now pressing close on the frontiers of the Third Reich. The Spitfires left, and Biggin Hill became a base for No. 168 (Heavy Transport) Squadron of the Royal Canadian Air Force. Britain's premier fighter station was now a post office!

This squadron had been specially formed to run a regular transatlantic airmail service for the Canadian forces in Europe. Its home base was Rockliffe, Ontario. From here the 'Mailcan' Fortresses carried the mail to Gibraltar for the Mediterranean zone and to Biggin Hill where it was transshipped to Dakota aircraft for distribution to France, Belgium, Holland and Germany.

For a station whose aircraft during the second World War had accounted for 1,400 of the enemy, it was, perhaps, appropriate that the last operations to be flown were missions of mercy, the transport of penicillin to Warsaw to combat an epidemic in Poland. On 19th October, 1945, a Fortress of 168 Squadron left Rockliffe with the first consignment of the drug which it landed at Prestwick two days later. There was a delay to secure clearance from the Russians for flights over Poland; then, on 25th October, a Dakota from Biggin Hill picked up the penicillin and flew it into Warsaw, via Berlin, on 1st November. A second flight a few days later ended in tragedy when the Fortress carrying another load of penicillin crashed near Halle in Germany; all five members of the crew were killed. A third trip was then made with another Fortress. Leaving Rockliffe on 16th November, it reached Biggin Hill on the 18th. Five days later, after waiting for the necessary clearance, it was flown on to Warsaw, and returned to Biggin Hill the following day.

In August, 1946, when the fury of war had abated, Biggin Hill was handed over to Reserve Command. Not until November, 1949, did it revert to Fighter Command. Two squadrons of the Royal Auxiliary Air Force, Nos. 600 and 615, re-formed at the station in 1946 and remained the sole flying units until 1951 when a Regular squadron, No. 41, joined them to give Biggin Hill first-line status for the first time since V-J Day.

Formed in 1925 as a day-bomber unit, 600 (City of London) Squadron was the senior squadron in the Auxiliary Air Force. During the Battle of Britain it saw intense fighting by day and night, and became the first night-fighter squadron to use Beaufighters. From 1942 until the end of the war 600 Squadron operated in North Africa and Italy and, with 179 claims to its credit, boasted the highest score at night in the Royal Air Force. After re-forming at Biggin Hill it flew Spitfires until 1950 when it converted to Meteor jets. In July, 1949, the Squadron was greatly honoured when Queen Elizabeth (now Queen Elizabeth the Queen Mother) graciously accepted the appointment of Honorary Air Commodore.

The squadron was also awarded the freedom of the City of London and traditionally took part in the Lord Mayor's Show.

615 (County of Surrey) Squadron was formed in 1937 as an Army Cooperation Unit but soon became a fighter unit during the expansion of 1938. It was proud to have an old friend and neighbour of Biggin Hill, the Rt Hon. Sir Winston Churchill, for its Honorary Air Commodore. During 1940 the squadron fought gallantly to stem the German advance into the Low Countries and, on its return to Britain, saw action daily in the Battle of Britain, claiming 27 enemy aircraft destroyed in August alone. From 1942 onwards, until the end of the war, the squadron served in the Far East. As with its brother squadron, No. 600, Spitfires were flown after it was re-formed until 1950 when Meteors were taken into service.

No. 41 moved to Biggin Hill in 1951 with its new Meteor VIIIs, now replaced by sleek Hawker Hunters, and with its arrival the station was brought up to full squadron strength. And so it remained, until the sad day in 1957 when the Royal Auxiliary Air Force was disbanded in the interests of national economy.

Today Biggin Hill has but one squadron, No. 41, and in a world overshadowed by rockets and guided missiles it future as a fighter station is uncertain.

Its tradition lives on. Battle of Britain Day at 'Biggin on the Bump' now rivals the great pre-war flying displays at Hendon in its attraction for the people of London. Rightly so, for they owe their lives and freedom to the sacrifice of some of 'the Few' who fought from Biggin Hill twenty-eight years ago.

EPILOGUE

IT is perhaps fitting that the last aircraft to see squadron service at Biggin Hill was the Hawker Hunter, a descendant of the legendary Battle of Britain fighter, the Hawker Hurricane. In fact No. 41 Squadron operated Hunters from Biggin Hill until 1959 when the station was taken over by Flying Training Command and its metamorphosis from a front-line fighter base to the Royal Air Force Officers and Aircrew Selection Centre was begun. The Ground Officers Selection Centre was the first to move to Biggin Hill, from Uxbridge, in April, 1959. The Aircrew Selection Centre followed, from Hornchurch, in 1962 when the present purpose-built headquarters building had been completed. The third major component of the Officers and Aircrew Selection Centre was added in 1964 when the Royal Air Force Selection Board moved from Cranwell to Biggin Hill; it was known initially as the Cranwell Board, but later was renamed the Cadetships Board when the former Cranwell cadetship system gave way to the present University Cadetship Scheme. Today, the Officers and Aircrew Selection Centre consists of the Cadetships, Air and Ground Boards, supported by a Medical Board, an Aptitude Testing Section and a Personnel Selection Training School.

As to the famous airfield, in 1964 it was relinquished to the Board of Trade. Later, it was sold to the London Borough of Bromley for use as a civil aerodrome, but has been handed back regularly to the Royal Air Force for annual Battle of Britain At Home Day flying displays. Other links with past Royal Air Force operational use of Biggin Hill are St George's Chapel of Remembrance standing in gardens beside the A233, and the Spitfire and Hurricane flanking the gateway giving public access to the Chapel.

An earlier chapel was dedicated in 1943, but completely destroyed by fire in 1946. To replace it, the present chapel was financed by public subscription. Fittingly the foundation stone was laid by Air Chief Marshal Lord Dowding, the Commander-in-Chief of Fighter Command during the Battle of Britain, and the dedication was by the Lord Bishop of Rochester on 10 November 1951. The altar is flanked by wooden reredos on which are listed the names of 453 pilots of 52 Royal Air Force, Commonwealth and Allied squadrons who were killed during World War II while flying from Biggin Hill and the other airfields in the Biggin Hill Sector. On either side of the altar and reredos are the flags of those Commonwealth and Allied countries whose airmen served in the Biggin Hill Sector. One of the chapel's most treasured possessions is a Book of Remembrance, which contains a day to day record of the pilots who lost their lives. By tradition a page of the book is turned each day; whatever the future holds for Royal Air Force, Biggin Hill, it is to be hoped that at least this tradition will be carried on.

Gordon Landsborough

Battery From Hellfire

North Africa. The desert, June, 1942. Rommel battering his way through a reeling Allied army towards Alexandria. In his path a mobile ack-ack column, new to the desert . . .

'It has everything, knowledge of the desert and of mechanised war, supremely good characterisation, descriptive brilliance, and a 'special idea', masterly in its simplicity – a major's insistence, at the risk of mutiny, on saving a mobile gun.'   *Birmingham Post*

40p

Patrol to Benghazi

A man-hunt in the Western Desert . . .

Hour after hour the trucks of the Desert Patrol crawled in the heat of the dry African sun. Time after time the men had to clear the track, manhandling their heavy, laden lorries. Time after time they went wrong, running into impassable wadis or cliff faces. They were desperate men on a desperate mission behind the enemy lines – and one of them might be a traitor.

'. . . the background authentic, the adventure brilliantly imagined.'
Birmingham Post

40p

Long Run to Tobruk

From the heart of the Libyan desert the daring marauders struck, destroying Rommel's air fleet on the ground. But the S.A.S. could not be allowed to get away with it, and Rommel ordered them to be pursued, and killed or captured. So began one of the greatest man-hunts of the war – a small patrol of British guerillas hounded over the vast Sahara, doubling and turning in their tracks to throw off the relentless pursuers.

'Use any means,' ordered the Field-Marshal, and they did – flying columns, Stuka dive-bombers and even paratroops.

45p

War in Tandem editions

Barry's Flying Column Ewan Butler 25p
The story of the I.R.A.'s Cork No. 3 Brigade, 1919–21.

Marshal Without Glory Ewan Butler and Gordon Young 40p
The life and death of Hermann Goering.

At War With the Bolsheviks Robert Jackson .. 45p
'Bizarre and desperate battles, rescues, failed rescues, intrigue and treachery.' – *Books and Bookmen.*

Betrayal At Arnhem A. Laurens 35p
Was there a traitor behind the fiasco of the Arnhem operation?

G Patrol Michael Crichton-Stuart 45p
The story of remarkable irregular warfare in the North African campaign.

Pocket Battleship Theodor Krancke & H. J. Brennecke 50p
The exciting account of the famous German raider, *Admiral Scheer.*

U Boat 977 Heinz Schaeffer 45p
A rare first-person account of submarine warfare from the German side.

Name ....

Address ....

Titles required ....

....

....

....

....

....

....

....

The publishers hope that you enjoyed this book and invite you to write for the full list of Tandem titles.

If you find any difficulty in obtaining these books from your usual retailer we shall be pleased to supply the titles of your choice upon receipt of your remittance.

Packing and postage charges are as follows:
1 book – 15p per copy, plus 5p per copy for each additional book ordered. 8 or more books – 50p.

WRITE NOW TO:
    Universal-Tandem Publishing Co. Ltd.,
    14 Gloucester Road,
    London SW7 4RD